Film and Television Genres of the Late Soviet Era

Film and Television Genres of the Late Soviet Era

Alexander Prokhorov and Elena Prokhorova

Bloomsbury Academic
An imprint of Bloomsbury Publishing Inc

B L O O M S B U R Y
NEW YORK • LONDON • OXFORD • NEW DELHI • SYDNEY

Bloomsbury Academic
An imprint of Bloomsbury Publishing Inc

1385 Broadway	50 Bedford Square
New York	London
NY 10018	WC1B 3DP
USA	UK

www.bloomsbury.com

BLOOMSBURY and the Diana logo are trademarks of Bloomsbury Publishing Plc

First published 2017

© Alexander Prokhorov and Elena Prokhorova, 2017

All rights reserved. No part of this publication may be reproduced or transmitted in any form or by any means, electronic or mechanical, including photocopying, recording, or any information storage or retrieval system, without prior permission in writing from the publishers.

No responsibility for loss caused to any individual or organization acting on or refraining from action as a result of the material in this publication can be accepted by Bloomsbury or the author.

Library of Congress Cataloging-in-Publication Data
Names: Prokhorov, Alexander, 1965- author. | Prokhorova, Elena, author.
Title: Film and television genres of the late Soviet era / Alexander Prokhorov and Elena Prokhorova
Description: New York : Bloomsbury Academic, 2016. | Includes bibliographical references and index.
Identifiers: LCCN 2016023096 (print) | LCCN 2016035443 (ebook) | ISBN 9781441177292 (hardback) | ISBN 9781501324093 (ePub) | ISBN 9781501324086 (ePDF)
Subjects: LCSH: Motion pictures–Soviet Union. | Film genres—Soviet Union. | Television series–Soviet Union. | Television program genres—Soviet Union. | BISAC: PERFORMING ARTS / Film & Video / History & Criticism. | PERFORMING ARTS / Film & Video / General.
Classification: LCC PN1993.5.S65 P75 2007 (print) | LCC PN1993.5.S65 (ebook) | DDC 791.430947—dc23
LC record available at https://lccn.loc.gov/2016023096

ISBN:	HB:	978-1-4411-7729-2
	PB:	978-1-4411-3428-8
	ePub:	978-1-5013-2409-3
	ePDF:	978-1-5013-2408-6

Cover design by Dan Stiles
Cover image (insert on the TV screen) © Anzhela Dzherih, *Shtirlits nashego dvora*

Typeset by RefineCatch Limited, Bungay, Suffolk

Contents

List of illustrations	vii
Acknowledgments	x
Introduction	1
Approaches to film and television genres	2
Why television?	6
The difficult fate of genre studies in the USSR and Russia	7
Overview of chapters: from socialist realism to film genres	15
1 Prestige Productions: Epic Film as a Tool of Hard and Soft Power during the Cold War	21
Syntax and semantics of the genre	21
War and Peace: art cinema on state service	27
Liberation: war spectacle and the politics of memory	43
Postscript: the revival of prestige productions under Putin	59
2 The Socialist Television Police Procedural of the 1970s and 80s: Teaching Soviet Citizens How to Behave	67
Syntax and semantics of the genre	67
The Investigation is Conducted by Experts: the Soviet police procedural is born	80
The Meeting Place Cannot Be Changed: the romantics of the criminal underworld	90
Postscript: streetwise cops meet the Russian mafia	104
3 Late-Soviet Comedy: Between Rebellion and the Status Quo	107
Syntax and semantics of the genre	107
El'dar Riazanov: the trappings and traps of private life	116
Mark Zakharov's television films: between the romance and the sitcom	128
Postscript: the living and the (un)dead	146
4 Reinventing Desire: Late-Socialist Melodrama	149
Syntax and semantics of the genre	149

Television melodrama 158
Cinematic masculinities 163
Late-Soviet "woman's film" 173
Postscript: televised passions 188

Conclusion 191
Bibliography 197
Filmography 207
Index 213

List of illustrations

1.1	Street advertisement for Iurii Ozerov's *Liberation* in East Berlin (1972)	25
1.2	Dancers in the Mass Ornament in *War and Peace*	31
1.3	Split screen in the scene after Natasha's first ball	32
1.4	Simon Ushakov's *The Tree of the Muscovite State* 1668	33
1.5	Oak Tree in Otradnoe as the Tree of the Russian Empire. The director's name is superimposed on the image of the tree	34
1.6	Prayer before Borodino, a harbinger of victory. No prayer before Austerlitz led to defeat	35
1.7	The victory bonfire	36
1.8	Liudmila Savel'eva as Natasha Rostova	39
1.9	Audrey Hepburn as Natasha Rostova	39
1.10	The number of Soviets killed in the Second World War confirms who made the major contribution	45
1.11	Tank stunts as visual attraction: T-34 tank jumps over obstacles	50
1.12	Promotional brochure for *Liberation*	56
1.13	Promotional brochure for *Liberation*	57
1.14	Promotional brochure for *Liberation*	58
1.15	The Imperial Army and Golden Domes of Orthodox Cathedrals meet each other in *Barber of Siberia* (dir. Nikita Mikhalkov 1999)	61
1.16	President Vladimir Putin on the set of *Burnt by the Sun-2*	62
2.1	The investigator (Mikhail Zharov) exposes the spy under Stalin's eagle eye in *Engineer Kochin's Mistake*	70
2.2	Interrogation as soul-searching in *The Investigation is Conducted by Experts* (1972)	72
2.3	Fashion show as a value-neutral consumer spectacle	77
2.4	The police team in *The Investigation is Conducted by Experts*	81
2.5	Garbage dump as a setting and metaphor in *The Investigation is Conducted by Experts*, Episode 10 (1975)	86
2.6	Soviet teenagers and the gun fetish in Episode 13 (1978) of *The Investigation is Conducted by Experts*	88

2.7	Stalin's portrait behind the protagonist in *The Meeting Place Cannot Be Changed*	93
2.8 and 2.9	Criminal types in *The Meeting Place Cannot Be Changed*	95
2.10	Intelligentsia on trial in *The Meeting Place*	99
2.11	Zheglov in action in *The Meeting Place*	100
3.1	Kalugina as the gloomy Soviet bureaucrat	110
3.2	A character mocks the humorless boss	111
3.3	The individual overshadowed by the body of a nameless working-class character	112
3.4	Collective identity only in a state of inebriation	123
3.5	Zhenia visibly suffers but recovers himself and makes a proposal to his fiancée Galia, a woman he does not love	125
3.6	Zhenia's mother observes the female "intruder"	126
3.7	The last frame of Zakharov's film: Munchausen departs into outer space from his oppressive community	132
3.8	Ilya Kabakov. *The Man Who Flew into Space from His Apartment*. Installation. Created in 1984	133
3.9	Ostap's eye gazing directly at the viewers opens every episode of Zakharov's *Twelve Chairs*	135
3.10	"And this is his dream as well"	136
3.11	Giant Glium, who was ordered by the city mayor to stop growing	139
3.12	Evgenii Leonov as the king in *An Ordinary Miracle*	141
3.13	The king's court, puzzled by characters who can have both agency and emotions	142
3.14	The king's three-cornered Napoleonic hat covers …	143
3.15	… a Russian babushka kerchief	144
4.1	Princess Volkonskaia's tear-stained face	155
4.2	Panagia Eleousa	155
4.3	Shura and her stepdaughter, with a church in the background	156
4.4	Revolution and love in *Shadows Disappear at Noon*	160
4.5	Russian community at the core of Soviet television melodrama *Shadows Disappear at Noon*	163
4.6	Sergei and Tania, the Soviet Romeo and Juliet	167
4.7	A TV cartoon character "looks" in amazement at the male protagonist who has undergone a dramatic change	169
4.8	The good Soviet life after the hero's death	169
4.9	Warrior paradise lost/exchanged for the good but uninspiring life	171

4.10 Watching the utopia in its final hour 177
4.11 Uvarova in search of utopia, with the church in the background 178
4.12 Uvarova mentoring her children 180
4.13 Tat'iana and Aleksei entering the monumental world of the
       communist paradise (*Radiant Path* 1940) 184
4.14 A Russian (not Soviet) male protagonist emerging from behind
       a Russian samovar 187

Acknowledgments

We would like to thank our mentors, Helena Goscilo and Vladimir Padunov, and our patient and supportive teachers, Mark Altshuller, David Birnbaum, Nancy Condee, Lucy Fischer, Jane Feuer, and Carole Stabile. We consider ourselves very fortunate to have worked and exchanged ideas with helpful and thoughtful colleagues at the University of Pittsburgh and the College of William and Mary. Continuous conversations, panels, and projects with our colleagues, Tony Anemone, Petr Bagrov, Marina Balina, Birgit Beumers, Eliot Borenstein, Katerina Clark, Fred Corney, Yana Hashamova, Beth Holmgren, Mikhail Iampol'skii, Vida Johnson, Lilya Kaganovsky, Arthur Knight, Ilya Kukulin, Mark Lipovetsky, Masha Maiofis, Anna Malguina, Zhenia Margolit, Viktor Matizen, Tatyana Mikhailova, Serguei Oushakine, Rima Salys, Elena Stishova, Alexei Yurchak, and many others greatly assisted our research, although they may not agree with all of the claims and interpretations provided in this book. We thank Emilia and Ilya Kabakov for their generous permission to use a photograph of the installation *The Man Who Flew into Space from his Apartment*. We also thank Anzhela Dzherih for her permission to use her image on our cover. During the writing process we benefitted from the enthusiasm and support of the editorial staff at Bloomsbury Academic, above all Katie Gallof. Finally, we would like to thank our mothers, Natalia Prokhorova and Valentina Shemonaeva, who brought us up and persevered through all the hardships of Soviet late socialism, and our daughter, Dasha Prokhorova, who is the love of our lives.

This research was supported by the grants from the Reves Center for International Studies, Film and Media Studies Program, and the College of Arts and Sciences of the College of William and Mary.

Note on Transliteration and Translation

This book uses the Library of Congress system of transliteration, except when alternate spelling is commonly used, e.g. Leo Tolstoy, Sergei Eisenstein. All translations from Russian into English are ours unless otherwise noted.

Introduction

This book examines film and television genres of the late-Soviet era, a topic and an era both challenging and important. Their importance lies not only in the necessity to conceptualize the tapestry of facts and fictions of, and approaches to, the 1970s, but also in the fact that contemporary Russian television and cinema bear hereditary features of late-socialist genres.

There is no agreement among film scholars on what genre is and which films do or do not belong to a particular theoretical genre. Even studies of the classical Hollywood studio system, with a long tradition of theoretical writings on the industry, audiences, and individual texts, have not established any consensus as to the body of films that constitute a particular genre or the function of the genre in culture, both inside and outside US borders. Genre studies of national cinemas, out of necessity, traditionally have relied on the methodologies and insights coming out of the scholarship of the Hollywood system, whose context—commercial, institutional, and ideological—is very different from that of other national film industries. In this Introduction we provide a very broad overview of three dominant approaches to film genre that originated largely in American film studies, before defining our own, and venturing into the difficult fate of "genre" in the land of late socialism.

One thing most film scholars agree on is that the concept of film genre is a useful tool to look for clusters of meanings and frameworks of understanding that were shared by producers and consumers of the most influential media of the past century: film and television. Genre is also a flexible category, accounting for the many forces at play in the production and consumption of visual texts, no matter how one theorizes the relationship of these "interpretive communities" in structuring the genre's meaning and the cultural work it performs.[1]

The methodology one brings to bear upon the texts, and the individual texts chosen as symptomatic of the patterns, largely define how that pattern is

---

[1] The term was first introduced by Stanley Fish in 1976. See Stanley Fish, *Is There A Text in This Class?*, Cambridge: Harvard University Press, 1980, 147–174.

constructed. But the admission that a genre is an analyst's construct makes the job harder, not easier. S/he is fully responsible for the fragile structure, when it works and when it does not.

Approaches to film and television genres

As an academic field in the US, contemporary film studies started in the 1960s, with the auteur theory, as one of its early theoretical platforms. Genre approach emerged as a response to this neo-romantic celebration of the author's original creation and the focus on individual filmmakers. In the 1970s, with the emergence of structuralism, two critical trends appeared: ritual and ideological. Inspired by the works of Vladimir Propp and Claude Lévi-Strauss, scholars such as John Cawelti and Will Wright studied narrative formulas in large groups of popular texts that conveyed shared meanings and structured cultural-industrial exchange.[2] Genre film studies started with the analysis of Hollywood narrative and ideological formulas. In the works of Thomas Schatz and others, the ritual approach responded to these initial examinations of textual structures with a broader conception of film genre. Schatz viewed genres as cultural problem-solving operations, where real societal problems are rehearsed and lead to a fictional resolution. In his works on the Hollywood genre system, Schatz contended that film audiences have a special investment in film genres because they "stroke[s] the collective sensibilities of the mass audience" (1981, 31).

Next to the interpretation of film genres as modes of ritual, there emerged the ideological approach, which was inspired by the Frankfurt School's analysis of capitalist ideology and focused on the genres' role in the reproduction of dominant structures and naturalization of the status quo. In this view, genres are ideological constructs designed to limit possible interpretations of social reality. Ideological criticism brings to film studies a view of genres as discourses, "systems of orientations, expectations, and conventions that circulate between industry, text, and subject" (Neale 1980, 20). Such film historians as Rick Altman and Jane Feuer write diachronic studies of film genres as manifestations of evolving social ideologies. For example, Feuer's study of television genres is historically grounded and appropriately titled *Seeing through the Eighties: Television and Reaganism*.

[2] John Cawelti, *The Six-Gun Mystique*. Bowling Green, OH: Bowling Green State University Popular Press, 1971 and *Adventure, Mystery, and Romance: Formula Stories as Art and Popular Culture*. Chicago: University of Chicago Press, 1976; Will Wright, *Six Guns and Society: A Structural Study of the Western*. Berkeley/Los Angeles/London: University of California Press, 1975.

Inspired by Cold War hostilities, the field of Slavic area studies unsurprisingly placed an extraordinary weight on discussions of the Soviet government's mechanisms controlling cultural production. At the same time, Slavists favored auteurist studies of those filmmakers who found themselves at odds with the regime, with Andrei Tarkovskii as the supreme example. Without denying the validity of findings by either of those methodologies, we propose a study of late-socialist cinema and television that tries to take into account the many, often competing, discourses that circulated among various interpretive communities. These included film and television administration (Goskino, with its Main Scripts and Editorial Commission, Gosteleradio,[3] the Ministry of Culture), critics, film audiences, and numerous institutions, such as the Central Committee of the CPSU, KGB, the Army, and the Police—all of which had a say in the formation of film and television texts. In fact, we claim that the formation of the late-Soviet film and television genre system, which in our view to a large degree has survived to the present, was a result of what Altman calls "the productive play of contradictory forces within a field" (1984, 10).

In our study of film and television genres of the late-socialist Soviet Union, we draw above all on Rick Altman's theory of genres, which tries to put to productive use the tools and findings of both the ideological and the ritual approaches, taking into account both synchronic and diachronic aspects of genre formation and evolution. In his influential 1984 article Altman proposes a semantic-syntactic model of genre, with syntax representing the dominant structure in which semantic elements are arranged. "The semantic approach thus stresses the genre's building blocks, while the syntactic view privileges the structures into which they are arranged" (Altman 1984, 10). The semantic approach has broad applicability, while the syntactic one has more explanatory power (Altman 1984, 11). Following other film scholars, in his 1999 book *Film/Genre*, Altman contends that genres represent discursive formations rather than purely textual phenomena.[4] As discourses they are put to different use by different interpretive communities. The latter idea leads Altman to add a pragmatic dimension to his genre model.

---

[3] Goskino was the agency supervising film production and distribution in the late Soviet Union. It was headed by Filip Ermash from 1972 till 1986. The Main Scripts and Editorial Commission was its main body, it reviewed and censored scripts and films. Gosteleradio, the agency supervising radio and television broadcasting, was headed by Sergei Lapin from 1970 till 1985.

[4] See, for example, James Naremore, "American Film Noir: The History of an Idea," *Film Quarterly*, 49.2 (1995–1996): 12–29: "[I]ndividual genre has less to do with a group of artefacts than with a discourse—a loose evolving system of arguments and readings, helping to shape the commercial strategies and aesthetic ideologies" (14).

Our study is also inspired by Katerina Clark's study of the socialist realist novel as a literary "total genre" of Soviet literature. We propose that socialist realist film likewise provided the basic syntax for Soviet film, no matter what thematic variation (pseudo genre) the filmmaker chose to follow. Socialist realist syntax includes the socialist realist master plot, the story of the protagonist who under the guidance of an ideological mentor undergoes the transformation from spontaneity to ideological consciousness, and the chronotope of "modal schizophrenia," the narrative constantly oscillating between the present and signs of the utopian future within the present (Clark 2000, 37). From the 1930s onward, Soviet cinema adhered to one artistic method (socialist realism), where production was organized on the basis of annual thematic plans that defined prioritized subjects, such as films about a kolkhoz village, films about war, films about post-war reconstruction, films about industrial production, etc.

In her analysis of the Stalin-era biopic Maria Belodubrovskaya contends that a film genre emerges and develops as a site of negotiation among various participants of film production and consumption. She comes to the conclusion that Soviet cinema used a mechanism of genre film production—through adjusting and replicating successful models—similar to that of the classical Hollywood model. Obviously, in Soviet cinema, the process of adjustment took a more overtly political turn. Belodubrovskaya argues that, because of censorship and political uncertainty, the Soviet film industry tended "to overcapitalize on previous film successes" (2011, 48), which led to uneven development of various genres and reduced the genre diversity of Soviet cinema.[5] We think that conceptually the issue is not so much a lack of genre diversity, but rather the gravitation of various thematic invariants to one Platonic ideal—the socialist realist masterplot.

In the eyes of the film administration socialist realist narrative continued to provide the core syntactic structure well into the 1970s and early 1980s. We argue, however, that in the late 1960s, new genre formations took shape and replaced the socialist realist syntax. Altman suggests that genres arise in one of two fundamental ways: "either a relatively stable set of semantic givens is developed through syntactic experimentation into a coherent and durable syntax, or an already existing syntax adopts a new set of semantic elements" (Altman 1984, 12). In our hypothesis we follow for the most part Altman's second model of genre formation, that is, new semantic elements redefine the old genre and coalesce into the new discursive formations, with new syntactic models at

---

[5] Maria Belodubrovskaya "The jockey and the horse: Joseph Stalin and the biopic genre in Soviet cinema," *Studies in Russian and Soviet Cinema* 5.1 (2011): 29–53.

their core. We believe that this is how the new genres of prestige film, police procedural, and late-socialist comedy took shape. In the case of late-Soviet melodrama we believe a stable set of semantic elements developed through syntactic experimentation into a new generic syntax.

We also draw on Mikhail Iampolski's[6] idea about a special ontology of the visual image in Russian culture, which stems from the tradition of Byzantine icon painting. Iampolski claims that, from its very birth, cinema in Russia "was drastically aligned to a set of pre-modern imperatives" (2006, 73) originating in the Platonic conception of the image not as mimetic representation of reality, but as an expression of pre-existing ideas, an external flat sign that points to the invisible depth, the intrinsic higher meaning. The formation of socialist realist aesthetics, in his view, was a movement away from the 1920s avant-garde experimentation to a traditional pre-modern vision. Iampolski writes that *Chapaev* (1934), which was declared a model socialist realist film, was striking in its simplicity and transparency. Unable to express the reasons for its success, Soviet critics declared that "[t]he strength of *Chapaev* lies in the profound *vital truth* of the film" (cited in Taylor and Christie (1998, 358)).

We suggest that this relationship to the image accounts not only for the evasiveness of Soviet critical discourse but also for the audiences' sensibilities. More often than not, both interpretive communities privileged a discussion of ideas/ ideals over the film style, etc. In fact, the discussion of acting often transformed into commentary on the (im)moral nature of the character and his/her actions. Melodrama in particular appeared under euphemistic names: "psychological drama," "moral quest" (*moral'nye iskania*), "film-confession," "scenes from private life," etc.

Finally, in our approach to late-Soviet genres we draw on the model offered in Paulina Bren's study of Czechoslovak television culture during the period of "normalisation"—an official designation of the post-1968 era. Bren contends that in order to understand late-socialist culture one has to study what kind of narratives circulated and defined the world of everyman, rather than explain socialist society in terms of binaries, such as dissident/official, private/public, true/false. She also insists on the persistence of late-socialist narratives in present-day Czech society and on a certain blurriness of boundaries between socialist and post-socialist Czech cultures. We, likewise, argue for the continuity

---

[6] Here we follow the spelling of the scholar's last name as it is used in the source we are citing. In *Theorizing National Cinema*, editors spell the scholar's name as Iampolski.

between late-socialist and post-Soviet Russian society, which manifests itself above all in the continuity of cinematic and television genres that dominate Russian big and small screens today.

Why television?

We write about *both* film and television genres because in the 1970s, television became the most important medium of popular culture and created a significant competition for viewers within the film industry. We argue that out of four major genres of visual propaganda and entertainment that we cover in our book, three were reconceived by television texts: police procedural, comedy and melodrama. By "redefined" we mean that films for television release transformed the genres' syntax. Television not only became the major rival of the film industry, but also influenced films' aesthetics as well as the industry's approach to thinking about genres. First, the serialized form of television mini-series affected the way Soviet films were being released. For example, previously film administrators were averse to releasing popular films, such as comedies or detective films, in several parts, this privilege being reserved only for big budget, state-commissioned films on important ideological topics. In the 1970s, a confluence of circumstances, including the rise of television and the growing importance of commercial imperatives, resulted in an increased numbers of multi-partite popular films for release in the movie theaters. And this, in turn, led to an evolution of genre models, with the increase in numbers of films produced according to the same generic syntax. Second, the more formulaic nature of television productions[7] and the broader spectrum of possibilities of experimenting with films for television (nobody expected highly artistic texts from this "low" culture form[8]), resulted in the consolidation of semantic elements around new syntactic structures, such as the emergence of the police procedural as an independent screen genre, first on television and subsequently on the big screen. Not surprisingly, for example, in 1969 Soviet filmmakers and critics discussed the

---

[7] While scholars agree that television series of the 1960s–1980s are generally more formula-driven and static in character development than cinematic ones, their interpretations of what this means vary depending on the approach. For some, this means that TV is inferior to cinema and/or is more culturally conservative; for others, the lack of psychological cues and realistic mise-en-scène (e.g., in a sitcom) prevents viewer identification with the characters and makes cultural conflicts in the plot more visible. See, for example, Feuer (1992).

[8] On the conflicted status of television in the Soviet media system see Kristin Roth-Ey (2011) and Ellen Mickiewicz (1981).

so-called adventure genre, drawing examples from both cinema and television films and treating these films as equal players.

Finally, we discuss both film and television productions because in the choice of texts and in the decision to address both media in the 1970s we are driven in part by a presentist approach, i.e. we look at the genres that survived the fall of communism and define the genre landscape of today, of present-day Russian cinema and television. There is a strong sense of continuity not only for us as researchers but also for the contemporary media makers' community. For example, before Fedor Bondarchuk undertook the production of his big-budget war films, he completed his father's unfinished film epic, *And Quiet Flows the Don* (*Tikhii Don*), but released it on two media platforms: as a seven-episode television drama (2006), which was then formatted into a 180-minute film (2009) for international release. Before Mosfilm started providing services for new Putin-era historical epics, the studio carefully restored two late-Soviet prestige films, which laid the foundation for the prestige film genre: *War and Peace* (*Voina i mir*) by Sergei Bondarchuk and *Liberation* (*Osvobozhdenie*) by Iurii Ozerov. Thus, the genres we examine in our book—prestige film, police procedural, comedy, and melodrama—bridge the transition from cinema to television as the main mode of popular culture in the late-Soviet Union and lay the groundwork for cinema and television genres of post-Soviet Russia.

The difficult fate of genre studies in the USSR and Russia

In our discussion of film genres we take into consideration three major film communities that made a significant impact on the formation of genres in late-socialist cinema: (1) film and TV critics, (2) film administrators and other institutional voices, such as those of party officials or experts from the government who had a stake in the production of films and television series, and (3) the viewers who consumed them. We see Soviet critics and film journals as the cornerstone of debates about genre. This community was far from homogenous in its ideological and aesthetic approach to late-socialist cinema and television. Some represented the views of the Communist Party, others kept close ties with various agencies, such as the KGB or the Ministry of Internal Affairs, while yet others, such as members of the intelligentsia, opposed the current political course of the government. Film administrators, including censors, also consisted of a mix of party functionaries and critics with a diverse set of views and agendas.

By the 1960s, two film journals defined domestic discussions of Soviet cinema: *The Art of Cinema (Iskusstvo kino)* and *The Soviet Screen (Sovetskii ekran)*. *The Soviet Screen* targeted mass audiences and familiarized them with new domestic and foreign releases; between 1957 and 1991 it also conducted audience surveys and published the results in the categories "Film of the Year," "Actor/Actress of the Year," etc. *The Art of Cinema*, in turn, functioned as both a scholarly and a trade journal. Created in 1931, the journal was not published during the Second World War, but was revived after it and had a major overhaul in the late 1950s. For the first issue of 1957 a constructivist artist, Solomon Telingater, redesigned the journal's cover and layout. Most importantly, the modern look, evoking avant-garde journals of the 1920s, packaged the new ideas of the Soviet intelligentsia, writers and film critics, about post-Stalin Soviet cinema.

After Stalin's death, the journal was at the forefront of changes in the film industry, publishing discussions of "new cinema" and the "new contemporary film hero." However, one of the problems of Soviet film criticism was its inability to speak directly. Just like *Cahiers du cinema*, *The Art of Cinema* defined the field, but, unlike their French counterparts, Soviet critics more often than not resorted to Aesopian language. Thus, for example, the seminal article by writer Viktor Nekrasov in the 1959 issue of *The Art of Cinema* was titled "Lofty and Simple Words," which cautiously argues for a diversity of styles and scales of representation in Soviet films. Next to epic films familiar from Stalin-era cinema, Nekrasov writes, filmmakers have a right to make films focusing on smaller-scale issues. The model for the new filmmaker favoring understatement, focusing on the everyday life and non-heroic characters, is Marlen Khutsiev.[9]

In their rejection of Stalinist cinema, most Soviet critics looked for inspiration in literature, theater, and European modernist cinema, with its cult of the film author (*auteur*). The filmmaker-innovator was viewed as the opposite of both the director fulfilling a state commission and of the one producing formulaic socialist realist cinema. Hence *The Art of Cinema* critics of the 1950s and 60s were, for the most part, hostile to the study of film genres.

The interest in genre cinema came in the late 1960s and early 1970s, largely indirectly, through scholarly studies of Western popular cinema and Russian pre-revolutionary cinema. Maia Turovskaia's pioneering *Geroi bezgeroinogo*

---

[9] Nekrasov, Viktor. "Slova 'velikie' i prostye." *Iskusstvo kino* 5(1959): 45–61. The article triggered a discussion in the Soviet press. Many contemporary critics denounced Nekrasov as a proponent of small-scale representation in Soviet literature and cinema, incapable of understanding the value of epic forms. See a summary of the polemic: n.a. "O khudozhestvennykh printsipakh, vzgliadakh i vkusakh." *Iskusstvo kino* 10(1959): 41–46.

vremeni (*The Hero of Non-Heroic Times* 1971) discussed, for example, James Bond films as a genre of mass culture. Ianina Markulan wrote *Zarubezhnyi kinodetektiv. Opyt izucheniia odnogo iz zhanrov burzhuaznoi massovoi kul'tury* (*Crime Film. A Study of a Genre of Bourgeois Mass Culture* 1975). The leading Soviet film historian Neia Zorkaia perhaps illustrates best the shift in methodology from the 1960s auteurist approach (*Portrety/Portraits,* 1966) to the study of popular culture genres, specifically film melodrama, in pre-revolutionary Russian culture (*Na rubezhe stoletii: u istokov massovogo iskusstva v Rossii, 1900–1910 gg,* 1976). Notably, Zorkaia avoids discussing Soviet cinema within the context of her popular genre approach.

More orthodox critics, associated with the film administration establishment, addressed Soviet film genres as thematic variations of the socialist realist film. For example, Kira Paramonova, who for many years worked as one of the top managers of the Soviet film industry, wrote extensively on Soviet cinema for children as a subtype of socialist realist cinema.[10] Rostislav Iurenev examined the genre of Soviet film comedy in his 1964 monograph *Sovetskaia kinokomediia* (*Soviet Film Comedy*). Comedy, cinema for children, and adventure films were frequent topics of discussion on the pages of the leading Soviet film journals.

Melodrama, however, remained a problematic genre or at least a problematic term. In 1978 Markulan published a monograph about the genres of melodrama and horror in Western cinema, thus implying that these genres were not part of the "healthy" Soviet cinematic tradition. A book-length study of Soviet melodrama did not appear until the height of Gorbachev's perestroika.[11] In 1987, Nina Dymshits "discovered" the fact that for several decades the Soviet film industry had been producing melodramas under the guise of "tragedy," "psychological drama" or "films about our contemporaries." Dymshits's monograph appeared during the glasnost era next to the recently rediscovered novels by Boris Pasternak and Aleksandr Solzhenitsyn.

A fresh voice among the scarce discourses on genres is an article by film director Andrei Mikhalkov-Konchalovskii, which he published in *The Art of Cinema* in 1975.[12] In it he notes that attempts to create Soviet genre cinema are quite recent. Neither filmmakers nor audiences have a "culture of genres;" more often than not, both communities judge and define films using the criterion of "life-like" (151–152). In Konchalovskii's view, the case of comedy is telling. On

[10] Kira Paramonova. *V zritel'nom zale deti.* Moscow: Iskusstvo, 1967.
[11] A notable exception to this denial of the existence of melodrama in Soviet cinema is Irina Shilova's article "O melodrame" in *Voprosy kinoiskusstva,* vol. 17 (Moscow: Iskusstvo, 1976).
[12] "V poiske," *Iskusstvo kino* 9 (Sept 1975): 145–157.

the one hand, this is the only genre that is formally recognized in the Goskino thematic units, which encompass "contemporary theme, historical-revolutionary theme, cinema for children and comedy" (152). On the other hand, comedy is treated as an "inferior" genre; it is neither historical nor contemporary—because it is not serious. Comedies are not nominated for serious competitions and are not awarded prestigious prizes (153). In a surprising move—and anticipating his Hollywood career in the 1980s—Konchalovskii referred to the Hollywood film industry and its genres in positive terms, as a model for Soviet cinema's thinking about genres. Meanwhile, in talking about his own two pictures, *A Lovers' Romance* (*Romans o vliublennykh*) and *Siberiade* (*Sibiriada*), the director never calls them melodramas. Another exception that confirms the rule is Iurii Tsivian's book *Istoricheskaia retseptsiia kino v Rossii, 1895–1930*. Examining Russian film viewership, the monograph was published in 1991 in Riga, Latvia, and almost immediately part of it was translated into English.[13] It is not surprising that Tsivian's approach to cinema as a discourse constructed by various communities found a more welcoming home in Western scholarship.

Post-Soviet Russian studies usually define cinema and television of the 1970s as the "cinema of Stagnation" and rely on the same binaries: dissident or freedom-loving filmmakers vs filmmakers and film administrators following the official line. Two of the most notable publications during this period include a collection of articles titled *Posle ottepeli: kinematograf 1970-ykh* (*After the Thaw: Cinema of the 1970s*, 2009), edited by Andrei Shemiakin and Iu. Mikheeva, and Valerii Golovskoi's memoiristic monograph, *Mezhdu ottepel'iu i glasnost'iu* (*Between the Thaw and Glasnost*, 2004).

As is obvious from the titles, the dominant approach to late-socialist cinema has been political and ideological. Its nickname, "cinema of Stagnation," although problematized, is the default designation of the period. Its most typically invoked temporal frame, 1968–85, positions it between significant political events: the crushing of the Prague Spring and Mikhail Gorbachev's ascent to power. The years "after the Thaw" or "between the Thaw and Glasnost" emerge as at best a lost time, at worst as *davil'nia*, a period of destruction of artists and their creative output.[14]

The 2009 volume *Posle ottepeli* tries to take a neutral approach in evaluating the 1970s. While attempting to negotiate the dominant pessimistic picture of Stagnation cultural crackdown with the view of the 1970s as the "golden age" of

---

[13] *Early Cinema in Russia and its Cultural Reception*. New York/London: Routledge, 1994.
[14] As a term describing the atmosphere in the film industry of the period, *davil'nia* was introduced by Valerii Fomin in his book *Kino i vlast'* (1996).

Soviet cinema,[15] the volume still divides cinema into "high" and "mass" strata, claiming that *the site most seriously and deeply affected by 'stagnating' tendencies was not the upper layers of the cinematic process, but above all the bulk of the general repertoire*" (Kosinova 2009, 15, emphasis added). In his introduction to the volume, Andrei Shemiakin calls *auteur* (avtorskoe) cinema the key genre of the 1970s–1980s (2009, 6). It is not surprising, then, that this authoritative study avoids genre as either a taxonomic or epistemological phenomenon, with two telling exceptions that feature as separate chapters: literary adaptations and comedy. The former provides evidence of a ray of light in the otherwise gloomy picture, while the latter selects films that "address" the intelligentsia through irony.

Television criticism started focusing on genres of television film only in the 1970s, when television became an established form of mass media. In the 1960s, pioneers of television criticism, such as Vladimir Sappak,[16] and other Soviet critics of the late 1950s–mid-1960s approached television as a new art form, with an enormous aesthetic and social potential. Discussions of television during that time centered on a search for a specifically televisual language, as analogue to "literariness" and "cinematographicity." Such a unique characteristic was found in television's ability to produce a "reality effect." In the round-table discussion organized by the journal *Art of Cinema* in 1965, TV producers and critics mention such features of television broadcasting as improvisation and spontaneity (56), as well as its participatory, active nature (58), and formal eclecticism (61).[17]

The end of the Thaw's attempts for liberalization of cultural life also brought to an end debates on the advantages of live versus recorded and fictional versus documentary, television. By the late 1960s-early 1970s, many genres of live television broadcast had disappeared. With the virtual disappearance of live broadcasts, the quest for an authentic tele-language lost its object of study. Notably, Soviet critics also started treating television as a low cultural form. Until the late 1960s, *The Art of Cinema* maintained a permanent rubric for the discussion of television theory and practice. By the 1970s, this rubric had disappeared, to re-emerge in the 1990s.[18]

At the same time, the growing number of television mini-series and their popularity with audiences opened up a new area of critical inquiry. The 1970s were

---

[15] The main proponent of a more nuanced look at the 1970s was Neia Zorkaia (*Istoriia sovetskogo kino*, 2006). See Kosinova (2009): 10–11.
[16] *Television and We* (*Televidenie i my*), Moscow: Iskusstvo, 1961.
[17] "Za kruglym stolom – televizionisty." *Iskusstvo kino* 3 (1965): 53–67.
[18] See Kristin Roth-Ey (2011) on the conflicted status of television in Soviet culture.

marked by a surge of interest in specific TV forms and genres. In 1975 the journal *Soviet Screen* organized a discussion of mini-series or "multi-episodic productions"—an umbrella term for any fictional television show that exceeded two episodes by leading film and television critics. The critics agreed that such productions were the most "organic" form for television, privileging stable and predictable formats. In attempting to explain the success of mini-series with audiences, critics traced the form's cultural lineage back to literature and film. Some concluded that mini-series revitalized epic forms of narratives; hence, the success of literary adaptations on TV (Vartanov 1975).[19] Others drew a parallel between TV series and serialized popular literature of the turn-of-the century (Zorkaia 1975).[20] Zorkaia also discussed some of the formal features of TV mini-series: length, discreteness, a permanent cast of characters, and a predictable structure.

In several respects this discussion was quite revolutionary. First, even though literary models continued to serve as the major point of reference for TV productions, the purpose of such a comparison was to establish structural parallels between verbal and visual narratives rather than to pass the familiar judgment that television was a "low art" or simply non-art. Second, several of the critics (for example, Viktor Demin) focused on issues of the audience, in particular the integration of serial television broadcasts into viewers' daily routine, creating an effect of "parallel existence."[21]

A collection of articles, *Bol'shie problemy malogo ekrana* (*Big Problems of the Small Screen*, 1981), addressed issues of television aesthetics and programming, and specific problems of TV genres and forms. Andrei Plakhov discussed made-for-TV films that dealt with contemporary "production" issues. He positioned such films midway between documentary reportages and "openly conventional forms" of the TV spectacle (1981, 76). Contemporary television films, according to Plakhov, suffered from predictable and banal scripts that recycled the schema of the Soviet production novel. The importance of Plakhhov's argument lies in the link he established between socialist realist novels[22] and a new "epic" form of serialized productions. In TV series, Plakhov argues, this schema was artificially

---

[19] Vartanov, Anri. "Otmenno dlinnyi, dlinnyi, dlinnyi fil'm," *Sovetskii ekran* 6 (1975): 14.
[20] Zorkaia, Neia. "Otmenno dlinnyi, dlinnyi, dlinnyi fil'm *Sovetskii ekran* 1 (1975): 18.
[21] Demin, Viktor. "Otmenno dlinnyi, dlinnyi, dlinnyi fil'm." *Sovetskii ekran* 16 (1975): 7.
[22] The "production novel" was a model genre of socialist realist literature. It typically centered on a factory collective fulfilling production plans and overcoming various problems. In the process, the protagonist matured into a conscious member of the collective; hence, the genre effectively linked economic production goals with the production of Soviet consciousness. For a detailed discussion of the production novel, see Clark, *Soviet Novel: History as Ritual*, Bloomington: Indiana UP, 2000. 69–77. Also see Mary A. Nicholas, *Writers at Work: Russian Production Novels and the Construction of Soviet Culture*. Bucknell UP, 2010.

lengthened to accommodate topical themes without integrating them into the plot. The lower prestige and the lower pay for TV scripts in comparison to both film scripts and literary texts led to uniform products to fill broadcast slots.

Another community that made a major impact on the formation of late-Soviet film and television genres are different institutions of the state apparatus, above all Goskino, led by Filipp Ermash, and Gosteleradio, led by Sergei Lapin. The major sources for the analysis of this community's role for us are Russian archives and studies such as Valerii Fomin's *Kino i vlast'* (*Cinema and Power* 1996). Fomin notes that film administration played a major role not only in defining the type of a particular film but also in providing a discourse to talk about it (1996, 63). In the case of big-budget epics, which we call prestige productions, the official review established the limits of the permissible. In the case of war films, the army and KGB consultants changed films' scripts and controlled their style, in order to represent better the institution's role in the events depicted in the film. An internal studio review process was designed to rescue whatever could be salvaged. The role of official rhetoric on this level was very different. Studio officials tried to protect projects from unnecessary changes by "at least a hint at socialist realism, even a fake connection to the officially approved themes" (Fomin 1996, 63). Such often insignificant elements would then be pulled out and paraded as being the gist of the film.

The police, the KGB, and the army all had a stake and a say in cinematic matters, and not only about the representation of their respective departments. For example, letters from Army General N. Liashchenko (who at the time was Commander-in-Chief of the Central Asian army district) to the Minister of Culture, Petr Demichev, and then Central Committee Secretary Mikhail Zimianin contained devastating criticism of El'dar Riazanov's comedy *Irony of Fate* (*Ironiia sud'by* 1976), which outraged the general by its purported immorality: "[under the guise] of harmless and typical acts [this film] represents a philistine lifestyle, promotes drunkenness, rudeness, profiteering, and debauchery".[23] In response to such letters, the filmmaker and the studio usually had to make changes in films or somehow to explain their behavior and protect their production.

If Soviet filmmakers from time to time had an opportunity to negotiate and bargain with industry administrators, Soviet television, along with radio and press, was viewed as a form of Mass Media and Propaganda (SMIP) and was under the stricter ideological control of the Communist Party. As a result of the

---

[23] Fomin 1996, 106.

restructuring of the Soviet broadcast industry under Sergei Lapin, who directed Gosteleradio from 1970 until 1985, television adopted broadcast policies that were to define its content and form for the next decade. Among the basic principles of these policies were isolationism (jamming TV signals from abroad); central planning (including compulsory broadcasts of the news program Time [Vremia] on all channels); a drastic reduction of live television broadcasts; privileging interpretation over information; a reduction of television journalism to the "creative" retelling of pre-approved stories; and reliance on an "iron script" that facilitated censorship (Boretskii 1998 16–17).

While the ambitions of the film administration to determine the nature of Soviet visual culture were quite insatiable, the outcomes were often ambiguous. This is especially true of late-Soviet culture, which for all its conservatism also provided viewers with choices (Soviet and foreign films, television) while ticket sales also became a major revenue item in the state budget. More often than not, ideological orthodoxy, mass appeal, and artistic qualities proved to be poor bedfellows. An admirer of Hollywood, Ermash encouraged production of commercial cinema, yet, as George Faraday notes, "[f]or the officials in charge of production decisions, achieving box-office success took second place to fulfilling the quantitative target for the production of films on particular subjects established by the Ministry of Culture in consultation with Goskino (the *templan*)" (57).

Finally in our study we examine the role of film audiences in genre formation. This community is the least studied and information about it is scarce. In 2009, Sudha Rajagopalan published a pioneering monograph about the reception of Indian films in the post-Stalinist Soviet Union. We rely on her methodology in our work. We also use *Soviet Screen*'s surveys conducted in the 1970s of viewers' opinions to determine the most popular film of the year and excerpts from viewers' letters published in the journal, as well as Sergei Kudriavtsev's data about ticket sales for Soviet and foreign films distributed in the Soviet Union.[24] In addition, we use oral history interviews collected in Russia in the 2010s about Soviet-era movie-going experiences and genre preferences.

Rajagopalan argues that late-socialist culture allowed for modest manifestations of consumerist desires. Cinema going was one of the forms of what she calls austere consumerism (2009, 5). The film industry became one of the first areas of the socialist economy where the administration started

[24] See http://kinanet.livejournal.com/689229.html

experimenting with market-oriented forms of production and distribution. The appearance of television as a major competition pressured the film industry to pay greater attention to its audiences in order to keep them going back to the screening rooms. In the late 1960s and 1970s, argues Joshua First, we can also observe the resurgence of sociological studies of audience tastes, which acknowledged that the moviegoer is not the homogeneous spectator but a consumer whose tastes vary and must be taken into account if one wants her or him to continue watching Soviet films (2008a, 321). In the 1970s, Goskino became one of the major customers who ordered such studies from sociologists.

In our discussion of audience response to film and television genres we use data provided in Ellen Mickiewicz's *Media and the Russian Public* (1981) and the most recent study of Soviet television by Kristin Roth-Ey (2011). We also draw on viewers' letters and discussions published in *The Soviet Screen*, *The Art of Cinema*, and *Television and Radio Broadcasting*. Gosteleradio archives also provide overviews of letters from viewers (*obzor pisem*) for internal industry use.

Overview of chapters: from socialist realism to film genres

Chapter 1 examines the prestige film, a genre that emerged in Soviet cinema in the mid-1960s. It evolved from the semantic elements of historico-biographical, historico-revolutionary, and fictional-documentary film. The first two took shape in the 1930s and initially described the story of origins of the Soviet Union. The historico-revolutionary film paid special attention to Stalin as the heir of Lenin and the present-day leader of world revolution. The fictional-documentary is a film that combines the depiction of fictional characters against the background of truthfully depicted epic historical events.[25] All these subtypes of the socialist realist film followed the same syntax and explained how the Soviet state came into being. They legitimated and sacralized political and military leaders, above all consolidating the cult of Stalin. Monumentalism, especially in the late Stalinist films, became one of the distinctive features of these historical epics.

The prestige film of the late-socialist era at times looks similar to the Stalin-era epic, but the new genre fulfilled a different and more complicated set of functions

[25] For a more detailed discussion of these three types of films see Belodubrovskaya (2011).

determined by the changes in Soviet society and international relations. By the 1960s Soviet society had become more open. Since the Cold War was not only an ideological conflict, but also a technological competition, a rivalry of cultures and lifestyles, an indispensable part of it was about who would attract more viewers to movie theaters. In this context the prestige film had to deliver an ideological message internationally, showcase the sophistication of the Soviet film industry, function as an art object, and provide a spectacle that could entertain the global viewer. The socialist realist masterplot could hardly provide a syntactic structure to fulfill so many new ideological objectives.

We maintain that by the 1960s, out of the semantic elements of Stalinist epics emerged the new generic syntax of the Soviet prestige film. The main syntactic feature of prestige productions was still a focus on the statist message, at the expense of the individual. At the center of these pictures is a Russian male protagonist serving the state. However, in order to appeal to an average moviegoer, the prestige film complicates the plot with elements of melodrama and epic spectacle. These serve the function of commercial appeal, rather than any narrow ideological goal, such as legitimating the cult of the dictator. To increase the authority of the film as an art object and to ensure name recognition, the director of the prestige film often used the devices of international art cinema and employed the plot and title of a classical Russian novel. Our case studies focus primarily on two prestige films of the late-socialist era: Sergei Bondarchuk's *War and Peace* (1965–67) and Iurii Ozerov's *Liberation* (1968–72).

In Chapter 2 we discuss the police procedural, which emerged from Soviet adventure film. The semantic elements that influenced the formation of the late-socialist police procedural as an independent genre were a contemporary setting that treated problems of modern society (such as consumerism and economic crime) and the representation of police as a professional organization of experts. The Ministry of Internal Affairs (known in the USSR by its Russian acronym MVD), the security ministry in charge of law enforcement in the Soviet Union, directly sponsored the genre.

Brezhnev's predecessor, Nikita Khrushchev, believed in the speedy arrival of communism to the USSR and the demise of the state as an institution of legalized violence against citizens. In the early 1960s, in anticipation of the USSR's gradual transition to communism, he abolished the Ministry of Internal Affairs of the USSR. Under communism volunteer citizens would enforce the law themselves, rendering police force unnecessary. Communism never arrived, but under Khrushchev crime and the black market economy flourished. When

Brezhnev removed Khrushchev, he restored the Ministry of Internal Affairs, and appointed his personal friend Nikolai Shchelokov as the MVD chief. The minister received unlimited resources to build a security ministry that could flush out and contain economic crime, which included private entrepreneurship illegal under socialist laws and which served as a counterpoint to the all-powerful political police, the KGB. Shchelokov turned out to be a savvy public relations man who masterfully used the television and film industries to improve the public image of the *militsiia*—the Soviet police force.

The police procedural positioned the police as the institution defining the public sphere and mediating the relationship between the state and its citizens. If the prestige genre could be termed a "state genre," the police procedural was an "institutional genre." At its core was an interrogation scene that inherited the re-education agenda of socialist realism and which conveyed a message of trust towards the police on the part of citizens. The formation of the police procedural, especially as a serialized television genre with a professional police team at the center, fulfilled two functions. On the one hand, the genre provided a mediated structure for disciplinary control (which replaced the unmediated mass terror of the Stalin-era secret police), on the other hand, it greatly expanded its reach, policing not only citizens' public behavior, but also their consumption and morality.[26] In our close readings we focus on two television police procedurals: *The Investigation is Conducted by Experts* (*Sledstvie vedut znatoki*, Viacheslav Brovkin and others 1971–89; 2002–03) and *The Meeting Place Cannot Be Changed* (*Mesto vstrechi izmenit' nel'zia*, Stanislav Govorukhin 1979).

Chapter 3 analyzes late-socialist comedy. Unlike the other three genres, we examine film comedy as an independent genre designation in the Soviet Union dating back to the 1920s. But its dominant 1930s iteration—Stalin-era musical comedy—in many ways defined the syntax of socialist realism. In this respect comedy, in our view, is just another sub-type of socialist realist film, following the same generic syntax. Grigorii Aleksandrov and Ivan Pyr'ev, the two most famous directors of Soviet musical comedy, successfully replicated the model in many films: it entailed the community-validated romance along with the protagonists' maturation into conscious communists, set in the utopian "future-in-the-present"[27]

---

[26] For more on the late-Soviet and post-Soviet police procedural's narrative power to "explain" society to itself, see Chapter 2 and Conclusion.

[27] For a discussion of Soviet utopian temporality or "modal schizophrenia," see Clark 2000, 37.

and accompanied by joyous songs. This "life-affirming comedy"[28] provided the syntax for the genre for several decades.

In the 1950s–1960s, the introduction of contemporary life onto the screen (even if in an idealized version), on the one hand, and parodic and stylized elements, on the other, started to change Soviet comedy. Late-Soviet comedy was a paradoxical phenomenon. While it was a predominantly romantic comedy (with the exception of Leonid Gaidai's slapstick films)—hence a more conservative subgenre, validating the status quo—its syntax bore so little relation to classical Soviet comedy as to usher in a new genre. Its inspiration came from Hollywood, specifically the classical screwball comedy of the 1930s. Its new semantic elements were the reification of private life (in fact, an almost complete withdrawal from the public sphere) and the supremacy of ironic discourse. In the new Soviet comedic syntax, the heterosexual romance usually involved a strong female and a weak/conformist male, who both belong to the Soviet professional/middle class and find comfort in the pleasures of the "good"/private life. Though often set in the present, late-Soviet comedies avoid commenting on the public sphere except in songs or ironic double entendres. And it is precisely romantic comedy that dominates post-Soviet film and television. For specific examples we focus on the work of two directors, El'dar Riazanov and Mark Zakharov, with a close reading of their most famous films, *Irony of Fate* (1975) and *Ordinary Miracle* (*Obyknovennoe chudo* 1978), respectively.

Chapter 4 examines melodrama, which we consider the most important genre of late socialism, and at furthest remove from socialist realist syntax. An "invisible" genre in Soviet cinema, melodrama was also the most radical in the late-socialist period, both in re-defining the boundaries and relations between private and public spheres, and in articulating individual agency. The rise of the urban middle class, the centrality of the nuclear family, and the changing role of women comprise the semantic elements of melodrama.

Unlike comedy, which retreated into private life and treated conformism with an ironic smile, melodrama's syntactic core is the suffering protagonist, the crisis of human emotions, and failed social connections at the intersection of private and public spheres. Late-socialist melodrama sets its pathos-driven situations in the context of the nuclear family's disintegration under the pressures of socialist modernity. As opposed to the melodrama of the 1960s, which tried to reconcile the utopian drive of socialist realist cinema with the crisis-driven plot of

[28] Kovalov 2004, 596.

melodrama, the 1970s variant of the genre constructed the scene of individual crisis and solicited an empathetic response from the viewer by portraying the disturbing results of failed utopian dreams and the resulting social apathy. Finally, many melodramas of the 1970s moved beyond Soviet identity tropes, either articulating a Russian identity or documenting a gap in its place. In this respect melodrama is essential not only for the construction of late-Soviet femininities and masculinities, but also for their post-Soviet Russian descendants. In our close analysis we focus on three major visual texts: Gleb Panfilov's *I Want the Floor* (*Proshu slova*, 1976), Andrei Konchalovskii's *A Lovers' Romance* (*Romans o vliublennykh* 1974), and a television mini-series *Shadows Disappear at Noon* (*Teni ischezaiut v polden'* 1971) by Vladimir Krasnopol'skii and Valerii Uskov.

Our major reason for choosing these four genres is their continuing relevance, as both narrative and ideological models, to contemporary Russian television and cinema. In short, we address those film and television genres that took shape in the USSR in the 1970s and that remain relevant for Russian cinema and television today.

1

Prestige Productions: Epic Film as a Tool of Hard and Soft Power during the Cold War

It seems that only among our people exists the proverb: "Company in distress makes troubles less (literally "When it's collective, even death is beautiful-" EP and AP). How so? Death is horror. Not really. What is "collective"? It means death for one of your own, for thy folk or, in modern language, for your Fatherland. This is the source of our patriotism. From here comes the mass patriotism in times of military conflicts and wars, even self-sacrifice in peaceful times. From here [derives] our sense of camaraderie, our family values.
Vladimir Putin. Television dialogue with the nation. 17 April 2014[1]

Syntax and semantics of the genre

This chapter traces the production and distribution history of the late-Soviet state's most privileged genre: prestige films. These films occupied a special place in the Soviet film industry: they were under the direct patronage of the Soviet state and were designed to legitimate its charismatic power. Dealing with ideologically and politically important themes, they showcased the Soviet film industry at international film festivals and enjoyed preferential financing conditions. There were two major types of such productions: epic war films (*Liberation, Soldiers of Freedom, The Most Important Assignment, Front without Flanks, Front beyond the Frontline, Front beyond the Enemy Lines, Victory*) and big-budget historical epics and adaptations of literary classics (*War and Peace, Waterloo, Red Bells, The Steppe, Boris Godunov*).[2] We claim that these films

---

[1] Vladimir Putin "Dlia russkikh na miru i smert' krasna." See www.regnum.ru/news/polit/1792501.html#ixzz3G4IRkCrl. Accessed April 20, 2014.
[2] *Osvobozhdenie* (1968–72), *Soldaty svobody* (1977), *Osobo vazhnoe zadanie* (1980), *Front bez flangov* (1975), *Front za liniei fronta* (1977), *Front v tylu vraga* (1981), *Pobeda* (1984), *Voina i mir* (1965–67), *Vaterloo* (1970), *Krasnye kolokola* (1982), *Step'* (1977), *Boris Godunov* (1986).

constitute a distinct genre of late-Soviet cinema because they share a number of syntactic features, as well as the state's direct participation at every stage of their production, release, distribution, marketing, and critical responses. In fact, the state is the ultimate author of these pictures. While their epic style and high budget resemble those of many commercial blockbusters, the main *raison d'être* of their production was to serve as public relations vehicles for the state and its agendas.

Stalinist cinema favored big-budget epic productions that sacralized state power and, by the 1940s, just Stalin; it did not concern itself with recovering costs or making a profit. Among the most notorious examples of such pictures is Mikhail Chiaureli's epic film *Fall of Berlin* (*Padenie Berlina* 1949), about Stalin's winning the Great Patriotic War[3] and defeating not only Hitler but also the scheming Allies. The film's portrayal of Stalin as a demigod and the film's grand style provided the representational model for Brezhnev-era cinematic epics.

After Stalin's death, *Fall of Berlin* and similar films were denounced for their promotion of the cult of personality and lack of authenticity. In the 1950s and early 1960s, many Soviet filmmakers were influenced by European neorealist aesthetics. The opening of the country to the global economy and film culture stimulated a dialogue and a competition with Western cinema, especially with Hollywood. As media historian Kristin Roth-Ey points out, the Soviet cultural model positioned itself as global by definition—"a safe house for the world's best" (2011, 4). One outcome of the policy of peaceful co-existence and cultural exchange with the West introduced in the mid-1950s was that Soviet culture after Stalin found itself in *open* competition on its own terrain (2011, 9).

In his discussion of the epic film as a genre Robert Burgoyne contends that the "tension between the evolving global context of film production and reception and the particular provenance of the epic as an expression of national mythology and aspirations creates what Bakhtin calls a double voice" (2011, 2). In other words, Burgoyne argues that the epic film often aspires to use national narratives "for the collectivities that are not framed by nation" (2011, 6). In our discussion of the prestige epic film we draw on cultural historian Nancy Condee's

---

[3] The term Great Patriotic War refers to the war that Soviets fought against Nazi Germany between June 22, 1941 and May 9, 1945. In the USSR and post-Soviet Russia, this term has been preferred to the term Second World War. One key distinction is the fact that the Great Patriotic War does not cover the period of the Second World War in Europe between September 1, 1939 and June 22, 1941 when the USSR was a de facto ally of Nazi Germany and alongside the Third Reich participated in the partition of several Eastern European nations, above all, Poland. In this book we use primarily the term the Great Patriotic War because this is how Soviet cultural producers and audiences of the era referred to the war.

claim that Soviet cinema differs from European national cinemas in its lack of a strong national tradition (2009, 18–19). Instead, by the Stalin era, Soviet cinema became an art form of supranational imperial collectivity, with ethnic Russian male protagonists appearing in Soviet epics as the vanguard of the new supranational community.

The gradual opening of Soviet society after Stalin's death changed the ideological priorities and gave rise to the genre of the prestige production. This type of film was still in the business of sacralizing power and mythologizing Soviet history, but it also had to be commercially successful, ideally both at home and in international distribution, as part of the Cold War rivalry with the West. As scholars Tony Shaw and Denise Youngblood argue, this rivalry between the two superpowers was mostly about the USSR's catching up with the US advances in technology and adapting Western-style generic models to Soviet ideology. The Soviet film industry "had to prove their system worked, and then to persuade others to follow it" (2010, 218). Soviet cultural producers, in other words, developed prestige productions in response to Hollywood blockbusters.[4]

In the 1950s-early 1960s Soviet cinema participated in international film culture by successfully adapting the neorealist and New Wave aesthetics to native themes—most importantly the Great Patriotic War—and scoring a number of awards at the top international festivals.[5] The Brezhnev-era political leadership and cultural administrators, however, shared a more conservative but ambitious agenda: to produce big-budget epic films. Amidst the sagging Soviet economy, rising consumerism, and the alienation of the populace, especially youth, from ideological rhetoric, the shared victory in the Great Patriotic War remained the only legitimate foundation of Soviet identity. Accordingly, the Soviet state had a vested interest in producing films that mythologized the Great Patriotic War through epic style and a state-centered message. Such films re-evaluated not only the "cult of personality" and Stalin's role in Soviet history, but also cinematic developments of the Thaw.

---

[4] Shaw and Youngblood argue that the Hollywood and Soviet film industry parted ways in the 1970s, when the Soviets turned to patriotic epics. We see the Soviet epics as a reaction to Hollywood big production films of the 1950s and 1960s. Indeed, archival materials confirm that many Soviet epics were produced in response to those of Hollywood. For the most recent discussion see also Stephen Norris "Tolstoy's Comrades: Sergei Bondarchuk's *War and Peace* (1966–1967) and the Origins of Brezhnev Culture." in Lorna Fitzsimmons and Michael A. Denner, eds, *Tolstoy on Screen* (Evanston, Illinois: Northwestern University Press, 2015), 155–178.

[5] Among the films that received top festival awards during the Thaw are *Cranes Are Flying* (*Letiat zhuravli*, 1957), *Ballad of a Soldier* (*Ballada o soldate*, 1959), *Ivan's Childhood* (*Ivanovo detstvo*, 1962).

Between 1966 and the early 1970s, the Main Scripts and Editing Commission (*Glavnaia stsenarno-redaktsionnaia kollegiia*) of Goskino rejected a number of film scripts dealing with the war, even those endorsed by the studios and official reviewers. The scripts' purported "flaws" varied: "abstract humanism and pacifism;" pessimistic and overly naturalistic treatment of the last, "victorious" years of the Great Patriotic War; and excessive focus on individuals at the expense of the panoramic, heroic picture of the war.[6] The writing on the wall was clear: Thaw liberal politics was out, together with stories of individuals and their physical and moral suffering and dilemmas.

The main syntactic feature of prestige productions was the revival of the Stalin-era focus on the statist message and collectivist agenda, at the expense of the individual. At the center of these pictures is a Russian male serving the state. The Army provides the major institution where the protagonist can find his community and become an honorable and patriotic citizen under the guidance of a patriotic mentor. The story of Russia's imperial expansion told as a tale of the liberation of smaller nations from the power of other, oppressive empires provides the plot of most patriotic epics of the Brezhnev era.

In short, the narrative of prestige productions adhered rather closely to the socialist realist master plot. However, in their bid for spectacle, these works borrowed devices and entire scenes from diverse, often incompatible, sources. Starting with *War and Peace*, devices of art cinema become important for these epics' display of the Soviet film industry's sophistication and for international marketing. However, their major inspiration was totalitarian cinema. Evocations of Stalinist epics and Leni Riefenstahl's *Triumph of the Will* (1935) are ever-present reference points in films as seemingly different as *War and Peace* and *Liberation*. The breathtaking aerial shots of diminutive human subjects, observed from above, re-stage the spirit of the imperial sublime for new audiences.

Whether adaptations of literary classics or war epics, these films were massive productions: *War and Peace* (4 parts, 403 minutes), *Red Bells* (2 parts, 274 minutes), *Liberation* (5 parts, 445 minutes), *Blockade* (*Blokada*, 4 parts, 337 min), *Soldiers of Freedom* (4 parts, 390 minutes); also a trilogy about

---

[6] For example, Efraim Sevela and Grigorii Chukhrai's 1966 script *People!* told the story a Soviet and a Finnish pilot who, after being downed, are forced to fight together for survival. After three years of recommendations and revisions, the script was rejected. Aleksandr Rodozhkin used the story in his 2002 film *The Cuckoo* (*Kukushka*). In the1970s, Fridrikh Gorenshtein's and Iurii Klepikov's script *The Trial* about an orphaned boy's wanderings through a town received a categorical rejection, especially from Sergei Iutkevich, who criticized the script for being written in the style of "naturalistic descriptiveness" (Fomin 2009, 327–435).

Figure 1.1: Street advertisement for Iurii Ozerov's *Liberation* in East Berlin (1972)
Source: Creative Commons Attribution 3.0(CC BY-SA 3.0 DE), image from the site Wikimedia Commons, the free media repository, https://commons.wikimedia.org

Soviet partisans and military intelligence *Front without Flanks, Front across Front Lines* and *Front behind Enemy Lines* (1975–1981, 6 parts, 472 min), etc. Most of these films were co-productions, often involving the Eastern Bloc countries, which ensured additional resources, facilitated the films' international distribution, and provided filmmakers (and their official "curators" from the Party, the Army, and the KGB) with a chance to travel abroad (see Figure 1.1). These films were directly commissioned by the state and received preferential treatment in terms of financing, material support (e.g., use of historical artifacts from museums), unlimited extras for battle scenes, and marketing and distribution in the USSR and abroad.[7]

---

[7] In order to improve movie theaters' attendance, from 1981 the Soviet film industry practiced All-Union premiers of ideologically important big-budget films. These massive simultaneous releases in all major movie theaters in the Soviet Union ensured higher ticket sales for state-sponsored films, such as *The Most Important Assignment, A European Story* (*Evropeiskaia istoriia* 1984), and *Victory*. The practice of All-Union release was revived in post-Soviet times by Nikita Mikhalkov. The first post-Soviet film to be released this way was the patriotic epic *Barber of Siberia* (*Sibirskii tsiriul'nik* 1999).

The choice of theme for these prestige productions was as much a matter of state interest as of competition with Hollywood. In fact, many Soviet films responded directly to specific American titles. Since the vast majority of Hollywood films mentioned in internal memos were never screened in the Soviet Union and were not present in public discourse, one has to conclude that the state assigned certain people to monitor new American releases, especially those which "infringed" on contested terrains: Russian literary classics, the official Soviet story of the Great Patriotic War, and space exploration. For example, the internal reviews for the film *The Taming of Fire* (*Ukroshchenie ognia*, 1972) about Sergei Korolev, the official founder of the Soviet space and missile program, repeatedly emphasized the urgency of the project because "Americans (Kubrick) have already created their space epic, steeped in historical pessimism" (10).[8] These strategic projects could always count on generous funding, superior filming technology (widescreen, stereophonic sound), and any other resources that the state-controlled economy could provide: army and navy units, special rocket launches, access to hard currency, etc.

The production of these epics was a very lengthy process, not only because of their scale but also because such close state supervision meant extreme control and often conflicting interests of various agencies. Scripts underwent a long process of reviewing and rewriting to eliminate any ideological ambiguity and to ensure that each major institution – the Central Committee of the Communist Party, the KGB, the Army, the Navy—received their own epic tribute. Highly positioned representatives of these agencies served as consultants on prestige productions and often directly influenced scriptwriting. For example, General Semen Tsvigun, Deputy Chairman of the KGB and Leonid Brezhnev's friend, served as consultant on three productions: *Front without Flanks* (also the scriptwriter),[9] *The Taming of Fire*, and the TV series *Seventeen Moments of Spring* (*Semnadtsat' mgnovenii vesny* 1973).

Finally, prestige productions were dual-use texts. While their primary purpose was to represent the state agenda on the big screen, after their release they found

[8] "Ukroshchenie ognia," RGALI, fond 2944, op. 4, ed. khran. 2202. Reference to Stanley Kubrick's *2001: A Space Odyssey*, released in 1968. The film was not screened in the USSR, but just like American and British Second World War films mentioned later (also never released in the Soviet Union), it prompted the Soviet film industry to respond with its own epics on these strategic Cold War themes.

[9] *Front without Flanks* was also based on the novel written by Tsvigun himself. Using the pseudonym S.K. Mishin, Tsvigun also appeared in the credits for the television series *Seventeen Moments of Spring* (dir. Tat'iana Lioznova 1973). The series chronicled the adventures of a Soviet super-spy Maksim Isaev, who has infiltrated the Nazi military and intelligence establishment as Standartenführer Otto von Stierlitz.

a permanent home on Soviet television, where they were ritualistically screened around official holidays: Victory Day and May Day. Soviet television also revived neo-Stalinist aesthetics in its own biographical mini-series which presented hagiographic portraits of key political figures of Soviet leadership and the Marxist canon. Perhaps the most interesting of those was the seven-episode series *Karl Marx. The Younger Years* (*Karl Marks. Molodye gody*). This Soviet-GDR co-production, which premiered on television in 1980, tried to appeal to viewers via a melodramatic plot, focused on Marx's family and personal relationships—a creative approach that caused resentment on the part of the more orthodox East German Marxists.

In this chapter we focus on two major late-socialist prestige productions: Sergei Bondarchuk's *War and Peace* (1965–1967) and Iurii Ozerov's *Liberation* (1969–1971). Bondarchuk developed a pseudo-art cinema aesthetic, combining Soviet ideological syntax with interpolations of modernist cinematic devices. The material was allegedly non-political, and thus could be marketed to Western audiences as Russian art cinema. Ozerov specialized in epic films about the Great Patriotic War, co-authoring with various state agencies a dozen pictures that shaped memory of the war for several generations of viewers. *Liberation* provided late- and post-Soviet audiences with a spectacular illusion of historical authenticity for the heroic myth of the past.

War and Peace: art cinema on state service

As part of the policy of relaxing tension between the two countries, in 1958 the USSR signed an agreement on cultural exchange with the US, which included the exchange of films between the two countries.[10] On the eve of signing the agreement, the Soviet government purchased a US-Italian adaptation of Leo Tolstoy's *War and Peace* (dir. King Vidor and Mario Soldati 1956). The film captured the imagination of both viewers and film administrators because it not only sold a lot of tickets but also was viewed as the Cold War foe's invasion into "our" cultural canon. The Soviet government decided to respond to the challenge with a bigger and better *War and Peace*. The result was an eight-hour long, four-part monumental project.

Three interpretive communities emerged as competing for the meaning and structure of the Soviet version of *War and Peace*: (1) the state, (2) the filmmaking

[10] "Protokol sovetsko-amerikanskikh peregovorov," 33–34.

community, and (3) the viewers. Viewers became vicariously involved in the debate about the shape of this prestige production by buying an impressive number of tickets for the American production.[11] If Soviets wanted to have similar ticket sales domestically, it made sense for them to adhere to the contours of the Hollywood melodramatic narrative that sold so well in the late 1950s.

Hollywood blockbuster style was not the only model for the Soviet production. After Stalin's death, Soviet filmmakers were exposed to Italian neorealism and later to the French New Wave and developed their own style of modernist filmmaking. Films by Mikhail Kalatozov, Grigorii Chukhrai, and Andrei Tarkovskii competed successfully on the international film festival circuit. Art cinema devices became part of the Soviet cinematic aesthetic. Appropriated successfully by the state, this new cinematic language allowed Soviet cultural administrators to promote Soviet films on the international market. It was no coincidence that this was the moment when Soviet co-productions appeared.

Two filmmakers competed for the right to make the Soviet *War and Peace*: a producer of Stalinist musicals, Ivan Pyryev, and a younger generation actor and filmmaker, Sergei Bondarchuk, who previously had made only one film, *Fate of a Man* (*Sud'ba cheloveka* 1958), a neorealist tale of a Russian POW during the Great Patriotic War. The film was not only distributed abroad but also received the Grand Prix at the first Moscow International Film Festival. It is very telling that Soviet film administrators voted for Bondarchuk, who could interpret *War and Peace* for international audiences and art critics in a more accessible and less dogmatic way.

As it was such an ambitious project and a matter of national pride for the Soviet film industry, the state played an unprecedented role in the film's financing, production, and promotion. The Council of Ministers of the USSR decided when production would begin, and, anticipating huge expenses, the Central Committee closely supervised the project. Moreover, the Ministry of Culture and its head, Ekaterina Furtseva, helped the director every step of the way. The film received *goszakaz* status, "a state-ordered picture that guaranteed good distribution and a lot of prestige" (Youngblood 2014, 11–19, Roth-Ey 2011, 52). In fact, the *War and Peace* production was planned as a strategic military operation. First, like the latter, it was top secret. The screenplay carried the seal "restricted for official use," as though it were a secret weapons blueprint.[12] Second, whereas the

---

[11] The film was released in the USSR in 1959 and sold 31.4 million tickets (Kudriavtsev).
[12] See, for example, the cover page of the film's shooting script, kept at the Museum-Panorama "The Battle of Borodino" in Moscow.

average budget of a Soviet film in the 1960s was 300–400K rubles, the final budget of *War and Peace* turned out to be over 8 million rubles, or "an estimated $700 million in today's dollars" (Youngblood 2014, 1). Notably, the Council of Ministers allotted 2 million rubles directly to the Soviet Ministry of Defense to provide tens of thousands of extras as well as weapons, explosives, fuel, and sundry services. Minister of Defense Marshal Rodion Malinovskii ordered the General Staff to open its archives to the film crew (Youngblood 2014, 19), while the Ministry appointed several military consultants for the film, including General V.V. Kurasov, the head of the War Academy of the General Staff and a Soviet hero as the main consultant. A special consultant, Lieutenant General Nikolai Oslikovskii, supplied expert advice on cavalry operations (Ivanov 2003, 144). In his article "Film about the Glory of Russian Arms," General Kurasov wrote:

> We recently saw the scenes of the Battle of Borodino in an American adaptation of *War and Peace*. American producers failed to convey the main thing that happened at Borodino—Russia's victory. When a viewer watches the film, he does not understand how the battle ended. Kutuzov's troops continue to retreat toward Moscow. Meanwhile, during the Battle at Borodino the victory of the Russian army became reality. And Tolstoy expresses this idea clearly (4).

According to the main consultant, the new film's main mission was to correct the historical mistakes of the 1956 *War and Peace*. Notably, and tellingly in the context of the Cold War-era cultural wars, the fact that Vidor had an Italian co-director and the film was a US-Italian co-production was not even mentioned.

Bondarchuk's film combined three narrative modes: melodrama, art cinema, and the totalitarian epic film. Melodrama put the family and its struggles at the film's center and provided most of the narrative interest for an average movie goer. Art cinema conventions made the film *auteur* the center of a fragmented and complex narrative, the main narrative form of post-war film modernism (Bordwell 1999, 718). The totalitarian epic met the expectations of the film's main sponsor—the Soviet state. In his fusion of these three narrative modes, Bondarchuk exercised the ultimate control of the text in three major ways: (1) as the actor playing one of the lead roles, (2) as the film's ultimate *auteur*, and (3) as the film's demiurgic voiceover, reading Tolstoy's philosophical comments on the meaning of history and life.

As is well known, Tolstoy's novel focuses on families and individual lives set against the background of the Napoleonic wars. The US-Italian adaptation simply followed the syntax of Hollywood melodrama.[13] The narrative syntax of the Soviet prestige production focused on the male protagonist's service to the empire, above all, military service. Service defines the male protagonist's desire, gives positive meaning to his quest, and makes death the ultimate resolution of the melodramatic conflict. In Part I, Bondarchuk depicts Andrei Bolkonsky's search for his life's meaning as a series of melodramatic conflicts. First, Andrei (Viacheslav Tikhonov) decides to join the army to escape his boring society life and find a worthwhile goal through his individual quest for glory. For both Tolstoy and Bondarchuk, this is a false romantic scenario because it is about individual agency, devoid of communal experience. Second, after Andrei realizes that personal glory is a false path, he embraces romance as an alternative. Here Bondarchuk and Tolstoy diverge. For Tolstoy, family is central to the individual's existence, even if the family is part of a larger community. For Bondarchuk, family is a part of the imperial state and auxiliary to it. There is nothing that the family can provide for a man if he does not serve the state directly. Hence, if in Tolstoy's novel the death of Andrei's wife during childbirth is a critical and tragic event, in Bondarchuk's adaptation, the birth of Andrei's son, a future servant of the empire, overshadows the death of a young woman who has already fulfilled her function.

The prestige production uses art cinema devices as semantic elements. Art cinema's conventions are about loosening the continuity of the cause-and-effect narrative by inserting authorial motivation into it. This motivation often manifests itself via visual excess and narrative flash forward because the *auteur* plays the role of the overarching consciousness in art cinema narrative. In the Soviet *War and Peace* we see moments of art cinema discourse in self-reflexive narrative instances, such as occasional jump cuts, complex montage sequences, wipes, superimpositions, etc. However, these editing devices are not central to the prestige production's displays of *auteurist* ideology. Instead, the agenda is to display the state-financed film studio and its technological and financial power. Hence, the most common and striking use of modernist discourse happens in epic spectacles, such as the aerial shots that punctuate the film's narrative.

War and Peace appropriates elements of the art cinema aesthetics—long takes, mobile camera, etc.—for a radically different agenda. For example, long shots of

---

[13] For a detailed discussion see Youngblood 2014, 106–109.

a battlefield, an aristocratic ball, or a military parade downplay the role of close-ups of individual faces. Close-ups are rare, and when they do occur, they often display Russians' stoic endurance of suffering or pain, or submission to a ritual. The mobile camera likewise foregrounds the expensive mise-en-scène, the elaborate staging of large groups of geometrically arranged human figures, or an epic point of view. Such devices do not bring people closer to the viewer but, rather, make them a part of intricately arranged settings of aristocratic estates and palaces. For example, in the scene of the Rostov women getting ready for the ball, the mobile long take (normally a self-reflexive art cinema device) is used to display the imperial luxury of the Mosfilm Studio sets and the craft of the studio technicians. In this self-indulgent visual tour, even medium shots of individuals are rare. We are not supposed to identify with the characters but, instead, to venerate and admire the production values of this sequence.

Visually represented subjectivity is one of the main claims of post-Second World War modernist cinema. At her first ball, as Natasha (Liudmila Savel'eva) hopes to get asked to dance, the camera switches into the subjective mode, expressing the blurred vision of the young girl desperate to be noticed. This moment of psychological insight, of an identification recalling Hollywood narratives, is abruptly interrupted by the camera's sweeping panorama of the dance floor from an extreme high angle crane shot in which people are portrayed as ornaments in the best traditions of Busby Berkeley musicals (see Figure 1.2).

In the novel, the ball is the high point of Natasha and Andrei's romance, after which they confide their feelings to their closest friends and family. Bondarchuk

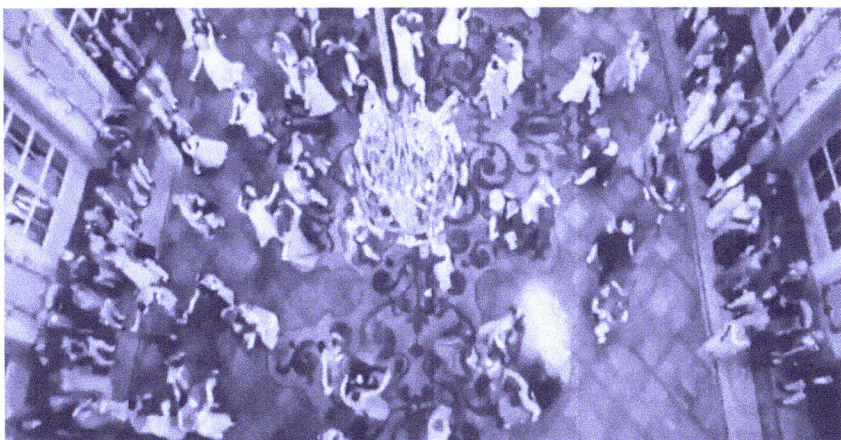

Figure 1.2: Dancers in the Mass Ornament in *War and Peace*

Figure 1.3: Split screen in the scene after Natasha's first ball

chose to use the split screen technique to display these confessions within one frame, with cross-edited dialogue. The effect of the divided screen makes it impossible for the viewer to identify with either. Instead of Hollywood suspense, we have a paternalistic omniscience about the outcome of the romance. The desire to display technology hijacks the novelistic polyphony of Tolstoy's *War and Peace* (see Figure 1.3).

The filmmaker deploys these various devices with no concern for either continuity or identification with an individual character; the concern is to display what the Mosfilm-funded epic production can do. These sudden shifts display Bondarchuk's omniscient and formalistic approach to storytelling and the ubiquity of a surveying point of view, which was completely alien to the spirit of modernist art cinema after 1945.[14]

One of the most famous sections in the novel is Prince Andrei's visit to the Rostovs' estate in the spring. He is experiencing a profound crisis as he struggles to come to terms with the death of his wife and, more importantly, his disillusionment in his personal quest for glory. Immersed in his thoughts, he

---

[14] In fact, Bondarchuk created the tradition of Soviet "white telephone" films or an idyll, set in nineteenth-century aristocratic estates, designed for dual distribution (domestically and internationally), and selling Russian imperial culture globally. A series of expensive film adaptations set in nineteenth-century aristocratic estates followed suit: widescreen, 143-minute *Anna Karenina* (1967, listed to compete at Cannes), *The Nest of Gentlefolk* (*Dvorianskoe gnezdo* 1969), *An Unfinished Piece for a Mechanical Piano* (*Neokonchennaia p'esa dlia mekhanicheskogo pianino* 1977), etc. All of them sold an idyllic depiction of the Russian past, where aristocratic estates serve as a microcosm of Russia. The estates might be poorly managed because Russian masters are too emotional and impractical, rather than rational and cold, but the serfs who live there are organically connected to their masters and form an idyllic community with them. The late-socialist Soviet Union that marketed these films represented itself as a faithful heir of this organic tradition.

passes an ancient oak tree, the only tree that has not yet bloomed. It stands apart against the background of the spring forest. At the estate he overhears Natasha for the first time and, without noticing it, he rediscovers an interest in life. On the way back from the estate he notices that the old oak tree is covered with green leaves. For Tolstoy, the tree is symbolic of personal transformation. In fact, you see the world the way you feel. In Bondarchuk's film, instead of a close-up of Andrei, which would make the viewer identify with the character coming back to life, the filmmaker uses a low angle shot to emphasize the enormous size of the tree, with Andrei's point of view represented by a rather impersonal voiceover, reading the character's thoughts in third-person narrative. Andrei's subjectivity is irrelevant here; what is significant is the epic size of the tree and Andrei's return to the loins of Russia, which he will serve and for which he will die. Bondarchuk's oak tree is not a metaphor for the individual's transformation but a doppelgänger of Simon Ushakov's famous seventeenth-century icon, "The Tree of the Muscovite State," where state power is sacralized and every human being in the image is just a small twig serving the glory of the rising empire (see Figure 1.4).[15]

Figure 1.4: Simon Ushakov's *The Tree of the Muscovite State* 1668

[15] For an insightful discussion of Ushakov's work see Merridale (2014, 12).

Figure 1.5: Oak Tree in Otradnoe as the Tree of the Russian Empire. The director's name is superimposed on the image of the tree

Not surprisingly, the central third part of the epic film dedicated to Russia's 1812 war against the joint forces of *the armies of Europe* (the point emphasized in the film) opens with the image of a gigantic imperial oak tree (see Figure 1.5).

While the above visual association was most likely accidental (which only confirms the continuity of Russian state iconography across centuries and political regimes), the generous representation of religious images and rituals in the communist *War and Peace* was a matter of choice. Tolstoy's novel, especially through Pierre's spiritual journey, portrays organized religion as alienating and barren, having nothing to contribute to the seekers of life's meaning. By contrast, Bondarchuk's film revels precisely in the luxury and abundance of gold in Russian Orthodox icons and religious paraphernalia. On the level of the film's narrative ideology, the display of the church's power serves to augment the nation's imperial power; on the level of the film's production value, these scenes offer spectacle under the guise of Russian spirituality. The communal prayer before the battle of Borodino illustrates the representation of this imperial vision of religion as the power legitimating and sacralizing the state and its glory of war (see Figure 1.6). As a side benefit and in its bid for international prizes, the film also promotes the Soviet state as being tolerant of religion and as heir not only to military glory but also the cultural traditions of the Russian empire—a message targeting Western film critics and the cinematic community.

The ending of such an epic work bears a particular ideological weight, for this is where the meanings of the work are made especially clear. Not surprisingly, here Bondarchuk and Tolstoy decisively part ways. For Tolstoy, open-endedness is of paramount importance because his is a novelistic narrative. Equally

Figure 1.6: Prayer before Borodino, a harbinger of victory. No prayer before Austerlitz led to defeat

important is the family, and the novel's conclusion portrays the prose of everyday life, devoid of unnecessary hyperbole about heroic exploits, which are left behind together with the war. The main characters—Natasha, Pierre, Nikolai and Maria—go to bed while Andrei's son wakes up, disturbed by a dream about his departed father. His path is as yet unclear, but his peaceful everyday life, pregnant with possibilities, is a major miracle of life.

Post-Second World War European cinema experienced a Tolstoyan moment of its own, in rejecting the epic monumentalism and pictorialism of totalitarian cinema and embracing the quasi-documentary aesthetics of neorealism as a rough visual equivalent of a Tolstoyan celebration of everyday life. Yet neither this visual language nor the philosophy of the everyday is of any interest to Bondarchuk, or his producer, the Soviet state. The film ends with the victory of the Russian Army over the "united armies of Europe," which froze to death in the midst of the snowy empire. Everyone gathers around a huge bonfire in the middle of a snow-covered field, under the fraternal supervision of the victorious and generous Russians. The camera rises in a crane shot and cuts to an aerial shot (see Figure 1.7). Ordinary humans dissolve into one big circular shape, a human mass around a gigantic bonfire. It is a pagan celebration[16] of victory in war. And war is not the Tolstoyan senseless slaughter and a pageant of false goals and ambitions. In this film, the army, the war, and victory are all beautiful, and in the midst of this spectacle one cannot be seduced by the

---

[16] The aerial shot emphasizes the circular structure of the gathered community. In Russian folklore, the magic circle protects the hero against evil forces.

Figure 1.7: The victory bonfire

boring minutiae of everyday experience. The epic point of view overwhelms the novelistic discourse.

Not surprisingly, Michelangelo Antonioni reacted unfavorably to Bondarchuk's film, noting that "the international filmmaking community had been fighting for 20 years to eliminate from films such nonsensical scenes as we find in *War and Peace*" ("Krieg um 'Krieg und Frieden'"). The two decades mentioned are no coincidence. Antonioni grew up watching Italian fascist cinema and defined himself as a filmmaker who opposed this tradition. His comment not only derides the unnecessary formalistic embellishments of Bondarchuk's film, but amounts to a political statement about the perceived return of the Soviet movie industry to totalitarian aesthetics.

As an afterthought, the film has Pierre (Sergei Bondarchuk) meet Natasha when he returns victorious from the war. But the narrative logic of this brief scene is that of a traditional Russian folktale, when a hero gets the girl after the battle with a (here) French dragon. Perhaps it is even closer to the Stalinist war film where the hero fulfills his duty to the state, and the girl, as always, waits for her hero. This stylistic eclecticism and a certain narrative incoherence are endemic to the entire genre of the prestige production because of its multiple priorities, the biggest of which is to showcase the Soviet film industry's superiority to any national—or one specific global film industry—competitor. In this uphill battle, the end justifies the means. Bondarchuk's *War and Peace* uses stylistic devices and direct references from multiple, and at times incompatible, cinematic traditions and filmmakers. It employs mise-en-scènes from Andrei Tarkovsky's *Ivan's Childhood* (e.g., burnt-down structures resembling crosses), episodes of melodramatic coincidence from Soviet quasi-neorealist cinema

(Pierre's saving a child instead of killing Napoleon borrows from Mikhail Kalatozov's *Cranes Are Flying*), battle scenes from Stalinist totalitarian epics, and aerial shots lifted from Leni Riefenstahl's *Triumph of the Will*. This list would be incomplete without the Soviet fantasy/fairy-tale film. When the Russian army and the Russian winter defeat the European invaders, and half-frozen French soldiers assemble around the bonfire, one of them is personalized for us. Georgy Milliar, a male actor who made a career playing the witch Baba Yaga in Soviet folktale film adaptations, speaks in *War and Peace* in the same characteristic voice, but represents a French prisoner of war sharing food with Russian soldiers. One could consider this a knowing and comic wink to the Russian audience because no foreigner would ever understand the reference. However, a more plausible explanation is in the genetic makeup of the prestige production. In its desire to make a spectacle that is better than Hollywood's, resources and devices were indiscriminately thrown together in a collage to demonstrate the industry's global reach and power. As an Austrian newspaper citing Western jury members at the Moscow International Film Festival in 1965 noted, the result is a *"Monsterspektakelfilm"* (monstrous film spectacle) ("Krieg um 'Krieg um Frieden'").[17]

Bondarchuk's prestige production drained resources (both financial and discursive) from competing projects that represented different cinematic traditions, and in this case, different views of Russo-Soviet history. Andrei Tarkovsky's auteurist portrayal of Russian history through the life of the Renaissance-era icon painter Andrei Rublev was slowed down and deprived of funding, before being shelved. Fedor Razzakov, a Russian media historian, notes that cultural administrators argued about which version of Russian history and which aesthetic vision the Soviet government should promote domestically and in the West. Should it be an auteurist, black-and-white vision, focusing on human endurance in the face of the medieval state's violence and barbaric invasions or a glorious epic of imperial vision, power, and eventual victory, shot in color on wide screen? Officials predictably chose the latter.[18]

---

[17] The Soviet film administration hurried the crew to finish the first two films of the epic in time for the Moscow Film Festival in 1965. Bondarchuk fulfilled the state assignment but suffered a heart attack and was declared "clinically dead"—his second attack during the making of *War and Peace*, according to his daughter. See Natal'ia Bondarchuk, "Na s"emkakh 'Voiny i mira' otets perezhil dve klinicheskie smerti"; www.trud.ru/article/30-09-2005/94416_natalja_bondarchuk_na_semkax_vojny_i_mira_otets_pe.html

[18] Razzakov, (2008) vol. 1, 438–439.

The seven years of the epic's production played a major role in stopping any public debate about who is authorized to commemorate the Russian imperial and Soviet past—and the right way to do it—as well as about the role of the imperial state and the individual's agency in Russian and Soviet history. The film helped to re-establish the state as the only agent of Russia's history and the monopolist of its meaning.

War and Peace also redefined the role of the film press in the promotion of a big-budget film. At the pre-production stage, both the trade journal *The Art of Cinema* and the popular magazine *Soviet Screen* started to publish positive reviews of the yet-to-be-shot Soviet adaptation of Tolstoy's novel. In 1962, when *War and Peace* existed only as a script, Iurii Khaniutin wrote a long article outlining Bondarchuk's cinematic career, both as an actor and as a director.[19] The barrage of positive reviews continued through the production of the epic and peaked during the release of the first two parts at the Moscow International Film Festival in 1965. Unsurprisingly, the film garnered the Grand Prix of the Festival, but not without an internal controversy, which for obvious reasons was never reported to Soviet audiences. Many of the Western members of the jury categorically objected to awarding the Grand Prix to Bondarchuk's film, which they considered an anachronistic spectacle without much artistic value ("Krieg"). Under pressure from the Soviet head of the Jury and his Eastern European allies, a compromise was reached and two Grand Prix were awarded: one to *War and Peace* and the other to the Hungarian art cinema film *Twenty Hours* by Zoltán Fábri.

Thereafter, the Soviet epic marched triumphantly across the movie theaters of the Soviet Union and its allies; it was also released in Japan, France, Italy, the UK, Denmark, and most importantly for Soviet competition, in the United States. The international distribution of *War and Peace* was framed by two traditional discourses of Soviet achievements: space exploration and ballet. Soviet cosmonaut Aleksei Leonov, who had just returned from the first spacewalk in human history, attended the film's premier in Paris (Zorkaia 2001). For the role of Natasha, Bondarchuk chose a professional ballerina from the Kirov (Mariinsky) Ballet Theater in Leningrad— Liudmila Savel'eva, who projected an aura of the imperial ballet tradition onto the Soviet state epic. Savel'eva's physical resemblance to Audrey Hepburn—the American Natasha—played a role too (see Figures 1.8 and 1.9).

---

[19] Khaniutin, Iurii, "Sergei Bondarchuk," *Iskusstvo kino* 7 (1962): 90–100.

Epic Film as a Tool of Hard and Soft Power during the Cold War 39

Figure 1.8: Liudmila Savel'eva as Natasha Rostova

Figure 1.9: Audrey Hepburn as Natasha Rostova

In 1969, the American Academy of Motion Picture Arts and Sciences awarded the four parts of *War and Peace* an Oscar for Best Foreign Film. Reviews in the Western press repeatedly invoked the "Russian spirit and soul" of the picture, and at the awards ceremony Jane Fonda mentioned Russia, and not the Soviet Union, as the country of the epic's production. The film, therefore, was interpreted as a pleasantly lavish and orientalist tale of Russia that the West loved and remembered from nineteenth-century Victorian classics. It was a smart move on the part of the Soviet film industry to match Jane Fonda with the only member of the crew who was receiving the award—Savel'eva/Natasha, sporting a nineteenth-century, virginally white dress. It was the soft 1969 face of hard Soviet power, who a year earlier had visited its Czech friends in tanks. The ambiguity was not lost on the organizers of the Oscars ceremony. Before introducing the winner, Fonda made a joke about the occasional poor synchronization of voice over translation of foreign-language dialogue—a point that was delivered by Walter Matthau's voice to which Fonda lip-synched.

Unlike the American Film Academy, Woody Allen did not buy the soft power camouflage of the prestige production. In 1975 he released his spoof of *War and Peace*, titled *Love and Death*. While it is an ironic and loving tribute to social urgency and lack of humor in the Russian literary canon, the immediate negative inspiration is Bondarchuk's "monster film" and its disregard for individuals and their agency. In contrast, it is precisely the frail and touching human played by Allen who is the focal point of *Love and Death*.

Having found a successful model for producing marketable epics, the Soviet state could not let anyone question the status picture. Yet, after all the domestic and international triumphs of Bondarchuk's film, and with a virtual state monopoly on the discourse about it, the debate flared again in 1968–1969—to be laid to rest together with the last traces of Thaw-era culture. An article by U. Gural'nik published in the August 1969 issue of *The Art of Cinema*, after the release of all four parts of the epic formulates its agenda in the title: "Epic Mission Accomplished. *War and Peace*. The Film and its Critics ("Dostizhenie eposa. *Voina i mir.* Fil'm i ego kritiki"). The author's goal is not so much to pass judgment on the film—with an Oscar and successful distribution both in the USSR and abroad there was no need to defend it—but to re-establish the idea that the film is a faithful vehicle for Tolstoy's ideas and to quash those who disagree with this state-sponsored claim. One target in particular deserves discussion because the incident is suggestive of the changing cultural politics around 1968, as well as the status of *War and Peace* as a special, state-curated project. A few months earlier, critic Igor' Zolotusskii published an article titled "An Addendum to the Epic" ("Dobavlenie k eposu") in *New World* (*Novyi mir*), in which he looked at the film from the position of a literary scholar. Point-by-point, Zolotusskii takes the film apart as a monumental facade, which lacks any of Tolstoy's ideas: on human life, on war as an abomination, on God, on fake vs real values, etc. In the film, war is a beautiful, epic spectacle, and so are the balls and salons of nineteenth-century Russia, meticulously reconstructed and expertly recorded by the filmmakers. The author also insightfully notes that the success of Bondarchuk's *War and Peace* abroad largely stems from the interest of Western viewers in external features of life in old Russia: "One can understand those critics in France, Japan, and Mexico who enthusiastically write about [...] the Russian atmosphere [of the film]. For them these *panoramas* of Russia are Russia proper; [they constitute] its spirit" (Zolotusskii 1968, 272). As the titles of the film's reviews in the Western press suggest (e.g., "Eternal Rus"[20]), this is exactly what pleased Western film critics and viewers.

Zolotusskii's suggestion that *War and Peace* offers an orientalizing view of Russia, rather than a major technological achievement and equal participation in the cinematic competition with the West, enraged the Soviet establishment. A few days after the publication of the article, assistant editor of *New World* Aleksei Kondratovich received a call from Igor' Chernoutsan from the Department of Culture of the Communist Party Central Committee. Chernoutsan complained that the article mocks a film that "enjoys huge popularity abroad" and that the piece appeared in *New World,* which had a wide readership, unlike more specialized trade publications, such as *The Art of Cinema* (Kondratovich 1991, 273–74). The assistant editor's key question of whether it was even possible to criticize Bondarchuk remained unanswered—a clear indication that for the Soviet establishment, the film was much more than a "Bondarchuk picture"; it was a state-commissioned, prestige project, exempt from "personal opinions." It did not help that the publication happened during the Prague Spring, which would put an end to any illusions about the open discussion of matters political and cultural.[21] Over the next two years, concerted attacks on *New World* and its liberal-minded editor Aleksandr Tvardovskii forced him and most of his staff to leave.

While it is not clear how many people read Zolotusskii's critique of *War and Peace,* official party curators certainly did their homework. The article by Gural'nik in *The Art of Cinema* does damage control, with extensive quotes from Zolotusskii and detailed explanations of the merits of Bondarchuk's picture and its legitimate place on the cinematic Olympus. It is also no accident that the discussion of *War and Peace* followed a lengthy discussion of a Stalin-era socialist realist masterpiece, *Chapaev* (1934) in the same issue.[22] That placement implicitly

---

[20] Excerpt from *Kristeligt Dagblat* newspaper, November 3, 1967; Gosfil'mofond, delo 251.
[21] The Prague Spring was the reformist movement led by the communist President of Czechoslovakia, Alexander Dubček. Elected in January 1968, he tried to implement political and economic reforms that would grant more human rights and economic opportunities to the citizens within the limits of a socialist political system. In August 1968, concerned about the impact of Dubček's reforms on the Soviet-led "Eastern bloc," the USSR and its allies (GDR, Poland, Hungary, and Bulgaria) invaded Czechoslovakia, removed the government, and put an end to political and economic reforms.
[22] D. Shatsillo, "Klassika na marshe," *Iskusstvo kino* 8 (1969): 43–76.

designated Bondarchuk's film as an heir of Soviet film classics; *War and Peace*, in turn, could serve as a legitimating ancestor for a new generation of prestige films about the Great Patriotic War—including *Liberation*—a few years later.

Whatever the weaknesses of prestige productions, their positive aspects for the Soviet film industry included the introduction of new film technologies, new formats for greater revenues from exhibition, and the influx of foreign partners for co-productions. For example, *War and Peace* used the new widescreen 70 mm film stock; unique, newly developed equipment for mobile camera shots; and new high-quality sound technology equipment, which was fairly competitive with Western sound technologies until the introduction of Dolby digital in the early 1990s. The Broadway producer Mike Todd had founded the American Optical Co. and introduced the new 70 mm film stock format in the mid-1950s. In 1958 he traveled to the Soviet Union with a proposal to make a joint film production of *War and Peace*. The Soviets refused his offer, but kept the technology and reverse-engineered it as the Soviet 70mm film format. In the early 1960s they successfully applied the new technology to the eight-hour production of *War and Peace*. Not surprisingly, the unbridled enthusiast from Broadway is never mentioned in the credits.

The 1960s witnessed the height of moviegoing in Eastern Europe, whereas film attendance in the West began to decline, largely due to competition from television. Soviets developed or rediscovered the serialized format for movie theater release in order to keep moviegoers buying tickets. *War and Peace* led the way in the introduction of serial production for theatrical release. Soviet viewers watched the film in four parts, first as *War and Peace. Part 1,* then its three sequels. The first film, *Andrei Bolkonskii,* came out in two episodes, each selling 58 million tickets, the equivalent of $1 billion dollars today, for the Soviet film industry. Not surprisingly, attendance fell for parts 2, 3, and 4, but such is the fate of most film sequels.

Some smaller national film industries found attractive the relatively lower cost of labor and the technological sophistication of the Soviet film industry, test-run and showcased by *War and Peace*. Italy, for instance, invited Bondarchuk to direct the Soviet-Italian co-production *Waterloo* (1970), which employed some Soviet actors and, most importantly, recycled thousands of costumes and technology (such as camera cranes) originally created for the Soviet epic production. The film failed at the Soviet box office and with Western critics, "ending Bondarchuk's career as a European filmmaker before it had really begun" (Youngblood 2014, 110).

Liberation: war spectacle and the politics of memory

The technical expertise and the aesthetics of epic war spectacle became the foundation of a series of 1970s Soviet prestige films commemorating the Great Patriotic War, the most ambitious of which was Iurii Ozerov's five-part *Liberation* (*Osvobozhdenie*, produced 1968–1971; released 1970–72).[23] As Youngblood notes, Ozerov's epic "was intended to be the Great Patriotic War's *War and Peace*" (2007, 158). The narrative focused on the last victorious years of the Great Patriotic War, each part depicting a turning point in the canonical Soviet war narrative: *The Fire Bulge (Ognennaia duga)* is about the Battle of Kursk, *Breakthrough (Proryv)*—about the crossing of the Dnieper and the liberation of Kiev; in *The Direction of the Main Blow (Napravlenie glavnogo udara)* Soviet troops liberate Belorussia while the Allies land in Normandy; *The Battle for Berlin* (*Bitva za Berlin*) and *The Last Assault* (*Poslednii shturm*) tell of the war in Poland and Germany and the fall of Berlin.

Like *War and Peace*, the project was commissioned by the Soviet state. The Ministry of Defense, the Ministry of Finances, and the State Committee on Cinematography jointly signed the letter that authorized the beginning of production.[24] Originally, the Mosfilm studio even approached Hollywood with an offer of a Soviet-American co-production. The Americans agreed, but on condition that the film would have a Hollywood star playing one of the leads, which would ensure box-office success in the US. The Soviet film administration refused: having an individual-driven narrative conflicted with the Soviet view of the war as one of generals and headquarters representing the collective power of the Soviet state. Eventually, Italian producer Dino de Laurentiis stepped in, and the picture is, in fact, a massive co-production. Almost

---

[23] The original title of the film was *Liberation of Europe* ("Liberation of Europe" 1). The main military consultant on the film, General Sergei Shtemenko, suggested changing the title to *Liberation*. The final title also evokes Alexander Dovzhenko's Stalin-era documentary compilation film *Liberation* (1940), which chronicles the Soviet invasion of Eastern Poland in 1939, portraying it as a reunification of two divided nations: Soviet Belorussians reunite with Western Belorussians and Soviet Ukrainians with Western Ukrainians.

[24] "The experience of work on the film *War and Peace* shows that the creation of such large-scale (*masshtabnykh*) productions that require major expenses (the expenses that would be definitely reimbursed as the film would be profitable) demand government decisions on a number of organizational and financial issues that are beyond the competence of the State Committee on Cinematography and the Ministry of Culture of the USSR." Letter to the Central Committee of the CPSU, September 2, 1965; signed by the Chair of Goskino, Aleksei Romanov, the Minister of Defense, Rodion Malinovskii, and the Head of the Main Political Administration of the Soviet Army and Navy, Aleksei Epishev. "Osvobozhdenie Evropy," RGALI, f. 2944, op. 4, ed. kh. 1294, 7.

all Eastern Bloc countries participated via actors, location shooting, and financing. For the East German DEFA and the Polish PRF-ZF *Liberation* was a major commitment in the late 1960s.[25] Italy was the only NATO nation to participate in the film's production.

Ozerov's saga had multiple agendas. Politically, its purpose was to counter Western cinematic representations of the final years of the Second World War. Letters from film administrators and Communist Party officials archived in the film's production file claim that Western films of that era "distort the course of the Second World War. The authors of these large-scale 'action movies' (*boeviki*) falsify history in trying to prove that the defeat of the German armies in Europe only began with the landing of Anglo-American troops in Normandy."[26] *Liberation* also polemicizes with Thaw films focused on the first disastrous years of the war. According to an official review in *The Art of Cinema*, those (unnamed- E.P. and A.P.) films are guilty of subjectivism and de-heroization in representing the war.[27] The third major task of *Liberation* was educational: to provide an epic visual document that would help the younger generation to connect with the heroic Soviet past.[28]

Countering US-produced visualizations of the Second World War became important in the late 1960s because what Soviets called the Great Patriotic War started to occupy a central place in the official history of the Soviet Union. By the late 1960s it was clear that the economic competition between socialism and capitalism was doomed to failure: with US astronauts on the Moon, the space race ended in at best a stalemate, confirmed in 1975 by the Apollo-Soyuz US-Soviet joint program. The defeat of Nazi Germany became the main historical event to construct the definition of "we" as the commonwealth of socialist nations and to substantiate the USSR's legitimate role as a superpower. In her analysis of the cult of the Great Patriotic War under Brezhnev, Nina Tumarkin contends: "From 1965 on, the Great Patriotic War continued its transformation from a national trauma ... into sacrosanct cluster of heroic exploits that had once and for all proven the superiority of communism over

---

[25] Youngblood 2007, 158.
[26] "Osvobozhdenie Evropy" 14.
[27] Iu. Lukin, "Kak eto bylo," *Iskusstvo kino* 7 (1970): 8–16.
[28] In fact, the main military consultant of the film, General Sergei Shtemenko, expressed concern about the original film title, *Liberation of Europe*: "During the war it was clear to everyone what was liberated and from whom. But since then ... a new generation has grown up ... The other side of the same question: the viewers must understand that no one, apart from the USSR and the Soviet Army *could* liberate Europe from the invaders." "Osvobozhdenie Evropy," RGALI, fond 2944, op. 4, ed.kh. 1294, p. 63.

capitalism" (1994, 133). No matter how far the Eastern Bloc would lag behind the West economically and technologically, the ultimate ideological competition was won in 1945 and sealed by blood. Notably, *Liberation* ends with an ideologically-freighted count of the number killed in the Second World War: "—What did fascism give the world?—In the Second World War perished: 520,000 French, 400,000 Italians, 320,000 English, 325,000 Americans, 364,000 Czechs and Slovaks, 1.6 million Yugoslavs, 6 million Poles, 9.7 million Germans, 20 million Soviets" (Fig. 1.10).

The final roll-call of deaths not only confirms who made the major contribution and who was mostly tagging along, but also lays bare important omissions in the story told by Ozerov. First and foremost, the extermination of European Jews is not mentioned in the tabulation. Instead, part of the Holocaust death toll is included in the number of people killed in Poland. Second, the film begins on 12 April 1943, after the victory of Stalingrad, and avoids two years of the Red Army's colossal defeats. The film also never mentions that the Soviet Union signed the Non-Aggression Pact with Nazi Germany and for two years had close economic and military ties with Hitler's Reich.

Finally, *Liberation* was an anniversary film dedicated to the twenty-fifth anniversary of Victory Day in 1970 (Youngblood, 2007, 158). The celebration of anniversaries of the October Revolution and of the birthdays of leaders, initiated in 1917, had become solidly entrenched as major Soviet festive events. On these occasions, cultural producers prepared special works that would correspond to the grandeur of the jubilees: artists and theater directors staged pageants that reenacted the storming of the Winter Palace in Petrograd, while

Figure 1.10: The number of Soviets killed in the Second World War confirms who made the major contribution

annual parades devoted to the anniversary of the Revolution had poets, playwrights, and writers addressing their panegyrics to the great leader (Lenin, Trotsky, Stalin, Khrushchev, etc.) and the revolution that opened Russia's new era. Cinematographers regularly created masterpieces for November 7 in celebration of the October Revolution (by the new calendar): *The End of St. Petersburg* (*Konets Sankt-Peterburga* 1927), *Lenin in October* (*Lenin v Oktiabre* 1937), *The Vow* (*Kliatva* 1946), *The Communist* (*Kommunist* 1957). Beginning with the festivities marking the twentieth anniversary of Victory Day in 1965, the calendar and hierarchy of sacred days changed. Victory Day became *the* major Soviet anniversary day, and by 1970, major prestige films productions focused on the cult of the Great Patriotic War.

While ideological and political concerns were central to the project, Mosfilm studio documents and reviews in *The Art of Cinema* suggest an element of Cold War competition not reducible to a fight over the meaning of the Second World War. Letters from the Mosfilm studio and Goskino to the Soviet of Ministers, the KGB, and the Central Committee of the CPSU repeatedly mention Ken Annakin's *The Longest Day* (1962), with John Wayne, and *Battle of the Bulge* (1965) (translated into Russian as *Bitva v Ardennakh*), with Henry Fonda. The driving force behind *Liberation's* epic scale was the desire to create a film spectacle capable of competing with Western productions internationally and of showcasing the Soviet film industry's—and thus the Soviet state's— power. In fact, in an article in *The Art of Cinema* following the release of the first two films in his series, Ozerov addresses precisely the larger generic and media shifts in international and domestic film markets:

> "[F]ilm giants" (*fil'my-giganty*) is exactly what contemporary cinema is. More and more television films are produced that people watch [...] slouched on the couch and drinking tea. Watch at home. That is why the West produces super films—colorful spectacles, grandiose, striking, entertaining. [...] And I think that our film industry should not derisively dismiss this competition [...] Wouldn't you agree that the international success of *War and Peace* is an argument in my favor?
>
> qtd. in Tsitriniak 1970, 9–10

Invoking the international success of Bondarchuk's film, both as a production model for later prestige productions and as an argument in the Cold War competition, was a standard feature of *Liberation*'s financing and promotion. The other, equally effective, strategy was references to the unlimited resources of Western blockbusters because of their anti-Soviet propaganda value. These references were carefully crafted and targeted specific people in the Soviet government whose particular agendas were at stake and who could provide leverage in the studio's requests for additional funding.[29]

Ozerov's epic films occupied a privileged position in the Soviet film industry. A letter from the studio to the chair of Goskino, Aleksei Romanov, noted that Mosfilm responded to the call to create a film of "heroic-epic character" and that "it seems reasonable to ensure this collective work *exclusive material conditions, different from the usual conditions of films' financing and production*" (emphasis added—E.P. and A.P.).[30] Indeed, already at the pre-production stage of the very first version of the film, the Council of Ministers authorized a payment of up to 30,000 rubles to the scriptwriters, up to 75,000 for "preliminary work" and 20,000 in hard currency for the purchase of footage from foreign archives.[31] As in the case of *War and Peace,* the creators of *Liberation* counted on getting a big budget from the government. The Mosfilm studio memo to their superiors made a point of mentioning that *Battle of the Bulge* cost over £3 million ("Liberation of Europe" 37). Thus the country should spare no expense on a film "telling the true story" of the Second World War.

While such films harked back to the epic representation of Stalin-era cinema, the filmmakers rethought the conventions of the "historical documentary film," the genre that appeared in late-Stalinist culture. One of the epitomes of this genre, Mikhail Chiaureli's *The Fall of Berlin* (1949), for example, was shot entirely in color, and although it features both historical characters (such as Stalin, Hitler, Roosevelt, and Churchill) and fictional ones (most famously the "star-crossed lovers" Alesha and Natasha) the epic style dominates both plotlines. *The Fall of Berlin* is uniform in its politics of representation, and its "interpretive community" was Stalin himself.

Liberation was conceived as the ultimate screen epic of the Great Patriotic War, a film that would embody an authoritative cinematic discourse about the war and finalize and "own" the meaning of that historical event. As a result, the series was over-determined by extratextual discourses and the diverse, often conflicting, demands of the parties invested in the production. Work on the

---

[29] For example, this argument is used in the Mosfilm studio letter to the Council of Ministers of the USSR and the Head of the KGB, Vladimir Semichastnyi, before the authors make the pitch for increased financing: "Gigantic resources are allocated for the production of such 'super-films' and the best forces of Western cinema participate in their creation. Further evidence of the propagandistic significance of the release of such pictures by certain circles is the fact that for their production NATO countries gladly provide large army, air force and navy units" ("Osvobozhdenie Evropy," 14).

[30] "Osvobozhdenie Evropy" 1.

[31] Ibid., 8–9.

script, co-authored by Oscar Kurganov, Iurii Bondarev, and Iurii Ozerov, took two years (1965–1967). The project underwent multiple revisions—from a two-part story titled *The Liberation of Europe*, scheduled to be released in 1967, to the 470-minute, five-film final version three years later. Additionally, repeated re-editing of the already completed material dragged on. Moreover, the films' release was delayed a year, to coincide with the twenty-fifth anniversary of victory in the Great Patriotic War, and in response to the world premier of another Hollywood military blockbuster, *Patton* (1970).

The role of Stalin (Bukhuti Zakariadze) in the film grew exponentially, as Brezhnev's leadership adopted a more and more conservative, imperial position; in the final version, Stalin's role as the mastermind of Soviet victory is clearly modeled on *The Fall of Berlin*. The script had to show both strategic decisions of the top leadership *and* the war of the people; the drama of the war *and* the relentless movement of the Red Army to Berlin. Furthermore, the films had to be both ideologically orthodox *and* commercially profitable; to offer a clear didactic yet exciting narrative for Soviet audiences *and* to be marketable in the West. The studio was under constant pressure from the military to represent "equally" various categories of the armed forces in major battles, while the party and the KGB pushed for the deletion of episodes that portrayed Stalin as a controversial figure.

On the one hand, then, the film's production history documents the formation of many key aspects of the late-Soviet war myth. On the other hand, the final cut of *Liberation* is fragmented and eclectic, with the state agenda dictating narrative motivations. With the genre of *Liberation* officially designated as an "historical chronicle" (*istoricheskaia khronika*), the films constantly shift between fictional and quasi-documentary modes of narration. The justification for calling *Liberation* a "historical chronicle" is its supposed objectivity and truthfulness of representation. To quote multiple official reviews, the film "simply tells the historical truth" (Orlov 1971, 18)—an assertion that the authors back up with both extratextual and textual authenticating discourses. Reviews repeatedly mentioned that many members of the production crew themselves fought in the Great Patriotic War (Ozerov, Bondarev, Kurganov, Slabnevich), while several prominent military leaders (e.g., Marshalls Georgii Zhukov and Ivan Konev) were mentioned as the films' consultants. While the Party did not particularly favor Zhukov, his popularity in the USSR and abroad was an asset in adding authority to the epic. Most reviews of *Liberation* quoted Zhukov's recently published memoir, *Reminiscences and Reflections* (1969), linking it directly to Ozerov's film.

Because *Liberation* is less about the Second World War per se than about the Soviet *victories* that confirm the USSR's superiority, back in the 1940s and under Brezhnev, this agenda determined the film's stylistic and narrative choices. Despite the discourse of authenticity framing official reviews of the film, its use of documentary devices is eclectic and opportunistic. While each film uses maps and alternates black-and-white and color sequences, the actual documentary material used in the films is rather scant. According to Ozerov, the filmmakers "watched hundreds of kilometers of documentary footage but, unfortunately, selected very little." Ozerov adds that such a film does not require a single style.[32] This statement is very revealing: while the "chronicle" is almost entirely staged, its claim to "historical objectivity" is based on conforming to the late-Soviet official discourse on the Second World War. Within this logic, the epic scale and spectacular sequences of battles only confirm the "truth," just as rhetorical devices enhance an argument. In the Kursk battle sequence alone, filmmakers used 500 units of weaponry, including 100 tanks, 18 planes, artillery, and 3,000 infantrymen (Tsitriniak (1970):17). In the technical and political competition with the West, the number of tanks, planes, and humans on the set serves as a visual demonstration of the power of the Soviet state, which alone owns the truth. Spectacle, or "panorama," (Lukin (1970):14) as the director and official reviewers preferred to call it, itself became a weapon in the Cold War, both in the battle over the meaning of the Second World War and in the more mundane cinematic rivalry with the West. Promotional materials for the first two films seamlessly transitioned from heroic Soviet tankmen in 1943 to their equally heroic heirs, staging stunts in 1968, while the "authenticity" (*dostovernost'*) of cinematic battle scenes worked as a cypher for the gigantic scale of the picture. Accordingly, a promotional brochure described the filmmakers' decision to repeat the jump of a Soviet T-34 over a German Tiger tank during the Soviet counter-offensive (see Figure 1.11).

The main value of this episode for the film is of a visual attraction, but the description in the brochure minimizes its cinematic meaning and instead conflates the past and the present as a continuous heroic narrative of Soviet victories. Likewise, the unlimited technical and human resources at the disposal of the state prestige production are framed by the discourse of loyalty and patriotism: "Marshals, generals, and GIs of the Soviet Army all wished to help the filmmakers in any way they could" (Komarov 18).

---

[32] *The Art of Cinema* 5 (1970): 13–14.

Figure 1.11: Tank stunts as visual attraction: T-34 tank jumps over obstacles

In a rather unconventional move, the epic begins with Hitler's (Fritz Diez) inspection of German tanks and his strategic meeting with Wehrmacht generals in the bunker. Consequently, the first few minutes of the film, even before the title or the credits appear, are dominated by German speech. The German headquarters are then paralleled to the Kremlin and Stalin's meeting with Zhukov (Mikhail Ul'ianov) and Rokossovsky (Vladlen Davydov). All these sequences are in black-and white, as is the subsequent scene at the concentration camp where Andrei Vlasov's Russian Liberation Army is recruiting prisoners to fight on behalf of Germany. The frequent insertion of maps and documentary footage authenticates these staged sequences. The montage is quite tendentious, its intended meaning naturalized by the consistent use of black-and-white film. For example, Stalin receives the news that the Germans want to exchange his older son, Yakov (Iosif Gogichaishvili), for Field Marshal Paulus, captured after the Battle of Stalingrad. Stalin pronounces his apocryphal verdict, "I will not trade a Marshal for a Lieutenant," and turns on the radio, which is playing Goebbels' speech. The film then inserts documentary footage of Goebbels talking about the imminent defeat of the Soviet armies, and from it cuts to Churchill (Iurii Durov) and his generals listening to the same speech. While Churchill orders the radio to be shut off, his evaluation of the frontline situation is almost identical to Goebbels'. The editing thus unambiguously links the British and the Germans in their dismissive attitude towards the Soviet Union's strength, and the rest of the episode sets out to prove them wrong.

The main stylistic feature of *Liberation*—the alternate black-and white and color sequences—is likely an after-thought of Thaw debates about authenticity and an attempt to recapture the international success of such war pictures as *Cranes Are*

Flying, Ballad of a Soldier and *Ivan's Childhood*. All these films and directors were influenced by Italian neorealism and European art cinema, which often associated color with the falsity and contrived narratives of totalitarian film. The visual memory of the Thaw and of Stalinism, however, is subordinated to state agenda by the creation of a new canonical narrative and a corresponding visual language about the Great Patriotic War. As a result, the film flips around the conventions associated with both. The *Liberation* films adopt a black-and-white, documentary style for scenes with Stalin, Hitler, Roosevelt, Churchill, and Mussolini. In addition, they incorporate documentary footage of key events of the war, including an American newsreel of the Normandy landing, often inserting parts of it in the middle of fictional sequences. All Thaw-inspired, "trench-war" scenes are shot in color, even when they directly quote Thaw-era films. Heads of state thus belong to a different realm than colonels and lieutenants: they tell the story of the past that claims to be "true" rather than "authentic." Marshals, such as Zhukov, move effortlessly from black-and-white when they are strategizing with Stalin, to color when leading an offensive from a command center. Every military leader is introduced by an intertitle identifying his rank and the specific army unit of which he is in charge.[33]

The primary function of color sequences of Soviet offensives, however, is to create spectacle. Each of the five films features technically sophisticated aerial and crane shots, split screens, complex sound mixing, massive battle scenes, and alternation of black-and-white and color sequences. The first tracking shot in *The Fire Bulge* lasts twenty seconds and is followed by a forty-second sequence of artillery fire tinted red. The Prokhorovka tank battle is represented via a panoramic tracking shot, followed by an aerial, fast-moving tracking shot and a rotating camera. Likewise quite complex is the music score: the credits sequence plays to a variation of "The Holy War"[34] melody; a modernist score accompanies the intense battle of technologies; the victorious Soviet offensive is set to symphonic music. All of these devices are deployed so as to convey the grandiose scale of the battle.

From the very beginning, the film establishes its vision of the war as a confrontation of leaders and headquarters. Accounting for the glaring lack of

---

[33] Extensive representation of Germans and the consistent use of intertitles to introduce military commanders of both sides of the conflict inspired the use of a similar quasi-documentary device in Tat'iana Lioznova's TV series *Seventeen Moments of Spring* (1973).
[34] "The Holy War" (music by Aleksandr Aleksandrov, lyrics by Vasilii Lebedev-Kumach) is one of the most famous Soviet songs of the Great Patriotic War. It was first performed on June 26, 1941, four days after the German invasion.

narrative and stylistic unity, Ozerov notes that "[a]t the basis of the story [*dramaturgii*] of our film is military strategy. In practice this means that the picture shows the work of headquarters" (qtd. in Tsitriniak (1970): 12–13). This tendency intensifies in the third film, *The Direction of the Main Blow*, which premiered on May 9, 1970, the twenty-fifth anniversary of Victory Day. The narrative is almost exclusively centered on the General Headquarters' search for the most efficient direction for the Soviet offensive in 1944. Sequences with Stalin, Zhukov, and Rokossovsky in front of a map alternate with telegraphically edited episodes of Soviet successes at the front. Epic style definitively takes over the film, while individuals become "people-symbols, people-signs, almost folk-song types, epitomes of Russian epic [*bylinnye*] heroes" (Orlov 1971, 23). As one Soviet critic noted:

> gigantic panoramas of gigantic battles, the movement of ... units and armies, masterfully filmed from the ground, from the air, from the water ... when even rows of planes darting through the sky at breakneck speed over the battle bursting with explosions are seen from above, [...] and tiny human figures [*chelovecheskie figurki*], cowering, are running and falling off the pontoons into the dirty water bursting from bullets.
>
> Orlov 1971, 23

This vision of the war is solidified by the authoritative voice-over. The Soviet state is both the source of historical knowledge and the ultimate author. The omniscient, authoritative, and solemn voice-over most clearly embodies a single "authorial consciousness." It is heard at the end of each episode to finalize the meaning of the events or, more precisely, to link the diegesis with the extratextual teleological narrative: "The greatest tank battle of the Second World War, the Prokhorovka battle, decided the outcome of the Kursk battle. This was the beginning of the end of fascist Germany." However, this teleological motivation is too broad to be able to provide coherence and continuity to individual parts of the narrative. The resulting product is a loose compilation of episodes where spectacle remains the only constant.

Liberation inherited not only the technical know-how and the financing model of *War and Peace*, but also the latter's eclectic style (quotes from Thaw war films, *Alexander Nevsky* [1938], *The Fall of Berlin*, etc.) and the uneasy combination of melodrama (involving the personae of Tsvetaev and Zoia) and the state-centered epic. The representation of the top commanders largely adheres to the iconography borrowed from *The Fall of Berlin*: a wise, unhurried Stalin; a hysterical, rodent-like Hitler; an indecisive and hen-pecked Roosevelt (his wife makes a brief appearance to boss him around; he is played by Stanislav Iaskevich); and a toad-like Churchill, who against his generals' counsel insists that the US and the UK delay opening a second front so that the Red Army will suffer as much as possible. At the same time, the films feature more than a dozen other historical figures (with no established canon of representation), some of whom appear in black-and-white, others in color. *Liberation* also includes some of the Soviet and Eastern European leaders and officials who were in power at the time of the films' release (Iosip Broz Tito, Panteleimon Ponomarenko, Andrei Grechko) – a trend that would come to full bloom in *Soldiers of Freedom* (*Soldaty svobody* 1977). The latter film features Leonid Brezhnev (Evgenii Matveev) and virtually all other post-war leaders of the Eastern Bloc countries during this period as their heroic and reasonably good-looking younger selves, helping the USSR to free Europe from fascism—and to establish socialist regimes in half-a-dozen countries.[35]

Meanwhile, the "trench war," so prominent in Thaw-era films, gets shortchanged. The director explained this decision by ideological imperatives: "While we were engaged in the psychological micro-study [of the tragic early years of the war], our Western colleagues 'corrected' the history of the war with their films" (Ozerov 1971, 2). The films make Lieutenant Tsvetaev (Nikolai Olialin), Captain Orlov (Boris Zaidenberg), and Colonel Lukin (Vsevolod Sanaev) permanent characters who intermittently appear on screen to fulfill their duty to the country—and to the audience. Their representation largely adheres to the iconography familiar from Stalin-era epics: they are infallible, ready to sacrifice themselves for their country, and are almost never occupied with everyday things or conversations. In a five-part film viewers learn very little about them, beyond their military valor. Because of the films' other, more pressing agendas (to show the work of headquarters, to stage spectacular battles), individuals' screen presence is "rationed" and designed to invoke Soviet cinematic clichés. For example, before a Soviet officer is shot by the Nazis, he rips his shirt open and yells to the enemies: "Shoot, you scum!" invoking many such scenes from 1930s–1950s films about the revolution and the Civil War. The only difference is that Ozerov's heroic officer does not invoke his Soviet identity, but

---

[35] If *Liberation* was informally dubbed a "generals' film," *Soldiers of Freedom* was called a "secretaries' film," because most central characters were acting First Secretaries of Eastern European communist parties. Razzakov (2008) vol. 2, 120.

instead says, "Shoot, and you will see how Russian Major Maksimov dies." In the last film Tsvetaev's heroic death while saving German civilians who are being flooded in the Berlin metro on Hitler's orders, simultaneously quotes *The Fall of Berlin* and showcases the ultimate sacrifice of a Soviet officer.[36] Unlike in *The Fall of Berlin*, where the military unit represented the ethnically diverse Big Family with a Russian man at the helm, in *Liberation* most individualized characters are ethnically Russian. In the late-Soviet culture "Russian" stood for the new, supranational community of "Soviet people."[37] National diversity *was* represented in the film: as a collaboration between friendly socialist nations, such as Soviets and Poles, fighting together against the common enemy.

Liberation pays lip service to the love between Tsvetaev and the nurse Zoia (Larisa Golubkina), who is practically the only woman in the film. They appear together for a few minutes in each episode, mostly in symbolic scenes familiar from the Soviet cinematic tradition: Zoia, in accordance with gender conventions, nurses her wounded beloved back to health; later the two accidentally meet after the Red Army liberates Kiev. The dialogue is minimal, especially when compared to the prolonged discussions of military strategy in the headquarters; Tsvetaev and Zoia are rarely together in the same shot, and when they embrace, the camera quickly zooms out to focus on a sea of people and vehicles.

Not only the personal dramas of individuals are abbreviated and dropped. The same logic of "pay tribute and proceed" is applied, for instance, to a quote from Sergei Eisenstein's *Alexander Nevsky*. When Zhukov is examining the terrain for a future attack, he comes across a group of soldiers and, as befits a people-minded leader, fraternizes with them. The soldiers joke about "the second front," by which they mean, of course, American spam, and then show Zhukov some ingenious footwear—*mokrostupy*[38]—which they use in the swamps. Zhukov immediately realizes that he can design something similar for his troops to go through the swamp and surprise the Germans. This is a reference to an episode in *Alexander Nevsky* in which a soldier suggests to the prince a way to lure the enemy into a trap. But the monumental, spectacular attack that follows

---

[36] This spectacular episode also features several German train cars brought to the USSR in 1945 as "reparations." See Artem Krechetnikov, "Trofeinaia Germaniia," http://news.bbc.co.uk/hi/russian/russia/newsid_6634000/6634155.stm.
[37] The film avoided references to any conflicts involving ethnicities comprising the Soviet Union. For example, in the episode about General Vatutin's death in an ambush his assailants are not identified. The viewer might infer that he was killed by Germans. In reality Vatutin was mortally wounded by Ukrainian anti-Soviet resistance fighters—a fact that the film carefully omits.
[38] Wicker footwear, with wide soles to walk on swampy ground; also a type of galoshes.

neither takes place in the swamp nor, indeed, offers a human-eye perspective, which would allow the viewer to appreciate either the episode or the reference.

Indeed, if there is a a star who stands out in *Liberation* it would most certainly be Comrade Stalin, who returned to Soviet screens for the first time after his 15-year-long absence during Khrushchev's destalinization.[39] As work on the script proceeded (1965–1967), all controversial issues, such as Stalin's refusal to allow the Red Cross to help Soviet POWs or his arbitrary reshuffling of commanding officers, which results in enormous human casualties ("Osvobozhdenie Evropy" 54), were smoothed over, while the style of the film became more and more pompous, approaching the representation of Stalin in *The Fall of Berlin*.

Yet despite the importance of this cinematic rehabilitation of Stalin as the mastermind of victory within for the Soviet state's cult of the Great Patriotic War, his major function in the film is that of a celebrity. He both legitimates the powers-that-be as heirs of the great leader and serves as a visual spectacle, an attraction on a par with aerial shots, massive battle scenes, symphonic music, sophisticated sound mixing, and other devices designed to *sell* the epic film to domestic and international audiences. A two-page insert in *The Art of Cinema* featured the scene of the 1943 Tehran Conference of the Allies, with Stalin at the table directly facing Churchill. Stalin is the visual attraction of the image: he is the only one wearing a symbolically light-colored jacket and is portrayed at the moment when all fifteen people in the room direct their glances at him.[40]

The film's advertising campaign in the USSR and abroad was unprecedented. For three years of the film's production both trade and the official press published reports "from the set," emphasizing the film's uniqueness and scale. Lavishly illustrated press releases, translated into a dozen languages (see Figures 1.12, 1.13, 1.14), highlighted the detailed and accurate recreation of battle scenes and strategic decision-making by leaders, while the overall promotional materials read like statistical reports.

The meaning of *Liberation* was entirely controlled by "the author's voice" in yet one more respect: through official discourses *about* the film. Dozens of internal letters, reviews, and reports to various agencies hone the language about the film and "refine" the discourse into its final modality. After this rhetorical

---

[39] Between 1953 and 1968 Stalin appeared as a character only in three obscure Soviet films: *Truth* (*Pravda*, dir. Viktor Dobrovol'skii and Isaak Shmaruk 1957), *October Days* (*V dni oktiabria*, dir. Sergei Vasil'ev 1958), and *On the Same Planet* (*Na odnoi planete*, dir. Il'ia Ol'shvanger 1965).

[40] *The Art of Cinema* 5 (1970).

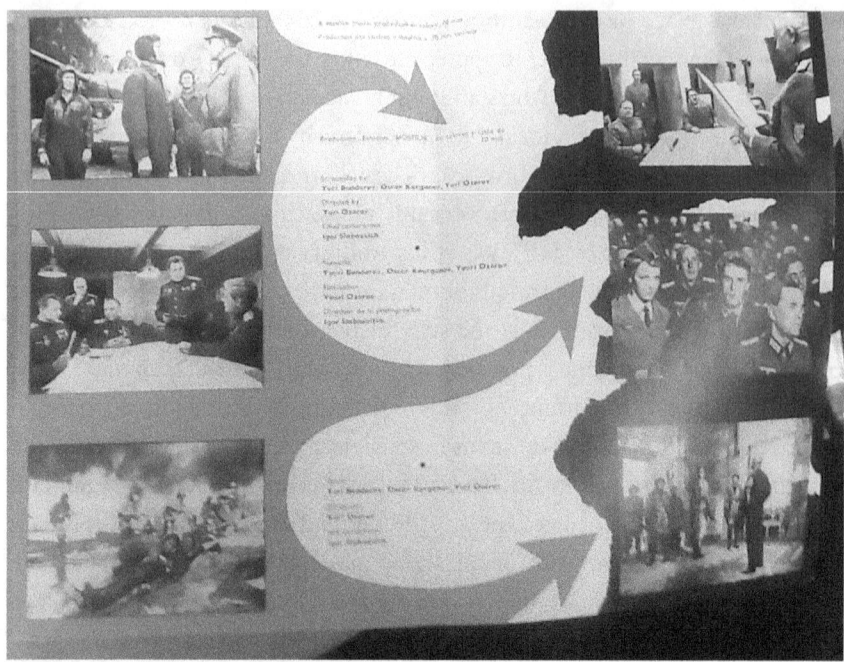

Figure 1.12: Promotional brochure for *Liberation*
Source: Gosfilmofond, National Film Foundation of the Russian Federation

labor, the films could not be criticized in the press or, indeed, discussed outside the pre-set parameters. All reviews in the press repeat the internal reviews almost *verbatim*, as if following a script. The narrative conforms to the newly-minted Brezhnev-era mythology of the Great Patriotic War and connects it both to the Soviet film industry and the Soviet state's self-promotion as a powerful player in the global film market. While the Soviet premiere of *Liberation* in Moscow, Leningrad, the hero-cities[41] and the capitals of the fifteen republics was a major cinematic and political event, equally, if not more, important was the evidence of the Soviet film industry's international success. As *The Art of Cinema* emphasized, *The Direction of the Main Blow* premiered in the "capitals of socialist countries, as well as in Paris, London, Rome, West Berlin, Tokyo, and one of the US cities. The well-known US company Columbia Pictures acquired the rights

---

[41] Hero-city was a Soviet honorary title awarded to the cities of the USSR where fighting with Nazis was especially fierce. The statute about the honorary title was issued by the Soviet government on May 8, 1965. Initially Leningrad, Volgograd (former Stalingrad), Kiev, Sevastopol, and Odessa received the honorary title.

Figure 1.13: Promotional brochure for *Liberation*
Source: Gosfilmofond, National Film Foundation of the Russian Federation

to show the first two pictures of the epic in 44 capitalist countries" (Tsitriniak 1970, 19). *The Art of Cinema* accompanied its multiple reviews of *Liberation* with excerpts from the foreign press praising Bondarchuk's epic, thus connecting the two productions as Soviet film triumphs.[42] *Soviet Screen* published a detailed account of a film essay competition for schoolchildren in Japan about the Soviet epic, with extensive quotes discussing both the "eye-opening" content and the technical superiority of Soviet filmmaking: "Only socialist cinematography can ensure participation of such a great number of tanks and people" (Kassis 1973, 15).

According to official statistics, the attendance at all five films of *Liberation* worldwide was 400 million, with many organized trips to the movie theater, inasmuch as Party members, soldiers, and schoolchildren were required to attend. Valerii Golovskoi reports on a story related to him by the director of a

---

[42] *The Art of Cinema* 8 (1969). Out of five quotes from the press, three are from American publications, in addition to a reminder that *War and Peace* received an Oscar.

Figure 1.14: Promotional brochure for *Liberation*
Source: Gosfilmofond, National Film Foundation of the Russian Federation

movie theater in rural Ukraine: everyone in the village had to buy a ticket, yet the majority did not go to the screening. When the regular schedule resumed they all showed up with their unused tickets and demanded to be admitted (2004, 215).[43]

The two prestige productions we analyze in this chapter were also released in over 2,000 prints (*War and Peace*—2,805 prints all over the USSR, *Liberation* in 2,202 prints)—two of only three Soviet films ever distributed this way, the third being Leonid Gaidai's blockbuster comedy *Diamond Arm* (*Brilliantovaia ruka* 1968). As with *War and Peace*, the Soviet state launched a massive advertising campaign for *Liberation*. Press reviews and promotional materials translated into a dozen languages teem with information about the numbers of troops who provided extras, of costumes made, weapons built or borrowed from museums,

---

[43] In fact, this incident is far from unique. One form of subsidizing certain films was the "transfer" of box-office receipts: show the Soviet film at one screening, while another ten screenings are of a popular comedy or a Western film, then claim box office profits for the prestige production (Golovskoi 2004, 215–216).

tanks and planes used in the production,[44] etc. Such efforts were not made in vain: Soviet attendance for the five films of the epic was over 200 million. However, by the third film, attendance had dropped from 56 to 35 million; as Denise Youngblood notes, "although the state could channel resources to a favored director, it could not control the audience" (2007, 162). The last two films try to fix the problem via drinking as visual humor. In an epic production, of course, warriors drank accordingly, and on their triumphant way to Berlin, Soviet and Polish soldiers located and bonded over an entire tanker of alcohol.

Liberation made an attempt to resuscitate the single ideological syntax of socialist realism while using spectacle for commercial attraction. Ironically, after its short theatrical run, the multi-partite epic found its permanent home on the Soviet small screen, where it premiered in summer 1972 and usually returned around the anniversary of victory in the Great Patriotic War.

After *Liberation*, Ozerov went on to make several other war epics, e.g., *Battle for Moscow* (*Bitva za Moskvu* 1985) and *Stalingrad* (1989), as well as a propagandistic and lavish documentary titled *Oh, Sport, You Are—Peace!* (*O sport, Ty—mir!* 1981) about the 1980 Olympic Games in Moscow, which were boycotted by almost 50 countries in protest against the Soviet invasion of Afghanistan. The official genre designation of this film duplicated that of Ozerov's war epics: "fictional-documentary film." A 200-minute spectacle, the film combined documentary footage and animation, interviews and the authoritative voice-over of Nikolai Ozerov, panoramic vistas of Moscow, aerial shots, and time-lapse photographs of Olympic records, keeping the visual memory of Leni Riefenstahl's *Olympia* alive.

Postscript: the revival of prestige productions under Putin

After the fall of the Soviet Union, epic productions disappeared from the struggling Russian film industry—only to re-emerge with a vengeance during Putin's reign.[45] Notably, two Soviet films restored and digitally remastered in the

---

[44] The Soviet Minister of Defense Malinovskii ordered the Soviet industry to support the filmmaker with 150 tanks and other vehicles. Using the original German blueprints, engineers of the Lvov Mechanical Plant built several dozen replicas of German tanks and self-propelled guns (Danilov 2012).

[45] After the fall of communism, with the collapse of the Soviet film distribution system, Ozerov reformatted all his war epics (*Liberation, Battle for Moscow, Stalingrad*) into a 24-part (45 min. in each episode) television series, *Tragedy of a Century* (*Tragediia veka* 1993–1994), for release on ORT Television Channel, the future Channel One of Russian Television (Sopin 2011–2012, 645). The mini-series was financed by Ganem-Film (Syria) and Mosfilm (Russia) and was broadcast in 1998. In 2000, the re-edited, more dynamic version in six parts was re-broadcast, again on Channel One.

early 2000s were *War and Peace* and *Liberation*.⁴⁶ Putin's regime manifests an affinity for 1970s culture and its visual texts, especially those dealing with the Great Patriotic War, which once again is portrayed as the story of origins of the great Russo-Soviet state. Sociologist Boris Dubin notes that the Putin era is about a "reconciliation with the Soviet" (Dubin 2006), partly based on celebrations of the Soviet victory over Nazi Germany. The special importance given to the Great Patriotic War in state-supported films and other commemorations helps to focus the national memory on one clear point. Opinion polls show, Dubin notes elsewhere, that Stalinism and other crimes of the Soviet era now mean little to post-Soviet Russians, while the victory in the Great Patriotic War remains the key positive event of the past century (2008, 6–21). Our research indicates that in addition to the focus on the Great Patriotic War, post-Soviet prestige productions integrate Soviet imperial endeavors into a larger frame—that of Russia's history as a global power. Hence, in 2002–2003, *War and Peace* and *Liberation* ended up in the same Mosfilm Studio shop for a digital facelift. Again, the Russian state does not spare expense and technology to capture domestic and foreign audiences with prestige productions.

An important bridge text from Soviet to post-Soviet prestige productions became *And Quiet Flows the Don* (*Tikhii Don* 1992–2006), a Russian-Italian co-production begun by Bondarchuk Sr. in 1986 and completed by his son, Fedor, two decades later. The demise of the Soviet film industry and the bankruptcy of its Italian partner complicated work on the film. Only in the 2000s was Fedor Bondarchuk, with the aid of Russian Channel One and, personally, Konstantin Ernst and Vladimir Pozner, able to recover the abandoned 160,000 meters of footage, which he edited himself for television release. Channel One premiered Sergei Bondarchuk's epic as a mini-series on November 6, 2006, linking the premiere with a significant date in the political history of Russia, the anniversary of the Russian Revolution.

The return of the undead (i.e., Soviet epics) inspired the efforts of Bondarchuk and Nikita Mikhalkov to revive the prestige production and its homosocial militaristic syntax as a major genre that narrates the official version of new Russia's collective memory. Mikhalkov, in fact, participated in the delayed release of *And Quiet Flows the Don*: his is the God-like voice-over explaining the events of the film and, by association, Russia's bloody history. Bondarchuk and Mikhalkov occupy two different niches within the genre of prestige

---

⁴⁶ *War and Peace* was restored in 2000 and *Liberation* was restored in 2002–2003, both at Mosfilm Studio (Sopin 2011–2012, 622–623).

production—the niches that re-enact the genre's late-Soviet history: Bondarchuk specializes in war epics, while Mikhalkov works primarily in the genre of historical costume epics.

In 1999, Nikita Mikhalkov released his *Barber of Siberia* (*Sibirskii tsiriul'nik*), a film that refurbished the prestige production syntax for Putin-era ideology. This big-budget French-Russian government-sponsored co-production revived the story of the male serving the empire and finding happiness in Siberia. Most importantly, as film scholars Stephen Norris (2012) and Birgit Beumers point out, the film reintroduced the imperial sublime associated with the Russian past. The film restored the spirit of militarism and proudly displayed new imperial acquisitions. In the case of *Barber of Siberia* it was the newly built replica of Christ the Savior Cathedral in the shots behind the tsar played by Mikhalkov himself. Initiated as a convention of late-socialist prestige productions by Bondarchuk in his *War and Peace,* the displays of Orthodox cathedrals, icons, and gold-clad priests became part and parcel of the new state ideology (see Figure 1.15).

In their discussions of *Barber of Siberia,* Beumers and Norris note that the film positions the male protagonist in the service of his country at the center of the film. The male protagonist, not so coincidentally carrying the name Andrei and the last name Tolstoy, sacrifices everything and goes to Siberia to serve and suffer for his country. The film is dedicated to "Russian officers, the pride of the nation," and Alexander III as played by Mikhalkov praises the courage, steadfastness, and endurance of the Russian army. As Condee notes, in Mikhalkov's films the army comprises the true imperial family—"a key producer

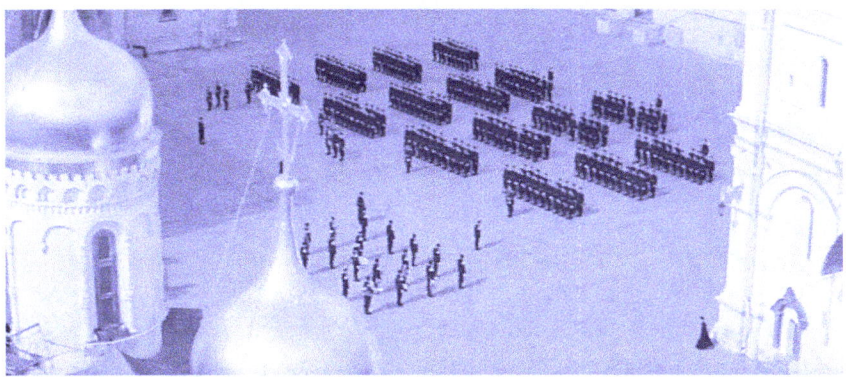

Figure 1.15: The Imperial Army and Golden Domes of Orthodox Cathedrals meet each other in *Barber of Siberia* (dir. Nikita Mikhalkov 1999)

of collective subjectivity"—where Russian men can bond, serve, and pursue their manifest destiny (91–92).

In 2010–2011, Nikita Mikhalkov released a two-part sequel to his 1994 Oscar-winning melodrama *Burnt by the Sun* (*Utomlennye solntsem*), titled *Exodus* (*Predstoianie*) and *The Citadel* (*Tsitadel'*). The sequel is the most expensive Russian film to date, costing an estimated $55 million. Vladimir Putin personally visited the set (see Figure 1.16), and the film was screened at the Cannes Film festival, but did not receive any awards and failed at the box office.

Mikhalkov's most recent film, *Sunstroke* (*Solnechnyi udar* 2014), based on two works by Ivan Bunin, manifests the Soviet-style close coordination of the ideologies of both the author and state and uses the melodramatic plot to provide some authenticity for the Putin-era mixture of imperialism and state-sponsored Orthodoxy. In her biography of Mikhalkov, Beumers notes that his films constantly perform a shift from nostalgia that is "openly constructed as a myth to a nostalgia for a past that pretends to be authentic" (2). One way to create this false sense of authenticity/pseudo-documentary moment in a staged film is to cast his own family in lead roles. In *Barber of Siberia*, for example, Mikhalkov's daughter Anna plays the true love of Andrei Tolstoy.

Figure 1.16: President Vladimir Putin on the set of *Burnt by the Sun-2*

Source: Creative Commons Attribution 4.0, image from the site of the Prime Minister of the Russian Federation, premier.gov.ru

In *Sunstroke*, the director excels in this practice of creating a pseudo-organic link across textual borders. Instead of his own family, he casts Russian-speaking citizens of the former Soviet republics and friendly Slavic nations, thus literally *embodying* in his film the state-sponsored dream of the greater "Russian World," expanding Russia's power beyond the official borders of the Russian Federation. The lead actor, Martins Kalita, a Russian-speaking Latvian actor, plays the male protagonist. A Russian-speaking Serbian actor plays one of his acquaintances. A Russian-speaking Israeli actress, Miriam Sekhon, plays the evil Jewish female commissar. Finally, Viktoriia Solov'eva, from South-Eastern Ukraine plays the female lead. At the film's premiere she talked about how the current events in Eastern Ukraine remind her of the atrocities addressed in the film.

Mikhalkov's post-Soviet prestige productions engage in remaking the state sublime via invoking extra-textual present day displays of state power in his films. In *Sunstroke* (filmed in Switzerland and Ukraine), the major display of state power is the newly annexed Crimea peninsula, depicted in the film as occupied and destroyed by evil Bolsheviks. Hence the extra-diegetic last-minute rescue by the Russian government of poor Crimeans and the ultimate sense of relief for Russian viewers.

As in the prestige productions of the Soviet era, ideological priorities trumped commercial considerations during the release of *Sunstroke*. The film received a non-refundable subsidy from the Russian Cinema Fund Board,[47] had a $21 million budget, and collected $2 million at the box office after its first month of release in Russia. According to a Russian film industry expert Oleg Ivanov, the public discussion triggered by the film might compensate for the box office losses. On October 3, Mikhalkov held the film's world premiere in Belgrade, Serbia, which was attended by the Russian Minister of Culture, Vladimir Medinsky.

On October 4, 2014 the filmmaker held the second premiere in Simferopol and Sevastopol, Crimea, and expressed his strongest possible support of Russia's annexation of Crimea, bluntly announcing, "Anyone who says Crimea is not Russian is the enemy." As ever, viewing his own activities as part of "Russia's destiny," the filmmaker sees a special significance in the film's opening in the newly acquired Russian peninsula. *Hollywood Reporter* noted that "Following a speech dedicated to the history of the Russian Empire, Mikhalkov joined a Cossack choir in singing the Tsarist-era imperial Russian national anthem" (Holdsworth 2014).

---

[47] See n.a. "Fond kino opredelilsia s proektami."

Finally, just as in the case of *War and Peace* in the 1960s, the Ministry of Defense of the Russian Federation helped the filmmaker and the film studio in work on the film. Specifically, the Ministry of Defense took over some of the expenses of the film's promotion in Crimea, and, according to *The Hollywood Reporter*, Mikhalkov and a press pool were flown from Moscow to Crimea in a Russian-made Tupolev 154 passenger jet chartered by the Russian Ministry of Defense (Holdsworth 2014). The flight on a Russian-made jet to the premiere of one's film is the ultimate moment of the great power sublime resuscitated.

While Mikhalkov has replaced Sergei Bondrachuk as the court artist in charge of visualizing the imperial sublime, Fedor Bondarchuk has established himself as the premier artist directing big-budget war films. His first feature, *The 9th Company* (*Deviataia rota* 2005) redefined the ignominious Soviet defeat in Afghanistan as the spiritual victory of a multinational military Soviet unit over its numerous enemies, including Mikhail Gorbachev, whose speech on the radio prevents the unit from keeping in contact with their commanders. Filmed in Crimea, the film became a self-fulfilled prophecy for the new imperial expansion.

The most recent Russian foray into the renewed competition with the West on the cinematic front is the 2013 film *Stalingrad* by Fedor, the son of Sergei, Bondarchuk. The first film in Russia shot in the IMAX 3D format, it proved quite successful in Russian movie theaters and received Putin's personal stamp of approval. During the Moscow premiere of the picture in October 2013 cosmonaut Aleksei Leonov was among the celebrities invited to the grand opening of the patriotic blockbuster,[48] yet another symbol of continuity with the Soviet tradition of prestige productions. Russia had great hopes for an Oscar— like father like son—but the film was not nominated. Ironically, the focus on the demonstration of the technical superiority and the power of the state-financed Russian film industry blurred the sacred line between the Soviets and the Germans. Some war veterans were outraged by what they saw as the picture's "heroization" of the Nazis.[49]

---

[48] See www.spletnik.ru/events/45379-premera-dramy-fedora-bondarchuka-stalingrad-v-moskve.html
[49] Petr Morozov. Petition to the Ministry of Culture, Russia, to Ban Fedor Bondarchuk's film *Stalingrad*. 1 November 2013. "To ban the exhibition of F. Bondarchuk's film *Stalingrad* in the Russian Federation; to ban the distribution of this film abroad; to withdraw the bid for Oscar." Change.org

Prestige epic films remain a peculiar case of continuity between the Soviet, state-run and the post-Soviet market-driven film industries. These epics still shape the visual image of Russia as a supranational great power for millions of viewers in Russia and on a more limited scale worldwide, interpreting history via a combination of expensive production, epic scale narrative, quality cinematography, and the use of popular actors. Writing about Hollywood epics, Gilles Deleuze remarks that "the American cinema constantly shoots and reshoots a single fundamental film, which is the birth of a nation-civilization ... each prefiguring America."[50] In a similar vein, Soviet and post-Soviet prestige productions depict key moments of the country's history in anticipation of Russia as a global power to come.

---

[50] Cited in Burgoyne, "Bare Life and Sovereignty in *Gladiator*"(83).

2

The Socialist Television Police Procedural of the 1970s and 80s: Teaching Soviet Citizens How to Behave

Syntax and semantics of the genre

Whereas late-socialist film epic focused on the male protagonist's service to the empire, either Russian or Soviet, the Soviet police procedural embodied a male community of professional investigators mediating the relationship between the state and its citizens. In contrast to prestige epic war films, which were exhibited primarily in the movie theaters, the police procedural articulated late-socialist ideology above all on the small screen and was present in every Soviet's living room every evening. Television police serials defined the syntax of the genre for both television and cinema and established television as the medium that could not only emulate the film industry's generic models but also establish conventions that cinema had to follow. The police procedural modeled the relations between the state and its citizens, and the desired behavior of socialist citizens.

In the late 1960s, various interpretive communities tried to define the ideological and aesthetic borders of the Soviet police procedural film. In 1969 the journal *Soviet Screen* ran a discussion of the adventure film genre,[1] an umbrella term that referred to four quite distinct subtypes: the police procedural film (which Soviets called *detektiv*), the film about Soviet intelligence agents (*fil'm o razvedchikakh*), war adventure film (*voenno-prikliuchencheskii fil'm*), and the domestically-produced Western usually set during the Civil War. The participants included film critics, writers, and film directors, as well as representatives of law enforcement agencies: the KGB and the Prosecutor General's office.

---

[1] Soviet adventure film emerged in the 1920s under the influence of American and German action imports starring Douglas Fairbanks and Conrad Veidt. The typical plot involves a quest by a male protagonist, often in an exotic location, against the background of a particular historical period. The Soviet adventure film by default included an overt ideological message and often targeted children as its primary audience. For further discussion see Prokhorov (2014): 67–70.

The discussion was quite revealing in that underneath a hegemonic socialist discourse there existed strikingly different approaches to the issue. On the one hand, in view of the importance of the themes treated in these films (law enforcement, the Civil War and the Great Patriotic War) the overarching concern of some was that the formulaic nature of the genres and the unclear boundary between the "good socialist" and the "bad capitalist" threatened to trivialize the ideological message of the films. The KGB colonel, for example, criticized the mini-series *Major Whirlwind* (*Maior Vikhr'* 1967) for portraying officers of Soviet special forces simply as professionals, rather than carriers of Soviet ideology and, in this respect, indistinguishable from American or German intelligence and counterintelligence officers.[2] Critics also noted that the police film often fell prey to the tendency to romanticize the criminal underworld, skewing the entire ideological message of the film in favor of Western genre conventions.

On the other hand, while the participating filmmakers tried to distance themselves from the accusation of commercialism, they often argued from the position of intimate knowledge of Hollywood genre conventions.[3] Moreover, in some critics' arguments, narrative considerations decidedly trumped ideological ones. For example, critic Vsevolod Revich noted that where the police film centers on the investigation of crime, the Soviet spy film inverts this pattern: here the enemy investigates the activity of the Soviet undercover agent.[4] The critic thus implied that the police film provides the key plot structure while the spy film is just its structural variant.

While all subtypes of adventure film continued to exist into the 1970s, it was the police film that occupied the key position in late-socialist cinema and television, and influences Russian popular culture after the fall of socialism. It was the only genre with contemporary settings and contemporary conflicts. Even though consumerism was criticized as bourgeois or criminal excess, it provided motivations for characters' actions with which contemporary audiences could identify, in stark contrast to the artifice of ideological motivations in spy thrillers and war adventures.

---

[2] N.a. "Chto takoe prikliuchencheskii fil'm?" *Sovetskii ekran* 9 (1969): 7–9, 8.
[3] Vitautas Zhalakiavichus, for instance, noted that his *Nobody Wanted to Die* (*Nikto ne khotel umirat'*, 1966) was frequently called a western but, in his view, had nothing to do with this genre. N.a. "Chto takoe prikliuchencheskii fil'm?" *Sovetskii ekran* 9 (1969): 7–9, 9. Likewise, Vladimir Motyl' claimed that his *White Sun of the Desert* (*Below solntse pustyni*, 1970) transcended the triviality of the Hollywood western plot. N.a. "Chto takoe prikliuchencheskii fil'm?" *Sovetskii ekran* 10 (1969): 12–13, 13.
[4] N.a. "Chto takoe prikliuchencheskii fil'm?" *Sovetskii ekran* 10 (1969): 12–13, 13.

If in the 1930s the state prosecuted its subjects on screen directly, whereby any transgression was interpreted as a political and ideological crime against the state, by the 1960s political crime, such as espionage or treason, parted ways with crimes that were not implicated directly in undermining the Soviet state. The former became the subjects of KGB-sponsored spy films designated as films about Soviet scouts (*fil'my o sovetskikh razvedchikakh*), while the latter were depicted in the detective film about Soviet police (*militseiskii detektiv*).[5] Soviet critics used the term "the detective film" rather loosely. These films were not crime films, in which an individual professional or amateur detective investigated a crime. Soviet "detective films" focused not on the private detective or an intellectual puzzle but represented the Soviet police as an institution collectively uncovering crimes, which were supposed to be eventually eradicated from Soviet life.

If in the West the police procedural followed the long reign of the detective hardboiled noir film and, as Thomas Leitch claims, superseded it only with the appearance of television, Soviet culture almost entirely escaped the hardboiled detective craze. Because of ideological demands, the iconic "private eye" and the sensationalism of car chases and physical violence were not a welcome model for films about the police. The Soviet police film immediately adopted the institutional model, the conventions of which were established in American culture in the late 1950s–early 1960s: "the emphasis on the daily routines of a given group of police officers, rather than their rare dramatic breakthroughs, and on the presentation of several overlapping cases simultaneously" (Leitch, 2002, 215).

In our further discussion, therefore, we will use the term police procedural to designate films and TV series depicting a team of officers and the procedures they follow to conduct their investigation. Soviet police procedurals dealing with contemporary crime allowed few types of criminal acts to feature on screen, primarily crimes against property (personal and government) and juvenile delinquency. Violent crimes rarely appeared in Soviet police procedurals because they would indicate that acts such as murder or rape were part of Soviet life. If

---

[5] *Militisiia* was the name of the civilian police in the Soviet Union and Warsaw Pact countries. On 17 April 1917, the Provisional Government of the Russian Republic gave the name *militsiia* to the law enforcement force of post-tsarist Russia to emphasize that it derives its legitimacy from the self-organization of the people and to distinguish it from the tsarist imperial police. When Bolsheviks seized power in October 1917, they kept the name *militsiia* for their civilian police force. In post-Soviet Russia, *militsiia* was renamed *politsiia* on 1 March 2011.

Figure 2.1: The investigator (Mikhail Zharov) exposes the spy under Stalin's eagle eye in *Engineer Kochin's Mistake*

the crime was violent, it was usually historicized as a survival of the pre-socialist past or explained by foreign (usually Western) interference.

The first key syntactic element of the late-socialist police procedural is the interrogation scene. During this scene the investigator either unmasks the incorrigible villain or reeducates a wrongdoer capable of change. Brezhnev-era police procedurals inherited this scene from Stalin-era spy films, such as Alexander Macheret's *Engineer Kochin's Mistake* (*Oshibka inzhenera Kochina* 1939). In Stalin-era films the interrogation both concluded the investigation and sealed the result of the redundant trial, at least in the eyes of the viewer (see Figure 2.1).

Thaw cinema changed this model by placing greater emphasis on the courtroom drama, which could reverse the results of a sloppy investigation, which accused the wrong person.[6] The first episode of the major Brezhnev-era television procedural *The Investigation is Conducted by Experts* revisits this Thaw-era

---

[6] See for example *The Man Who Doubts* (*Chelovek, kotoryi somnevaetsia* 1963), directed by Leonid Agranovich and Vladimir Semakov.

collision in order to re-establish a neo-Stalinist ideological model. The episode begins during the end of the trial, in which the accused criminal is acquitted. The police team then picks up where the judges and prosecution dropped the ball, re-investigates the case, and successfully convicts the criminal who almost got away with it. Notably, the courtroom never reappears in the rest of the series because its convicting function is carried out by the police. In other words, if the police tell the viewer that the accused is guilty, there is no need to prove this on screen in a court of law. The government and its police force never make mistakes.

The moral and legal issues of late-socialist society became the content of the extended interrogation scenes. These scenes showcased the advantages of the socialist way of life. For example, criminals were usually people who could not consume moderately. Instead of driving Soviet compact Lada cars, they bought limousines; instead of eating in modest cafeterias, they frequented expensive restaurants. Because, according to the films and TV shows, Soviet life was plentiful, criminals usually stole luxury items, such as jewelry, not items of everyday consumption. Moderate consumerism, of private apartments and cars, for example, was showcased in police films and television shows to indicate an advanced socialist society.

The interrogation scene was also the time when an errant citizen could learn that the government, represented by the investigator, should be trusted. A key syntactic element of the socialist realist masterplot, the reeducation trope becomes a semantic—and increasingly anachronistic—element in the late-Soviet police procedural.[7] Late-socialist reeducation did not aspire to instill the character with communist ideology, but only hoped to regain the citizen's trust in state institutions. The interrogation built the suspect's trust and goodwill towards the system, something every viewer was expected to experience vicariously while watching the show. In fact, the police investigator not only exposed the suspect to impeccable legal procedure, but also provided psychological counseling, quasi-buddy smoking, and a quasi-religious opportunity to confess (see Figure 2.2). But

---

[7] In *Petrovka 38* (dir. Boris Grigor'ev, 1980) in the course of his investigation Senior Lieutenant Rosliakov (Evgenii Gerasimov) falls in love with the female (Liudmila Nil'skaia) who, conveniently, needs to be reeducated to be worthy of a Soviet police officer. The late-Soviet reeducation plot begins in a swimming pool, where Rosliakov's desire for a female's body is disguised as admiration of her perfect athletic skills. During their next meeting the girl thinks that Rosliakov simply wants to sleep with her. However, the Soviet police officer wants a serious and meaningful relationship. Instead of undressing her as she assumes he would, he uses his spectacular karate skills to open a bottle of brandy and declares that not all men want the same thing on the first date. Rosliakov's self-control is in total conformity with the police code of conduct and, most importantly, with the reeducation plot.

Figure 2.2: Interrogation as soul-searching in *The Investigation is Conducted by Experts* (1972)

while the private citizen under investigation was supposed to trust the state, the state never trusted its citizens. The presumption of innocence, which officially was reasserted in Soviet criminal law during the Khrushchev era, did not appear as an important concept in Brezhnev-era police procedurals. With so many issues at stake, it is not surprising that interrogation scenes occupy the bulk of screen time in Soviet police films and television police procedurals.

The second important syntactic feature of the Soviet police procedural that distinguishes it from its Western counterpart is the police squad: the epitome of social harmony amidst an urban setting aspiring to that perfection. In their study of the police procedural, *The Public Eye*, Robert Winston and Nancy Mellerski link the emergence of the modern police procedural after the Second World War with the shift from a market to a managed economy, which made the "corporate hero" into the ideologically central figure of cultural narrative. The authors see the rise of the police procedural as a response to the technological penetration and increased bureaucratic complexity of post-industrial society. Accordingly, the genre operates by proposing a squad of individualized detectives, each possessing certain crucial skills that enable them to work collectively in investigating the same systemic evil that the hardboiled detective nostalgically confronted alone (1992, 6).

The emergence of a more complex and diversified society in the USSR in the 1970s also manifested itself in such television and film police procedurals as *The*

Investigation is Conducted by Experts and a film cycle about Colonel Zorin (Vsevolod Sanaev) and his investigative team. In fact, one of the most famous film cycles based on the novels of Iulian Semenov carried the institutional identity on its sleeve: *Petrovka 38* was named after the Moscow Criminal Police HQ (MUR) and *Ogareva 6* was the address of the HQ of the Ministry of Internal Affairs.

The police squad is not simply homogenous with the Soviet state, as it used to be in the films of the 1930s and 1940s, but is rather an egalitarian group of professionals mediating between the state and the public.[8] Professionalism, rather than ideological mission, defines this community's identity and allows it to fulfill its service to the state and the public. Each team member has a particular specialization and contributes to the investigation in his unique way. Such a team points to the emergence of a complex and modern society consisting of individual professionals with a strong sense of agency. Moreover, the crime itself becomes more complex and requires forensic science, forensic accounting, and, depending on the nature of the crime, creative uses of various scientific expertise.

At the same time, the focus on the police team, at times at the expense of the built-in lure of any investigative drama, suggests the unit's other function—that of a miniature model for the ideal Soviet society. The team includes representatives of different ethnicities and, at times, even genders. After all, a way the police procedural manages "widespread public distrust and fear of surveillance by a faceless bureaucracy...and overextended police power" (Winston and Mellerski 1992, 6) is through particularizing police officers. The new corporate detective squad consists not of faceless cogs, parts of the institutional machine, but of fallible human beings and hard-working guarantors of public order and stability. The police squad serves as the model to be emulated by the rest of the society, with which the ideal Soviet cops interact in "humanized" disciplinary spaces, such as interrogation rooms, police offices, and jail cells.

Serialization is the third key syntactic element of the police procedural. As such, it has both ideological and industrial implications. While a focus on the routine of police work can be construed as familiarizing the general audience

---

[8] Along the way, the late-Soviet police procedural abandons another convention of earlier crime films, especially of the 1950s–1960s Thaw period: the reeducation of a rash young policeman by his older and wiser colleague. By the mid-1970s, this convention was coming under attack in the film press. According to one reviewer, "[An old investigator] is smart, in contrast to his young colleague. Every detective film surely has one young, spirited fool who, as soon as someone falls under suspicion, immediately asks: 'Will we arrest him right away or should we wait?'" Ol'ga Chaikovskaia, "I eshche neskol'ko tain," *Sovetskii ekran* 10 (1973): 2–4, 2.

with the public service of the police, thus making it more transparent and non-threatening, some authors argue convincingly that the very serialized format of the genre represents an ideal of disciplinary society in a Foucauldian sense: "a precise and repeated reproduction of the stages of interrogation, investigation, and judgement [which] maintain such discipline over time—in a conciliatory and therefore non-threatening manner" (Winston and Mellerski 1992, 8). It is certainly the case with the Soviet police procedural, with its pronounced didactic goal of crime prevention via viewers' acculturation into a society of invisible but ubiquitous surveillance. This new complex social organization with a friendly and ever-present police team in your streets and on your screens replaces the unmediated and visible terror campaigns of the Stalin era.

The late 1960s' discussions of the nature of the Soviet detective plot spearheaded increased funding and attention to the development of the genre for both big and small screens. In this chapter we argue that the television police procedural defined the syntax of the genre for both media. Most importantly, television's serialized format, case-by-case structure, and a permanent cast of police characters resulted in the long-running Soviet television series, *The Investigation is Conducted by Experts* (1971–1989). Cinema, in turn, adopted this model by creating a series of films unified by the same set of characters who investigated new cases. For example, Mosfilm's creative unit Ray *(Luch)* specialized in films about police Colonel Zorin made by two directors: first, Anatolii Bobrovskii (*The Return of St. Luke/Vozvrashchenie Sviatogo Luki*, 1970 and *The Black Prince/Chernyi prints*, 1973) and later Andrei Ladynin (*Colonel Zorin's Version/Versiia polkovnika Zorina*, 1978). Like genuine commercial genre films, these series of films were connected by the star actor, Vsevolod Sanaev, while the filmmakers' role was secondary.[9] Another example is a series of films based on Iulian Semenov's screenplays about a team of Moscow detectives, *Petrovka 38* and *Ogareva 6* (both 1980), followed by a television mini-series, *Standoff* (*Protivostoianie*, 1985).[10] Thus, for the first time, the television format defined the conventions of films made for theatrical release.

---

[9] Film officials praised the Ray Unit for writing scripts of police procedurals for specific actors, which implied the possibility of serializing the plot and bringing viewers back to film theaters to see the same lead actor. "Chernyi prints," RGALI, f. 2944, op. 4, ed. khran. 2396, p. 5.

[10] Before the 1970s, two-partite features were usually limited to films with "significant ideological content," such as war and historical epics. From the 1950s on, big budget prestige productions based on Russian and Soviet literary classics joined this elite financial category, such as Sergei Gerasimov's *Quiet Flows the Don* (1957–58), Sergei Bondarchuk's *War and Peace* (1965–67), and Alexander Zarkhi's *Anna Karenina* (1967).

Television influenced film production and exhibition not only on the level of narrative and visual conventions, but also in terms of economic models. With a decrease in the cinema audience in the 1970s, economic considerations made film administrators more agreeable to allow modest-budget, but action-packed police films to come out in two parts. Such films included *The Gold Mine* (*Zolotaia mina,* dir. Evgenii Tatarskii, 1977) and *The Sleuth* (*Syshchik,* dir. Vladimir Fokin, 1979). Of the slim pickings of film genres available to Soviet audiences, the police film was among the most popular. Even if these films were not always blockbusters they inevitably attracted young, especially male audiences, with the promise of the vicarious pleasures of violence, chase, transgression, and excessive consumption. For example, *Petrovka 38* sold 53.4 million tickets[11]; *Sleuth* sold 43.6 million[12]; *Black Prince* sold 24.6 million[13]; *Colonel Zorin's Version* sold 23.7 million,[14] etc.

By the 1970s, television had become a major competitor to cinema and an employer of Soviet filmmakers. Many popular crime film directors started their careers by making police films for the big screen and then migrated to the units within major studios, such as Telefilm at Mosfilm studio, which produced the television mini-series commissioned by Gosteleradio, State Committee on Television and Radio Broadcasting. Evgenii Tatarskii, for example, started a successful career with his film *The Gold Mine* and then switched to making crime miniseries for television (*Sharlotta's Necklace/Kol'e Sharlotty,* 1984). After making several adventure films, in 1979 Stanislav Govorukhin directed a very successful police television mini-series, *The Meeting Place Cannot Be Changed.* Scriptwriters such as Iulian Semenov and Arkadii and Georgii Vainer also worked more for television than for cinema in the 1970s and 1980s. A successful film, such as Ivan Lukinskii's 1968 *Village Detective* (*Derevenskii detektiv*), spawned two television sequels starring the same actor, Mikhail Zharov, in the lead role of an octogenarian village police chief and investigator (*Aniskin and Fantomas/Aniskin i Fantomas,* 1974 and *Aniskin, Yet Again/I snova Aniskin,* 1977).

The police procedural did not aspire to be a vehicle for an ideological message or an art masterpiece. Instead, these films had moderate budgets[15] and stable but

---

[11] See http://kinanet.livejournal.com/14172.html#cutid1.
[12] See http://kinanet.livejournal.com/14886.html#cutid1.
[13] See http://kinanet.livejournal.com/20119.html#cutid1.
[14] See http://kinanet.livejournal.com/20119.html#cutid1.
[15] *The Return of St. Luke, Colonel Zorin's Version,* and *Petrovka 38* each had a budget of about 360 000 rubles., as compared to with *War and Peace,* with its exceptional budget of 8 million rubles. "Vozvrashchenie Sviatogo Luki." RGALI, fond 2944, op. 4, ed. kh. 1755, "Versiia polkovnika Zorina." RGALI, fond 2944, op. 4, ed. kh. 2396, and "Petrovka 38." RGALI, fond. 2944, op. 4, ed. kh. 5300.

not spectacular attendance; thereby they performed the regular cultural work envisioned by the film industry and official supervisors. While some government officials suggested that widescreen spectacles about the Soviet police should be made and shot in studios, scriptwriters and filmmakers opposed such a change. They insisted on continuing to shoot the films on location, with modest budgets and a documentary feel. In their view, such products would avoid the staged official and glossy look of earlier films about the Soviet police.[16]

At the same time, the influence of film on television is by no means negligible. An episode of a TV series lasted up to 90 minutes, and episodes occasionally came out in two parts, totaling 150–180 minutes. In the absence of advertising, the series ran uninterrupted, much as did feature films. Moreover, as Soviet television struggled against the stigma of a popular (hence frivolous) medium, police series often were made at film rather than television studios, featured film stars and an elaborate mise-en-scène, had a well-developed narrative, well-defined characters, and good dialogue—in other words, television series tried to combine the best of literature, cinema, and theater. Notably, the most famous cinema and theater actors, such as Georgii Menglet and Armen Dzhigarkhanian, appeared in the roles of criminals.

By the early 1970s the police procedural had emerged as the major action genre, with a stable semantic and syntactic structure and interpretive community of producers, viewers, and critics sustaining its hegemonic position within Soviet cinema. There were multiple social and institutional reasons for the rise of the Soviet police film beyond the film and television industry's considerations. First, the Soviet Union had become a consumer society with an ideology that criticized excessive consumerism and felt uneasy about its abuses: "official rhetoric prescribed that consumerism must be rational and 'austere' for it to correspond to the spirit of the Soviet collective" (Rajagopalan 2009: 4).[17] A display of consumer goods and lifestyle, framed as the juxtaposition of "good" and "bad" consumption, becomes both an educational element and a visual attraction of the late-Soviet police film (see Figure 2.3). The police film served as a perfect vehicle for the safe and controlled channeling of consumer desires. Black-market

---

[16] "Petrovka 38," RGALI, f. 2944, op. 4, ed. kh. 5300.
[17] On the question of consumption under late socialism see also Susan E. Reid and David Crowley, "Style and Socialism" in David Crowley and Susan E. Reid (eds), *Style and Socialism: Modernity and Material Culture in Post-war Eastern Europe* (Oxford and New York: Berg, 2000), 1–24.

Figure 2.3: Fashion show as a value-neutral consumer spectacle
Source: Ogareva 6 (1980)

and economic crime emerged as central themes of the police film genre, with the spectacle of consumer goods tempered by the necessary punitive measures for "excessive" consumption.

Equally important for the genre was the rise to power of Leonid Brezhnev's close associate Nikolai Shchelokov, the Minister of Internal Affairs (MVD),[18] whom Brezhnev viewed as a counterbalance to Iurii Andropov's all-powerful KGB. Shchelokov established close relations with, and financially supported, many writers and filmmakers of crime fiction and cinema.

As opposed to Stalin era cinema, which was a more or less direct product of the Kremlin's ideological visions, the police procedural was under the patronage of the MVD. As a shrewd public relations person, Shchelokov considered cinema and, most importantly, television, useful vehicles for promoting his Ministry's influence, together with the positive image of the Soviet police force. To boost public opinion about the Soviet police in 1962 the government established November 10 as the Day of the Soviet (later Russian) Militiaman. In the 1970s, the television concert marking this day became a major nationwide musical event, second in popularity only to the New Year's TV line up. In 1982, when Leonid Brezhnev died, the government even postponed the announcement of

---

[18] During the Brezhnev era, MVD was the ministry in charge of the Soviet civilian police force. One of its major missions was to fight economic crime—mostly private business activity, which was illegal under the laws of the USSR.

the leader's death so as not to cancel the Militiaman's Day TV concert. After the fall of the USSR, this Soviet-style concert celebrating the police force still remains a staple of the Russian television schedule.

The MVD also sponsored several conferences on detective fiction and instituted awards for the best literary and cinematic works about the Soviet militia. In 1969, the first All-Union Conference, "Problems of the Contemporary Soviet Detective Story," was held in Baku and resulted in an official agreement between writers and the state. It established a working relationship between the Moscow Criminal Police (MUR) and individual writers, and instituted prizes sponsored jointly by the MVD and the Union of Soviet Writers. Clearly, with such close supervision on the part of the state, only a few authors were up to the task of creating both engaging and politically sound works—Iulian Semenov, the Vainer brothers, and Arkadii Adamov among them. Semenov's novels *Petrovka 38* (1962) and *Ogareva 6* (1972), referring respectively to the Moscow Police and MVD Headquarters, were among the first works to make a police team the protagonist and investigative procedures the structural core of the narrative.

Finally, all police film and television productions employed MVD consultants, and discussions in film journals included reviews of police films by high-ranking officers of the Soviet police force. Published scripts of the television series *The Investigation is Conducted by Experts* were accompanied by articles written by representatives of the MVD who served as permanent production consultants. Filmmakers and crews received gifts from the police authorities, including watches, radio sets, and film cameras—in other words, those consumer objects that it was hard to come by in Soviet stores.[19] In short, as an institution, the MVD had a major stake in supporting police film productions. As a result, in the 1970s, police procedurals quickly overshadowed and outnumbered films about heroic Soviet intelligence agents who were representing competing institutions, above all the KGB.

The two major television productions celebrating the work of the Soviet police were *The Investigation is Conducted by Experts* (1971–1989; hereinafter *ICE*) and *The Meeting Place Cannot Be Changed* (1979). Each in its own way crystallized police procedural conventions and the shift from the socialist realist

---

[19] See, for example, the report on awarding consumer goods to the writers and filmmakers of police procedurals in the official Goskino film file for *The Return of St. Luke*. "Vozvrashchenie 'Sviatogo Luki,'" RGALI, fond 2944, op. 4, ed. khran. 1755, p. 41.

master plot to the semantic and syntactic structure of the police film. While genre conventions came to dominate the plots, ideologically these TV shows remained rather orthodox. *ICE* especially offers interesting evidence of the contradictions of the era. On the one hand, because of their mass audiences, television productions were under an even tighter control of the MVD than police films. As a result, the show had a permanent team of police consultants headed by high-ranking officers, Lieutenant-Generals B.A. Viktorov and V.G. Novikov, who participated in every stage of the production and even wrote introductions for the published scripts. On the other hand, the show manifested a changed relationship between print and television media. Unlike the vast majority of Soviet police films that adapted existing literary works for the screen, *ICE* reversed this relationship: scripts were published in installments following the release of episodes. Moreover, these collections featured images from the show, confirming the primacy of the visual medium and essentially advertising the show. These publications also served as a forum for discussion of the plots: in addition to comments by police consultants, each collection also featured articles by the scriptwriters, Ol'ga and Aleksandr Lavrov,[20] comments by film critics, and viewers' responses.

To a large degree this need to frame and control the interpretation of the episodes may be ascribed to the revolutionary nature of the series. *ICE* was the only serialized television production of the 1970s with a contemporary setting and a sustained focus on the real ills of late-Soviet society: economic crime, mismanagement, alienation of young people and, in the perestroika episodes, corruption and organized crime.[21] From this point of view, at the time of production, *The Meeting Place,* while narratively and visually more daring and inventive, played it safer. Its action was historicized and displaced into the late-1940s, which allowed the filmmakers to indulge in representing violence and the criminal underworld without implicating the "radiant present" of developed socialism.

---

[20] The Lavrovs started their literary career by publishing a series of courtroom reportages in the *Literary Gazette* [Literaturnaia gazeta], based on documentary material and focused primarily on the social and psychological causes of crime. These essays already contained some of the plots for the future series. Later, the Lavrovs turned to documentary cinema and television. After writing the script for a two-part television film, *Special Investigator* [Sledovatel' po osobo vazhnym delam], the Lavrovs were invited to write scripts for a multi-episode television production.

[21] Oushakine, Serguei. "Crimes of Substitution: Detection in Late-Soviet Society." *Public Culture* 15.3 (2003): 427–451.

The Investigation is Conducted by Experts: the Soviet police procedural is born

The first installment of the scripts (six cases) was printed by Iskusstvo publishing house in 1974.[22] In the introduction to the collection, film critic Andrei Zorkii juxtaposed the show's characters to police in Western crime film, which, according to Zorkii, lacked social and ethical significance. In contrast, Soviet police investigators engaged in an argument with "the spirit of acquisitiveness (*stiazhatel'stvo*), cynicism, egoism, and disregard for norms of social life. [The show] is a resolute attempt [...] to arouse the dormant conscience, to find a healthy kernel in any person" (1974, 8). Zorkii defines the genre of the series as halfway between a documentary account ... and an emotional, imaginative narrative (1974, 6).

The episodes are connected through a team of police protagonists: Znamenskii (Georgii Martyniuk), Tomin (Leonid Kanevskii), and Kibrit (El'za Lezhdei). Their institutional identity is mediated by the personal nickname for the team, composed of their three last names: ZnaToKi, which translates into "experts." All three are individualized and each fulfills a particular narrative and social function. Znamenskii is a Russian male and the senior member of the team. He is the most "institutional" of the three; therefore his specialty of reeducating criminals is a function of the "humane" Soviet police as an institution. Other characters address him by his full name and use his patronymic: Pavel Pavlovich. Tomin, with his "southern" looks, is a streetwise ethnic cop. A master of disguise, he infiltrates criminal organizations and catches perpetrators red-handed. He is the only one of the three who uses his gun and is himself shot and presumed dead in one of the episodes. Other characters address him by his diminutive first name, Sasha or Shurik. Kibrit, the only woman in the team, is the crime scene investigator who works at the crime lab and represents the technical sophistication of the modern Soviet police force. Later episodes enhance the display of technology by the development of the television medium: beginning in 1975, episodes come out in color. Despite her technical expertise, she is primarily Zinochka, a diminutive term of endearment for a woman. In fact, ethnic and

---

[22] The show's twenty-two Soviet-era episodes appeared intermittently, sometimes with long pauses between releases. For example, the first seventeen episodes were produced between 1971 and 1982. After Brezhnev' death in 1982 and the firing and later suicide of Shchelokov (the Head of the Ministry of Internal Affairs and the show's official sponsor), *ICE* was put on hold and only resumed in 1985 during Gorbachev's perestroika. Since 1991, *ICE* has enjoyed multiple re-runs on Russian television, as well as in several post-Soviet countries (e.g., in Ukraine, Kazakhstan, and Belarus'). In 2002–2003 two additional episodes were produced, in which the team investigated the crimes in the new Russia.

Figure 2.4: The police team in *The Investigation is Conducted by Experts*

gender hierarchies are firmly in place despite the egalitarian pretenses of the series. Hierarchy and the official look become even more pronounced in the later episodes. The team members begin their careers as mid-ranking police officers. As the episodes unfold, Znamenskii gets promoted first, Tomin next, and Kibrit moves up only one rank. The experts also acquire a more institutional look: in the early episodes the team often appears in civilian clothes, while later they switch to police uniforms (see Figure 2.4).

Except for some technological changes, the series is made on the cheap. Its mise-en-scène is minimalist, limited to several, predominantly studio-set locations. There are almost no chases or shoot-outs, and in many scenes the camera is stationary while capturing "talking heads" during a conversation or interrogation. Likewise, the first nine episodes of *ICE* are entirely devoid of glamour: the fruits of criminal activity are not shown, and everyone lives a "good" but nondescript life. The low production values and the focus on dialog almost to the exclusion of the visual makes the series look theatrical, and in fact the show is classified as a "television play" (*televizionnyi spektakl'*) in the Gosteleradio's annual thematic planning.[23]

---

[23] "Tematicheskii plan Tsentral'nogo televideniia na iiun'-avgust, 1974." GARF, f. 6903, op. 33, ed. kh. 45, list 42.

As in most urban police films, the setting is identified as Moscow only through the protagonists, who work at Petrovka 38 police headquarters. Otherwise, Moscow is constructed as a generic city, an abstract "urban space." The action either takes place indoors (in police offices, jails, apartments, cafés, stores, warehouses, etc.), or in unnamed parks and yards. The only recognizable shots of Moscow are in the opening and closing sequences, when the police protagonists drive through the city's streets. Even in these sequences filmmakers avoid postcard vistas of Moscow and favor unremarkable urban mises-en-scène.

Despite its contemporary setting, *ICE* does not provide a broad social and historical context that would allow viewers to make any meaningful connection between the crime under investigation and the broader social milieu of the era. While the vast majority of crimes are economic, there is no mention of the population's general poverty, of the shortages of basic goods in the stores, or any other symptoms of social and political tensions of late-socialist society so familiar to the show's viewers at the time. This ahistoricism of *ICE* connects it with the tradition of the detective narratives of the Victorian era where the sleuth investigated a single crime and where, "by removing this single source of disorder, the detective restores the utopian society, which existed prior to the first page of the novel" (Winston and Millerski 1992, 3). Many *ICE* cases focused on economic crime do not have an identifiable and specific victim beyond the abstract a priori knowledge that in a "people's state" a loss of state property affected all citizens.[24] In the Soviet context, ahistoricism allowed one to avoid systemic criticism of socialist society and implied that screen-made developed socialism, despite a few exceptional crimes, was reasonably close to social utopia.

In its narrative focus and politics of representation, *ICE* falls into two more or less equal parts. Early episodes (those released in 1971–1974) reiterate the ideology of the Thaw. The three central elements of this model are the representation of the police investigative team as a family unit (both as the narrative center of the episodes and as a social mini-model), the representation of crime as an atypical deviation from the socialist norm (hence the diverse and random crimes, their visual and narrative localization, and the solution of every crime by each episode's end), and a belief in the reeducation of criminals. In contrast, later episodes, those released from 1975 to the late 1980s, represent the

---

[24] Moreover, as Serguei Oushakine points out, the production of illegal goods out of state-(mis)managed materials often produced a *surplus* of goods rather than a scarcity. See "Crimes of Substitution," 436–437.

police rather formulaically, shifting the focus to the criminals. The reeducation of criminals becomes secondary to their punishment, or even simply fails as a project. The main reason for the failure of state enlightenment is the emergence of organized crime. Praising the series, General Novikov noted the topicality (*aktual'nost'*) of many cases: according to him, quite often the broadcasting of a "case" coincided with the very same problem being discussed in the press. Novikov claimed that the show's social role was preventing crime, and he praised its "overcoming the conventions of 'puzzle'-style entertainment."[25]

The central concern of the early episodes is not so much the apprehension of the criminal—more often than not, this happens early in the plot—as the reaffirmation of citizens' trust in the Soviet police and the socialist state. As figures of state enlightenment, the police in *ICE* see their mission as one of mediating the relations between socialist law and the public. Lieutenant-General Viktorov, the chief consultant for the series, found the main value of the series in the idea that the viewers and readers could see that "any crime can always be solved, the guilty party can always be identified and undergo a well-deserved punishment. This gives people a feeling of peace and security."[26] Viktorov also commented on Znamenkii's patience and his perceived "softness" toward the criminals:

> Our criminal laws, based on the principles of socialist humanism, from its inception have rejected punishment for the sake of punishment. The primary goal of punishment is the re-education of the criminal (*pravonarushitelia*) ... But the re-education of the criminal cannot take place only after his sentencing and imprisonment. Already at the stage of the preliminary investigation Znamenskii's major goal is to begin the re-education of people who committed crimes ... It is necessary to understand the motives and reasons that prompted the person to commit a crime. And when he knows them, the investigator attempts to awaken in the criminal the capacity for self-condemnation, the desire to change, to reform one's life.[27]

In order to start his reforging into a law-abiding citizen, the criminal needs to trust his investigator, and this is where Znamenskii's patience and pedagogical skills become essential for establishing the dialog and emotional contact between

---

[25] Novikov, V.G. "Posleslovie." In *Sledstvie vedut znatoki*. By Ol'ga and Aleksandr Lavrov. Moscow: Iskusstvo, 1985. 269–270.
[26] "Interv'iu vmesto poslesloviia." Lavrova Ol'ga and Aleksandr Lavrov. *Sledstvie vedut znatoki. Sbornik telepes.* Moscow: Iskusstvo, 1974. 270–272, 270.
[27] Ibid., 270–272.

the criminal and his police-redeemer. "Trusting the police" in turn becomes tantamount to loyalty to the socialist way of life. This issue is of particular importance in relation to the younger generation, those who were born into a stable and relatively prosperous time and who therefore are liable to fall into the trap of consumerism and individualism. The police team assumes the function of a collective mentor, who, unlike their Stalinist or Thaw predecessors, cannot work miracles of transformation but can reveal the true essence of false friends and prevent new crimes. The resolution of a case is, above all, about preserving the status quo. Accordingly, the success of the police team prevents the system from collapse rather than propelling it toward the radiant future.

Meanwhile, the reeducation plot in its classic socialist realist version gradually disappeared from the show. Several early episodes still presented the police and the criminals as two forces competing for the souls and lives of weak and flawed characters. This disappearing breed of positive heroes usually included young people, often lacking a father figure ("Dinosaur," 1972), simple-minded people, who fall victim to amoral "educated" criminals (read *intelligentsia*), and women (often the criminals' spouses) ("The Black Dealer," 1971). For instance, in "Caught Red-Handed" (1971), an intelligent-looking ex-con nicknamed "Brain" [Bashka] uses his former prison "disciple"—a naive, bear-like man, Silin—to burgle a warehouse. The plan is a set-up to damage the alarm system and allow the real criminals to enter unhindered. Silin has to choose between this false "intellectual" friend and the true friend—the police officer Znamenskii and the state he represents. Even criminals guilty of large-scale embezzlement are still redeemable. The director of a restaurant (Leonid Bronevoi) in "A Fault Confessed Is Half Redressed" (1971) gets fifteen years in jail, but his chain-smoking, "bonding" conversations with Znamenskii, both at police headquarters and in the labor camp, miraculously transform the hardened criminal and set him eventually on a path to redemption.

Early episodes retain also some cultural memory of the Thaw by providing the police team with a private life. Occasionally, the team discuss cases at home; in the episode titled "Blackmail" a criminal (Armen Dzhigarkhanian) shows up at the apartment where Kibrit is babysitting for her sister and threatens to kidnap her nephew. Znamenskii lives with his mother and a younger brother, and Tomin's mother makes an appearance on the show when he is shot. Moreover, in several episodes both Znamenskii and Tomin flirt with their female colleague, and there is even a promise of romance between Kibrit and Znamenskii. Yet, in the end, she marries a different man whom we never see. Viewers were displeased at the prospect of Kibrit marrying "outside the team": "We are convinced that [Kibrit and Znamenskii] love each other. They just need to be left alone at least once and have a chance to talk heart-to-heart"; "you should marry Kibrit to Znamenkii, and in two–three episodes let them give birth to a girl" (qtd. in Viktorov (1977): 268). In his article, General Viktorov dispels these hopes for a more personal turn of the plot: "It happens of course that husband and wife serve in the same MVD unit, but for them to work together in a group investigating the same crime is out of the question. Investigation is a sensitive matter, and there should be no hint of any kind of nepotism ... I hope viewers will bravely endure Kibrit's 'infidelity'" (Viktorov (1977): 268–69). In later episodes even these traces of family life and romance disappear, turning the detectives into professional but impersonal figures of Soviet law.

The turning point of the show was the episode "Counter Strike" ("Otvetnyi udar" 1975), which introduced new stylistic and narrative elements. The episode came out in color, ending the quasi-documentary look of the mini-series, and established a new pattern of narrative exposition. The police team received their assignment from their superior, Colonel Skopin (Semen Sokolovskii), who until then had remained on the periphery. At this point the team's relative independence from police authorities disappeared, together with their quasi-domestic meetings. The office space lost its personal touch, Znamenskii cast off his civilian clothes, and interrogations turned into a routine procedure, the goal of which was not to defend the innocent and help those who made a mistake, but to punish the guilty.

Simultaneously with the establishment of hierarchy and institutional control, a new agency came to occupy a permanent place in *ICE*—the Directorate for Combating the Embezzlement of Socialist Property (OBKhSS),[28] signaling the emergence of organized economic crime as a major social problem, which the police team could contain but not eradicate. In "Counter Strike," the scale of embezzlement is not just a topic of discussion but an object of visual representation. The criminal syndicate steals metal from a factory, "launders" it through a recycling office, stores it at the city garbage dump, and sells it to underground factories and workshops producing black-market goods. The head of the syndicate (Georgii Menglet) poetically describes the garbage dump as

---

[28] The Directorate for Combating the Embezzlement of Socialist Property was established in 1937 as a part of the NKVD and later became a unit within the Ministry of Internal Affairs (MVD). After the fall of the USSR its functions have been fulfilled by the Division for Combating Economic Crimes (OBEP).

Figure 2.5: Garbage dump as a setting and metaphor in *The Investigation is Conducted by Experts,* Episode 10 (1975)

"nobody's land, a holy land, the only place where one can steal anonymously." Time and again the camera returns to the wasteland of garbage, a metaphor for Soviet society—a desolate place, which is periodically raided by the police (see Figure 2.5).

Furthermore, for the first time the episode spells out the punishment for economic crime targeting state interests. This information neither comes at the end of the episode, where it would strike a particularly grim note, nor is it voiced by the police. Instead, the head of the criminal syndicate ironically "enlightens" his terrified accomplices in the lingo of Marxist dialectics: "Quantity has transformed into quality. The amount of stolen goods has reached the point that changes the applicable article of the criminal code—up to capital punishment."

Simultaneously, reeducation receives a major blow. Midway through the narrative, the boss's aide (Valerii Nosik) kills one of the members of the syndicate—right after the latter repents and is ready to return to an honest life. His death, which the police are unable to prevent, marks the symbolic death of the reeducation utopia. The crime boss himself, who passes as a humble worker at the city garbage disposal, is confident, refined, and unrepentant. Though his girlfriend's naïve conviction that "[h]is job is absolutely secret. Probably he is working on a military or a space project," in fact, spells out the truth: no other legitimate activity provides a decent living in the land of developed socialism. In this respect, too, "Counter Blow" is quite revolutionary, if unintentionally so. The black-and-white images of the preceding episodes constructed a world where material concerns were of importance only to social degenerates. Everybody lived equally badly or "normally," following the principle of austere consumption. The simultaneous introduction of color and the switch of focus to the life of "the rich and the criminal" revealed the double standard of life in the Soviet Union, thus opening a visual can of worms.

Beginning with "Counter Strike," a criminal lifestyle appeared not as an anomaly but as an alternative, consumerist way of life, where spacious apartments, comfortable suburban houses, expensive cars and drinks, and fashion model girlfriends in furs existed. At times, these objects functioned as targets of criminal activity: theft of cars, jewelry, and electronics in "An Afternoon Burglar" (1985); forgery and black market operations with art masterpieces in "A Herdsman with a Cucumber" (1979). More typically, the camera simply reveled in these consumer fetishes. This visual paradigm culminated in the detailed exploration of the criminal's apartment in the perestroika-era episode "Without a Knife" (1988). By Soviet standards, the living quarters of the single mother and cleaning woman was a magical palace—literally so, because the walls contained hidden gold coins. Sof'ia Rashidovna (Lidiia Fedoseeva-Shukshina) is the widow of a large-scale counterfeiter and drug-dealer, executed ten years earlier. In her present life she is the right hand of a large-scale embezzler, the head of a housing management committee (Aleksandr Beliavskii).[29]

While in the earlier episodes the settings were semiotically unmarked, that is, they just signified a socialist urban space, in perestroika-era episodes this paradigm radically changes. Urban poverty, social stratification and economic mismanagement make their appearance. Law-abiding Soviets discover that they dwell in a less-than-perfect environment: run-down buildings, dirty yards and overcrowded communal apartments. One of the residents spells out the

[29] The woman's patronymic is a hint at Sharaf Rashidov, the First Secretary of the Communist Party of Uzbekistan under Brezhnev. During his 23 years of unchallenged rule in the republic, he maintained absolute control over state subsidies, pocketing huge revenues from cotton production. Maintaining a relationship with the Kremlin by means of feudal loyalty and bribes, the Rashidov clan *de facto* replaced Soviet law within Uzbekistan. The anti-mafia campaign directed against Rashidov, known as the "Cotton Affair," was started by Iurii Andropov and continued under Mikhail Gorbachev. Late-Soviet rulers tried to explain economic decline and corruption by the economic crimes committed by non-Russian (Central Asian and Transcaucasian) party leaders.

crisis—of management and of trust: "You step over the threshold of your own apartment and it seems that Soviet power has ended."

Perhaps the most pessimistic aspect of the late 1970s episodes is the failure of the state to influence young people. In the episode "Before the Third Shot" (1978), a group of teenagers finds a gun hidden by a criminal. Znamenskii attempts to convince them to turn in the gun but when he succeeds, it is too late—a young woman, a local police inspector, is fatally wounded by the criminal, who also hunts for the gun. Despite the teenagers' rejection of adult consumerism and hypocrisy, they have trust neither in the humane police, nor in any positive ideals. Their fascination with the gun and the power it brings effectively neutralizes any illusions one might have about their potential for reeducation or the ideological meaning "the new man" carries in late-socialist culture: "I have never had such a real, such a strong thing. When I have it in my pocket—I am *a new man*" (emphasis added) (see Figure 2.6).

ICE triggered a discussion about the scope of crime in socialist society and its representation in the television show. In their evaluation of the series some viewers were holier than the Pope. "I am against showing this on TV ... Where do the authors find such big-time (*materykh*) criminals? All this is nonsense and

Figure 2.6: Soviet teenagers and the gun fetish in Episode 13 (1978) of *The Investigation is Conducted by Experts*

fairy tales (*vydumki*). Examples like these, which the authors are trying to force on us, do not and cannot exist in our socialist life. O. and A. Lavrov should stop going through garbage, which they have been doing for many years" (A.V. Iudin, Smolensk) (qtd. in Viktorov (1977), 269).

Film critics, in turn, addressed the disproportionate attention to the criminal lifestyle. The formulaic theatricality of scenes set in the police office clashed with the rich array of details, nuances of behavior and mood, and the particularized mise-en-scène of the criminal "pads." As Viktor Demin notes, this contrast was understandable: "[I]n this representational system 'the way it should be' does not allow variation, while the way 'it should not be' can be as varied as you want" (114). While this criticism explicitly targeted the narrow narrative schema that *ICE* set for itself from the very beginning, Demin's comment equally applies to the ideological and aesthetic representational limitations of the Soviet police film in general.

By the mid-1980s the pattern of idealistic policemen fighting conventional criminals could only fit a children's show.[30] In a way, the arrival of perestroika reforms provided *ICE* with new, previously taboo topics, such as corruption and big-scale economic crime. In his introduction to the last installment of scripts published in 1989, Novikov pointed to the link between the series and actual economic and social reforms in the USSR. For example, one of the episodes triggered improved oversight of the delivery of merchandise to vegetable warehouses, and the Ministry of Finances issued official gratitude to Central Television. "One occasionally hears that the series has stagnated in its development, risking turning its protagonists into masks. [...] In such a series, the authors have the right to use their characters as instruments to investigate certain social phenomena, at the expense of the development of the three protagonists. Znatoki ... continue to work for perestroika" (1989, 271).

The last Soviet-era episode, "Mafia" (1989), finally admits to the failure of the police to keep crime under control. As the professional police brotherhood is institutionalized and the natural family falls apart, the mafia takes on characteristics of both. The real protagonist of the episode is the drug syndicate, a well-organized professional unit and a family, with a Godfather at the top, a mother, and "boys"— hit men who grew up believing in guns as the only real value. Besides several well

---

[30] In 1983 Igor' Kovalev and Aleksandr Tatarskii produced an animation film for children, *Sledstvie vedut kolobki* (*The Investigation is Conducted by Bread Rolls*). A magic bread roll (*Kolobok*) is a character in a Russian folk tale. The cartoon's title parodied the title of the famous police serial, and two major characters—detectives—conducted a comic investigation of a theft from the city zoo.

planned and executed murders, there are a number of less violent, but more disturbing episodes: for instance, a woman who gives birth to a "crack baby" or a former scholar who is selling drugs on the street. Like the entire series, the last episode is an ambiguous cultural gesture: while opening up space for a discussion of previously unspoken social phenomena, it is quite conservative in interpreting them. The scale of organized crime, for instance, is directly linked to the "chaos" of perestroika. In struggling with its preset ideological and aesthetic limits, *ICE* in its own way documented the emergence of a consumer society in the Soviet Union and the demise of the myth of the socialist state as the guarantor of either public order or social well-being.

After the fall of communism, two more episodes of the show appeared. However, the show's true legacy lies elsewhere: it served as the model for the most successful post-Soviet police show, *Cops: Streets of Broken Lights* (*Menty: Ulitsy razbitykh fonarei*, 1998–2012, 14 seasons), which pioneered a new dystopian way of depicting the city, its authorities, the criminal underworld, and the police squad itself. Post-Soviet cops have to fight overwhelmingly powerful organized crime, receive little support from city authorities and negotiate their relationships with numerous city services and private businesses. The squad consists of flawed individuals who face countless problems themselves, including alcohol abuse, dysfunctional family relations, and tough living conditions. They constantly break the law in order to trap the criminals they fight. They by no means comprise a harmonious unit. The new realistic style of *Cops* was reproduced by sundry new police procedurals, such as *Deadly Force* (*Uboinaia sila*, 2000–2005) or *Kamenskaia* (2000–2011). The latter has a female lead investigator (Elena Iakovleva) as the protagonist and deals with issues unusual for Russian television, such as sexism and gender equality, among others.

The Meeting Place Cannot Be Changed: the romantics of the criminal underworld

In her 1980 discussion of Soviet police films and TV series, critic Inna Vishnevskaia wrote that they shared the convention of beginning with police operators receiving an emergency call. This opening suggests a new understanding of police work: these investigators are not Conan Doyle-style detectives, but professionals whose work, while very important, largely consists of phone calls and police reports, and only occasional action. The flipside of this sober approach to policing is the boredom of all those cool-headed reassurances, such as "don't worry" and "the police are on their way." Vishnevskaia suggests that there should be a synthesis of the new and the traditional, of Sherlock Holmes and the "ZnaToKi":

> As characters, znatoki aren't bad, but if we have only znatoki in the plot, then why would we go to theater or sit in front of the TV? They know everything about all things—let them, but what does it have to do with us? Police characters often ironically comment on the romantic image of the Baker-street detective who could catch the criminal by looking at the cigarette ash. But without mystery, fear, and unexpected turns there can be no good detective film.
> 1980: 12

Govorukhin's police series *The Meeting Place Cannot Be Changed* (1979) answered the critic's plea and introduced a number of new features in the representation of crime on the Soviet screen. The series combined the focus on the work of the police team with the "whodunit" narrative. The *Meeting Place* is a five-episode series commissioned by television but, like most Soviet series, produced at a film studio, in this case the Odessa studio. The series is set in the summer and fall of 1945, right after the end of the Great Patriotic War. A young Soviet Army officer, Vladimir Sharapov (Vladimir Konkin), returns home from the front and comes to work at Petrovka 38, the Moscow Police Headquarters. He is included in the group headed by Gleb Zheglov (Vladimir Vysotskii), which investigates murders and robberies committed by the single most dangerous criminal group, the Black Cat gang. Parallel to this investigation, Sharapov also participates in the investigation of the murder of an actress Larisa Gruzdeva. Although the police immediately arrest Larisa's former husband, a doctor (Sergei Iurskii), Sharapov continues to doubt his guilt. While working on these two big cases, the police arrest and interrogate several lesser criminals who name a certain Evgenii Foks, Larisa's lover (Aleksandr Beliavskii), as the true villain with connections to the gang. Despite the evidence, Zheglov continues to keep Gruzdev in jail. Meanwhile Sharapov tries to infiltrate the gang but is kidnapped. He spends a terrifying night in their hideout, yet manages to win their trust and deliver the entire gang to the police.

On the surface, *The Meeting Place* fit the ideological bill of a good Soviet police film to a T. For a start, it adapted an already published and thus ideologically sound novel by Arkadii and Georgii Vainer, *The Era of Mercy* (1975). Owing to its genre of a police procedural, it extols the heroic work of the Soviet police as an institution rather than following an individual detective.

The Great Patriotic War plays a key role in the narrative, and the series' release in 1979, a year before the thirty-fifth anniversary of the Victory, suggested an anniversary film.

But the narrative and visual politics of the series have nothing to do with Soviet collectivity or the law, despite Zheglov's repeated statements to his disciple about the importance of legal education. In her analysis of late-Soviet TV series, Neia Zorkaia pointed out that they hark back to traditional Russian *lubok* and dime crime novels in the structure of the narrative, the privileging of archetypes over characters' psychology, the polarization of good and evil, and the fascination with the criminal underworld.[31] Developing this argument, we claim that *The Meeting Place* is, above all, a commercial production that establishes continuity between the pre-revolutionary popular genre of a thieves' tale and post-Soviet romanticized gangsters/aka Robin Hoods, such as the hero of *Brigada* (*Brigade* 2002) Sasha Belyi or Aleksei Balabanov's *Brother* (1997).

Most importantly, Stanislav Govorukhin's *The Meeting Place Cannot be Changed* not only reiterates the major features of the police procedural, but also places them in a rich historical context. While attention to a socio-historical context often implies an exposé of an era's social issues, Govorukhin plays a more subtle game with the historical setting of his mini-series. The filmmaker sets his picture in the post-Second World War years in order to explain rampant crime, urban poverty, and the police's inefficiency as consequences of the Nazi invasion. For example, in contrast to *ICE* investigators, the police team in *The Meeting Place* investigates several crimes at the same time. They are overwhelmed by the number of cases, lack experience, and are constantly reprimanded by their superiors, who have little sympathy for them and provide no help. A similar film in a contemporary setting would be damning testimony about the crisis of late-socialist society and its law enforcement system. Historical distance and the invocation of war-era hardships gave Govorukhin more freedom to romanticize the criminal underworld and exploit nostalgia in his depictions of the period's urban life. This socialist police procedural acquired a complex and picturesque social milieu, but only at the cost of being set safely back in an historical past.

While polarizing the good and the bad guys in some parts of the plot, the series asserted their parallels in others. The Great Patriotic War mythology, which under Brezhnev became the basis of national identity,[32] provided a

---

[31] Zorkaia (1994) especially pp. 95–107.
[32] See, for example, Kelly (1998).

convenient framing for the "us" vs "them" opposition. At the same time, the polarization was foregrounded exactly where the series redefined the conventions of the late-Soviet police film. In lieu of the conventional and, by the 1970s, hardly convincing, trope of reeducation and the juxtaposition of criminal and perverse greed, on the one hand, and the "good Soviet life," on the other, *The Meeting Place* pitched criminal excesses against the staggering poverty of the population that had just survived a devastating war. Food rationing, a dinner of potatoes as a feast, over-crowded communal apartments, the flourishing of the black market and alcoholism are facts of life; against this background, commercial restaurants or even a table full of food instantly separated black from white.

The main role of the war myth was to contribute to the period-piece, nostalgic feel of the series, drawing on familiar images. At the beginning of the series we see Sharapov strolling through Moscow streets, which feature victory posters, men in uniforms, and even a portrait of Stalin in a shoe-polisher's booth (see Figure 2.7). For the 1970s Soviet viewer, the war mythology evoked nostalgia for the time of the great victory, a shared fate, and the ultimate transparency of

Figure 2.7: Stalin's portrait behind the protagonist in *The Meeting Place Cannot Be Changed*

conflicts, the time when everything was clear, including who was "us" and who was "them." In the series this longing was especially significant for Sharapov. During a police raid he has a face-to-face encounter with the main villain, Evgenii Foks, but lets him go, confused by the medal on the man's (stolen) officer's uniform. When Sharapov realizes that he has mistaken appearance for "essence," arresting Foks becomes for him a matter of honor above and beyond a police investigation. In Sharapov's eyes, Foks is more than a criminal; he is an impostor who uses a war medal and a military uniform—signs of a sacred, shared experience—as a cover for his nefarious deeds. The scene of Foks's arrest, which follows a car chase, a shoot-out, and Foks's car plunging into the river, is a moment of ultimate unmasking: the water of the Moskva-river instantly transforms good-looking Foks into a Hitler look-alike.

In all other respects, the series caters to popular Russian tastes, with its love for the culture of the criminal underworld (*blatnaia kul'tura*). The real crowd pleasers in the series are scenes where Zheglov and Co. venture into hide-outs, seedy gambling places, commercial restaurants, and movie theaters. These iconic scenes involve a parade of criminal types—prostitutes, cardsharps, and pickpockets. All of these colorful figures are played by major Soviet film stars: Leonid Kuravlev, Larisa Udovichenko, Evgenii Evstigneev, Stanislav Sadal'skii, Aleksandr Beliavskii, and Armen Dzhigarkhanian. Moreover, they come with nicknames, argot, and a host of memorable quotes. The series is a veritable celebration of the criminal underworld—its mores, its lifestyle, and its jargon (see Figures 2.8 and 2.9). The line separating the criminals and the police is quite thin. Zheglov is not just familiar with the ways of the underworld—he is personally acquainted with many of the criminals: he flirts with a prostitute, plays pool with a crook, and engages in a battle of wits with a con artist. The scenes of their interrogation by the iconic Vysotskii are pure spectacle, providing both viewing pleasure and comic relief.

The director Stanislav Govorukhin is a master of genre cinema. At the beginning of perestroika he accused captains of the Soviet film industry of snobbishly neglecting the box-office and of ignoring the "democratic tastes" of the public.[33] Prior to *The Meeting Place* he made several adventure films, mostly adaptations of such Western classics as *Robinson Crusoe* and *Tom Sawyer*. His

---

[33] For a detailed discussion of Stanislav Govorukhin's films released during perestroika see Eric Naiman and Anne Nesbet, "Documentary Discipline: Three Interrogations of Stanislav Govorukhin," in Nancy Condee (ed.), *Soviet Hieroglyphics: Visual Culture in Late Twentieth Century Russia* (Bloomington: Indiana University Press and BFI, 1995).

Figures 2.8 and 2.9: Criminal types in *The Meeting Place Cannot Be Changed*

most notable fiction film of the 1990s, *The Voroshilov Sharpshooter* (*Voroshilovskii strelok* 1999), deals with the gang rape of a 16-year-old girl by a group of young "new Russians." The girl's grandfather happens to be a decorated Stalin-era sniper. When he realizes that the police have all been bought by the new Russians, he gets out his trusty rifle and takes justice into his own hands. In one particularly spectacular scene he shoots at the genitals of the main offender.

It stands to reason that Govorukhin's most popular production, *The Meeting Place*, would likewise offer pleasures rare on Brezhnev-era TV: action, a straight adventure plot, a whodunit narrative (rare in Soviet cinema), and violence. Even more importantly, it responded to Russian cultural sensibilities and popular tastes: valuing justice over the law and communal ideology over individualism; a charismatic leader over freedom; and romanticization of the criminal underworld. The trick, of course, was that the series' protagonists are policemen, and Govorukhin's veritable tour-de-force was to cast Vladimir Vysotskii in the role of Zheglov.

A guitar poet (a Russian Bob Dylan) and a Stagnation cult figure, Vysotskii was 41 years old at that time, a year before his untimely death from alcohol and drug abuse. The popularity of the mini-series owed a great deal to his personal charisma and the association with the underworld and societal outsiders who constituted the multiple lyrical personae in his songs. The ultimate performer, he was so "authentic" in channeling these voices that many people believed in his war experience (which he couldn't possibly have) and his street upbringing. Vysotskii also modeled his cinematic persona on Charles Bronson's film characters, in particular Paul Kersey in *Death Wish* (1974), which celebrates vigilante justice for the sake of clearing the city of crime.

Govorukhin's series also thoroughly reworked the source novel to flesh out the contrast between the populist Zheglov and his younger "straight" colleague, Sharapov. In the novel, Sharapov constantly refers to his "peasant stinginess" and narrow-mindedness—the qualities that he finds hard to combine with fighting urban crime. In contrast, in the series he embraces the intelligentsia's 1960s ideals.[34] According to the director, writers were mistaken in making Sharapov, a typical idealized hero, the protagonist of the novel, while in Govorukhin's view the star was Zheglov, who consisted of contradictions (qtd. in Mashchenko 1986, 163). Zheglov favors popular justice over rule of law. He serves the Soviet

---

[34] A few years before, the actor Vladimir Konkin had played a revolutionary romantic Pavel Korchagin in the 1973 TV mini-series (dir. Nikolai Mashchenko) about the iconic hero of Nikolai Ostrovskii's 1932 novel *How the Steel Was Tempered* [*Kak zakalialas' stal'*].

state but despises the police uniform, which he never puts on. As an officer, he is part of the Soviet establishment, but feels more comfortable when he interacts with the representatives of the criminal underworld. Finally, the celebrity persona of the popular singer Vysotskii constantly surfaces through the television character of Zheglov. Not surprisingly, in an interview forty years after the series' release, actor Vladimir Konkin, who played Sharapov, complained that he had felt overlooked on the set, where Vysotskii had ruled.

In representing Zheglov's police team the series negotiates between the canonical Soviet-style diversity and non-institutional identity. On the one hand, the police squad offers a cross-section of society: a Russian, a Ukrainian, and a Jew; a wise old driver and a rash young man; a tough street-wise cop and a gentle policeman. On the other hand, none of them wears a police uniform, has studied law, or has knowledge of investigative procedures. There is little in their actions to suggest the disciplined, squeaky-clean, institutional professionals of the 1970s police film and plenty to offer emotional identification to the viewers. Namely, their main allegiance is to their own team. The first murder Sharapov witnesses is that of a young policeman who tries to impersonate a criminal so as to penetrate the gang. He gives a convincing if short performance and is killed with a shiv. Apart from the shown violence, rare on Soviet television, the scene elicits viewers' sympathy and also motivates the response of the team: revenge for their own.

More importantly, Zheglov himself neither looks nor acts like a cop. He appears in a police uniform once,[35] but only to perform a few lines of Aleksandr Vertinskii's 1910s escapist and decadent hit "Lily White Negro" ("Lilovyi Negr").[36] Zheglov's most natural outfit is a cross-over between a revolutionary commissar and a post-Soviet gangster. Zheglov has profound disdain for privacy, private property, or individual rights in general. Communal justice always wins over individualism, as evidenced by the plotline involving one of the policemen, Petiunia, who is put on trial by Zheglov three times. The first time Zheglov accosts Petiunia at his post where he is eating bread with lard and drinking tea

---

[35] According to the director, Vysotskii vehemently objected to wearing a police uniform in the series: "For him a policeman of the Stalin era was associated with the terrible lawlessness of those years" (Govorukhin 6). Even the interference of the MVD consultant could not change Vysotskii's mind.
[36] Aleksandr Vertinskii is one of the major figures of Russian popular culture of the 1910s and one of the few "continuity figures" of Russo-Soviet popular culture. His songs of lost love, decadent nostalgia, and exotic imagery dominated music halls, records, and movie screens before and during the First World War. Having emigrated after the revolution, Vertinskii returned to the Soviet Union during the Second World War and enjoyed another stage in his performing and cinematic career.

with sugar, the luxuries that the rest of the police cannot afford. Zheglov starts by pointing out Petiunia's "unfair" luck (his relative sent him the goods from Central Asia) and ends by requisitioning a large part of the food supplies. The second time Zheglov sees Petiunia surrounded by a crowd of excited policemen discussing his winning a lottery. Zheglov immediately asks what he is planning to do with the money and suggests giving it away to a volunteer organization because "it is shameful to keep the money in such a difficult time for the country." Petiunia retorts that the government organized this lottery to provide relief for people after their wartime deprivations, but his is a losing position because the charismatic Zheglov/Vysotskii here appeals to one of the main traits of the Russian national character: dislike of the rich, originating in the conviction that it is impossible to become wealthy in an honest way. This scene anticipates Petiunia's crossing the line separating a "greedy" individual from a traitor: he acts like a coward, allowing Foks to shoot another policeman and escape. The interrogation scene is constructed as a communal trial and ends with the traitor's expulsion from the police community.

Zheglov might rage against criminals, but it is clear that for him they are, to use a Stalin-era notion, kindred spirits (*sotsial'no blizkie*), unlike the intellectual Ivan Gruzdev. This plotline of the television series alludes to the Stalin-era "Doctors' Plot." The motif of treacherous intellectuals inherited from Stalinist culture and put to earnest use in 1970s film and television police films (cf. the Zorin cycle and *ICE*), in *The Meeting Place* is presented as Zheglov's sense of grass-root justice. While investigating the murder of a young actress, Zheglov interrogates her estranged husband and immediately becomes convinced of his guilt. This conviction is based solely on the husband's "class origins": to Zheglov, the doctor, Gruzdev, is an alien element, hiding his criminal nature under an educated veneer. The policeman is dead set on convicting the man, even though the evidence exculpates him. The interrogation scene mirrors Zheglov's trial of Petiunia, the policeman: the accused sit, while Zheglov towers over them or paces around the room pronouncing verdicts. Although he is proven wrong in his suspicions, he never apologizes to the man he wrongly accuses (see Figure 2.10).

The "doctor's plot" becomes the frame for a series of confrontations between Sharapov and Zheglov concerning the methods and ethics of police work. Another controversial moment is the arrest of a pickpocket who in the ensuing commotion drops the evidence—a stolen wallet. Zheglov picks up the wallet and secretly slides it into the criminal's pocket, blackmailing him into providing

Figure 2.10: Intelligentsia on trial in *The Meeting Place*

information about Foks. When confronted by Sharapov who says that the police have no right to play it dirty, Zheglov vehemently retorts:

> Was it you who pulled a woman, mother of three, out of the noose, from whom he [the pickpocket] stole her last money? Was it you who found butter and caviar in their homes, when the whole country was giving away its last slice of bread to the front? ... If it weren't for my lie, the recidivist Saprykin would be in a hideout now, and not in jail. But a thief belongs in jail! Let's ask a hundred people now what they like more: my lie or your truth?

Zheglov's argument eschews the entire issue of the law and legitimacy of police action, drawing instead on the notion of "popular justice." Whereas Sharapov's view is backed up by historical facts uncovered by de-Stalinization—the fabricated cases of the 1930s, 1940s, and 1950s—Zheglov's is supported by centuries-long Russian debate on law (always flawed and crooked) and popular justice. In the final analysis, however, historical or narrative logic is irrelevant. What really matters is Vysotskii's solo performance, his raspy voice as a strong and passionate "avenger of the people." The series pulls a veritable tour de force: while the narrative condemns his actions by pitching Zheglov against the law-abiding "humanist" Sharapov, it never undermines populist preference for justice over law or Zheglov's charisma (see Figure 2.11). The "era of mercy"—the title of the novel by the Vainer brothers on which the script is based—is nothing but an intellectual's dream.

In the final episode, Sharapov, in disguise, finds his way into the gang, whose hideout, albeit terrifying, mirrors the idyllic topos of the communal apartment. In both cases, the major occupation of the "dwellers" is conversation while sharing food and vodka. Both communities seem frozen in time and space, having a common goal—survival. This survival depends not on history or current ideology, but on the internal coherence and unwritten laws of patriarchal society. At the foundation of both communities—the police and the gang—is not the law, but *absolute loyalty* to the leader and the group. In both communities there is an unshakable hierarchy: the gang leader's (Armen Dzhigarkhanian) word is law for the rest of the criminals, just as Zheglov, once he moves in with Sharapov, becomes the judge within the apartment. Significantly, Sharapov's main antagonist—Foks—is marked as an outsider within the criminal community. He is an individualist and adventurer, whose "non-Russian"

Figure 2.11: Zheglov in action in *The Meeting Place*

habits—a love of restaurants, women, and risky escapades—expose the entire gang to danger and eventually lead to its demise.

Two scenes in particular are crowd-pleasers, testifying to the series' nature as popular entertainment. The gang leader's wife notices Sharapov's well-groomed hands, odd for the truck driver he claims to be. After he explains that he used to play in movie-theaters, he performs a virtuoso rendition of a classical piece on a piano, which satisfies the woman, but not the gangsters from the Black Cat gang. They order "real music,"—"Murka" (The Pussy Cat)—a song that emerged from the criminal subculture in the 1920s and became part of Soviet unofficial popular culture. As Sharapov plays, the camera slowly moves from one gangster to another—all of them (like the viewer) enjoying the performance—and finally lingers on a black cat. The song is Sharapov's ploy to gain the gang's trust and the production's ticket to popular success. Meanwhile, in the hope that his friend is alive and will succeed in leading the gang to the police trap, Zheglov scouts the basement of the store where the criminals will be apprehended. A storage door is decorated with images of Soviet movie stars, and Zheglov adds the picture of Sharapov's girlfriend, signaling to him that this is his escape route. In the dark labyrinth of the store basement the protagonist is saved by the image of his beloved—and by popular cinema.

The series closure also engages the war myth, but this time to exploit its melodramatic potential. One of the gangsters, Levchenko (Viktor Pavlov), is a soldier from Sharapov's unit, who recognizes his former lieutenant. After they are left alone, Levchenko tells Sharapov the sad story of his past-war life: after serving in a penal battalion and redeeming himself, he was detained by the secret police who sent him back to prison. Bitter and angry at this injustice, after his release, Levchenko joined the gang. Aware of the police trap, Levchenko nevertheless does not betray Sharapov: trench-war brotherhood trumps criminal camaraderie. The prospect of going to jail again is not an option, and while trying to escape Levchenko is shot by Zheglov despite Sharapov's plea not to shoot. "I killed a criminal," Zheglov tells the devastated Sharapov. "You killed a human being," Sharapov replies.

In contrast to earlier police procedurals and in anticipation of the late 1980s–1990s *chernukha*, *The Meeting Place* does not shy away from portraying violence, blood, and gore. The series begins when the rookie policeman Sharapov witnesses the brutal murder of a young cop who tries to infiltrate the gang. Observing from a distance, the police see the young man strolling cheerfully and eating an ice-cream. Two minutes later we see him, in a close-up, stabbed in the heart with a shank. Unlike *ICE*, *Meeting Place* is centered on crime against private citizens. In the episode of the store robbery, the gangsters kill not only the night watchman but also the watchman's little grandson, intensifying the melodrama, as children, traditionally, are viewed as helpless victims. While this violence is softened by displacement into the past, it juices up the plot and enhances viewers' emotions and desire for revenge onscreen.

In stark contrast to *The Investigation* and the vast majority of police films, *The Meeting Place* does not portray the police as simply a state institution. Recruited hodgepodge from the slim pickings of the surviving post-war men, members of the squad are neither professionals, nor do they have any identifiable police markers. They work on sheer enthusiasm and a desire to protect their community. By portraying the police as run-of-the-mill guys, blue-collar rather than intellectual, amateurs rather than professionals, the mini-series offers a state-centered narrative without the state, policing without any of its negative sides. Even crime-busting tactics—invading private apartments or raiding commercial restaurants—are normalized because they are stripped of their associations with power and grounded in the "necessary" violence of the post-war years. Moreover, policing is interspersed with scenes in which the squad participates in the peaceful and idyllically constructed life of the community: helping with potato harvesting, adopting an abandoned baby, or dancing with wives and girlfriends. The police also share the material deprivations of the community they protect, surviving on bread and tea or scrupulously counting money assigned for organizing a set-up in a luxurious restaurant.

The populist appeal to the shared past and ennobling suffering justifies and naturalizes other, more problematic, aspects of the series' "period-piece" ideology: the interrogation and expulsion of a traitor, a distrust of the intelligentsia as an "alien" class, the celebration of a charismatic group leader as the guarantor of justice, who is above the law. From the late 1990s and especially in the 2000s, these and many other signs of "value-neutral" Stalinism have become standard features of both television police procedurals and gangster sagas, where the professional criminal or law enforcement male community with a strong boss at the helm showed to the post-Soviet viewers how the ideal citizens of the new Russia have to behave in regards to the state and its leader.

A perestroika-era song by the soft-rock group Liube titled "Atas!" captures the populist appeal of the Zheglov-type street justice, with its class-mindedness reduced to a celebration of anarchic freedom: not freedom under the rule of law (*svoboda*) but vigilante justice (*volia*). The successful police show of the 1990s *Streets of Broken Lights,* discussed earlier in this chapter, quotes *The Meeting Place,* both directly and in appropriation of a vision of the Russian character and the normal Russian social order. The police characters may complain about social chaos and occasionally invoke the law, but they also happily break it (e.g., their office has a jar with the inscription "for bribes"), bond over vodka, and even allow an arrested man to have a conjugal visit on their office table.

In 2007 the 14-episode series *Liquidation* (*Likvidatsiia*) remade *The Meeting Place* for a new era. Since the series is set in post-war Odessa, the main attraction is the city's Jewish culture and criminal milieu. Instead of Zheglov, the chief protagonist is the streetwise policeman Gotsman (Vladimir Mashkov). Unfortunately, the Putin-era state-centered environment gets the better of the filmmakers, and they introduce a Soviet-style plotline of anti-Soviet conspiracy and Nazi collaborators, which completely kills the joy of watching the first few episodes.

The Meeting Place also became part of the post-socialist cityscape. On the one hand, its cult status is commercialized in the many restaurants and bars throughout Russia: The Meeting Place, Zheglov, The Black Cat, etc. On the other, several monuments have strived to immortalize it. For instance, the monument in Kiev, which features both Zheglov and Sharapov, was erected in 2009 in the courtyard of the local Ministry of Internal Affairs headquarters, which had just celebrated its ninetieth anniversary. According to the Ukrainian Minister of Internal Affairs, the monument should remind the police officers of Zheglov's words: "A thief should be in jail."[37] Originally the sculptor planned to include a figure of a cat as the symbol of the criminal world, but instead drew a silhouette next to Zheglov's boot. The word *davit'* (to crush) is prominently placed in the comments next to the photograph of the monument on the Internet.

It is no accident that Putin, and his PR service, has invoked two iconic heroes of 1970s television as his alter egos: Shtirlitz[38] and Zheglov. Putin's association with the former largely plays up his identity of an agent and has nothing to do

---

[37] "Pamiatnik Glebu Zheglovu i Volode Sharapovu v Kieve." See http://toursdekiev.com.ua/ru/monument_Geglovu_i_Sharapovu. Accessed 12 April, 2015.
[38] Shtirlitz (Viacheslav Tikhonov) is a character in a 12-episode spy series, *Seventeen Moments of Spring* (*Semnadtsat' mgnovenii vesny,* dir. Tat'iana Lioznova, 1973). The title character is a Soviet agent who infiltrated the German high command during the Great Patriotic War. For a discussion of the series see Prokhorova (2003).

with the characters' metaphorical potential.³⁹ Mark Lipovetsky argues that Shtirlitz's dual identity of a Nazi and a Soviet officer became a cypher for the 1970s intelligentsias' self-positioning: the need to compromise while continuing to imagine oneself as the conscience of the nation.⁴⁰

Putin and his regime's affinity with the character of Zheglov runs deeper. In December of 2010, just before Mikhail Khodorkovsky's second trial and conviction, which sentenced him and Platon Lebedev to 14 years in prison, Vladimir Putin participated in a direct line, during which callers could ask the Prime Minister questions. One of the callers asked Putin whether he considered it just that Khodorkovsky was still in prison. The woman noted that she did not expect an answer because such direct lines usually focus on calls from grateful old ladies. Putin, however, did answer. "Just like the famous character played by Vladimir Vysotskii, I believe that a thief should be in jail. Khodorkovsky stole several hundred billion rubles. In the US the jail term for an analogous crime is 150 years."⁴¹ The rather coy analogy to the US aside, by quoting Zheglov, Putin basically admits that the legally collected evidence means nothing. After all, in the eyes of state power, Khodorkovsky's real offense was not stealing money. It was challenging the leader of the gang.

Postscript: streetwise cops meet the Russian mafia

After the collapse of the Soviet Union and the disintegration of the Soviet film industry, audiences wholeheartedly embraced previously inaccessible Western cinema and television productions that in the early-to-mid-1990s constituted the bulk of Russian TV's fiction offerings. Television recovered from a slump much faster and more vigorously than cinema. Not surprisingly, police procedurals and crime dramas paved the way for the TV renaissance and post-Soviet police shows have been using successful Soviet productions as their

---

³⁹ For a detailed discussion of the uses of popular Soviet film and television iconography to boost Putin's public image see Helena Goscilo, "Putin's Performance of Masculinity: The Action Hero and Macho Sex-Object." *Putin as Celebrity and Cultural Icon*. Ed. Helena Goscilo. New York: Routledge, 2013. 180–207.

⁴⁰ See Mark Lipovetsky, "Iskusstvo alibi: *Semnadtsat' mgnovenii vesny* v svete nashego opyta," *Neprikosnovennyi zapas* 3 (2007): 131–146.

⁴¹ Putin, Vladimir. *Priamaia liniia s Vladimirom Putinym*. Channel Russia-1, Broadcast 16 December 2010. *The Priamaia Liniia (The Direct Line with Vladimir Putin)* is an annual Q&A Show starring President Putin, broadcast in December by television channels: Russia-1 and Channel One, Russia and supported and directed by the Kremlin Press Secretary. The 2010 program was the ninth broadcast of the "direct line."

models while adjusting the plots and characters to the new social environment. The two most successful 1990s projects, *Streets of Broken Lights* (1997–) and *Kamenskaia* (1999–2011), each adapt the syntax of the Soviet police procedural to their vision of contemporary Russian society. *Kamenskaia* followed the more institutionalized and idealized view of police work of *ICE*, but made a female detective the protagonist and the driving force of the narrative. *Streets of Broken Lights* adopted the populist model of *The Meeting Place*, but deployed its overworked, cynical, and law-bending heroes in contemporary St. Petersburg, rather than in the distanced and ideologically safe post-Great Patriotic War past.[42]

Streets became the harbinger of the genre's unchallenged rule on Russian television since Putin's first term as president. But whereas the first seasons of the show moved beyond the Soviet model by engaging social problems of Russian society in transition—corruption, economic collapse, poverty, alcoholism, drug abuse, etc.—Putin-era television has been increasingly moving away from social issues of present-day Russia while reverting to the concept of a strong and benevolent state protecting its citizens. As Vera Zvereva points out, the multiplication of shows featuring police, special forces, prosecutors, FSB and other law enforcement agencies (*silovye struktury*) works to project an image of a strong state and reassure audiences that it has complete control over not only Russia, but also the post-Soviet states and former Cold-War rivals. These police procedurals share many features of *ICE*, such as its focus on the police team's collective identity (Zvereva notes that interrogations are often conducted by several detectives) and its downplaying of the detective plot (the criminal is known from the beginning). Unlike the classic Soviet-era police shows, however, new Russian series are populist in imitating—and reproducing—informal and often semi-criminal language, behavior, and ideas about social norms.[43]

In a way, post-Soviet police procedurals and gangster sagas are located at the symbolic center of a unified television universe in contemporary Russia, while sharing a number of key features with other genres: an obsessive representation of state power, which, as critic Andrei Arkhangel'skii writes, can be channeled through either law enforcement or the criminal milieu, with the same message that people's everyday lives are at the mercy of these competing proxies of state

[42] For a discussion of the two models see Prokhorova (2003).
[43] Vera Zvereva, "Zakon i kulak: 'Rodnye militseiskie serialy,'" *NLO* 78 (2006); http://magazines.russ.ru:81/nlo/2006/78/zver20.html.

power. In the narrative universe of these crime shows, a successful business and individual agency, autonomous from the Russian state, are inherently criminal and the search for these enemies of Russia's safety and unity is the reason for the existence of ideal male communities, be they organized crime groups or the police squad.[44]

---

[44] Andrei Arkhangel'skii, "Rodnee nekuda: o chem govoriat i progovarivaiutsia rossiiskie serialy?" *Colta* 15 April 2015; see www.colta.ru/articles/media/7020.

3

Late-Soviet Comedy: Between Rebellion and the Status Quo

Syntax and semantics of the genre

If late-Soviet melodrama is by its nature transgressive and articulates values that question the status quo, romantic comedy as a genre celebrates the status quo and examines non-systemic problems against the background of stagnant but generally prosperous society. Soviet film comedy was one of the few film genres acknowledged by Stalin's film administrators and actively promoted after Boris Shumiatskii's famous dictum that the film comedy embraces "the laughter of the victors" and should combine the ideological message with a good dose of entertainment (1935: 249).[1] Stalinist filmmakers such as Grigorii Aleksandrov and Ivan Pyr'ev established key syntactic features of the Soviet film comedy. At its core was the socialist realist masterplot, which implied state-sponsored satire about surviving elements of the bourgeois past; the dependence of romance on the ideological narrative; fantasy sequences illustrating the communist utopia; the centrality of the so-called mass song in articulating the ideological meaning of the film; and the female protagonist as a carrier of state agency and the best proof of the advantages of the socialist way of life. There were also several glaring absences driven by state censorship and the syntax of Stalinist comedy. For example, Stalinist comedy avoided formal experimentation, such as intellectual montage or theatricality in mise-en-scène and acting, as well as any allusions to sexuality and bodily humor. Most importantly, Stalinist comedy favored the temporality of the utopian future over contemporary life; hence, the bucolic collective farm or Moscow as the exemplary socialist city of the future were the prime locales of Stalinist comedies.

---

[1] For further discussion see Richard Taylor "Ideology as Mass Entertainment: Boris Shumyatsky and Soviet Cinema in the 1930s," in Richard Taylor and Ian Christie, (eds), *Inside the Film Factory*, London: Routledge, 1991, 193–216.

Influenced by neorealist aesthetics, Thaw cinema (post-Stalinist cinema of the Khrushchev era) brought back contemporary life to the screen. Usually the utopian sequences depicting the transformation of backward Russian life under the influence of Soviet modernity were relegated either to the end of the film or to short dream sequences.[2] Most importantly, the romantic plot started competing in its relevance with the socialist realist masterplot. Thaw comedy also became more diverse. Next to the musical comedy of El'dar Riazanov (*Carnival Night/Karnaval'naia noch'* 1956), which updated the syntax of Stalinist comedy, the viewers enjoyed romantic comedies, such as *Behind the Department Store's Window* (*Za vitrinoi univermaga* 1955), *She Loves You!* (*Ona vas liubit!* 1957), *A Girl without an Address* (*Devushka bez adresa* 1957) and the slapstick comedies of Leonid Gaidai.[3]

By the late 1960s and 1970s comedy had caught up with contemporary Soviet life and focused on such phenomena as consumerism, private life, sexual desire, and many other features of modern consumer-driven and increasingly individualistic society. In a parallel fashion, comedy protagonists lost their idealistic aura as characters capable of transforming society and its traditions. El'dar Riazanov's Detochkin from *Beware of a Car* (*Beregis' avtomobilia* 1966) is the last survivor of this Thaw-era breed of social dreamers. The rest of the film's characters are already seduced by the ultimate consumer object of the era—the automobile. In a way Detochkin (Innokentii Smoktunovskii) is the last bona fide socialist mentor who tries to reeducate the entire Soviet community. The philistine community is way beyond any possibility of reeducation or redemption, while Detochkin's expropriation of cars purchased with the money earned via illegal activities is considered a crime or eccentric quixotic acts. Even the characters who sympathize with Detochkin constantly question his normalcy, and he carries a medical certificate confirming his sanity.

While in the 1960s Soviet comedy splintered into multiple subgenres—romantic comedy, slapstick, comedy parodying serious genres, such as crime film—by the 1970s, the major syntactic feature of the Soviet film comedy had become a romance between the strong female protagonist and the male lead,

---

[2] In Stanislav Rostotskii's *It Happened in Pen'kovo* (*Delo bylo v Pen'kove* 1957) a brief dream sequence about communist future is framed by a story of romance between two main characters. When the female character tells the male lead about computerized tractors, he falls in love with the speaker herself rather than the communist tractors of the future.

[3] In this chapter we do not discuss Gaidai's eccentric comedies, which topped Soviet box office charts in the 1960s. While he continued making films into the late 1980s, both the quality of his filmmaking and his cultural relevance declined. For a discussion of Gaidai's and Riazanov's parallel careers as comedy filmmakers see Prokhorov (2003).

who initially lacks the desire to commit to the relationship. Most importantly, when characters in comedy refer to the public sphere (the domain of Soviet ideology) they adopt an ironic discourse, which serves as a defensive screen protecting the privacy of the protagonists' relations. Closer to the film's end the display of a private household appointed with modest furniture and often a car at the building's entrance confirms the emotional and financial strength of the relationship. The socialist realist re-education narrative provides semantic material for late-socialist comedy, but stops playing a lead role in the ideological make-up of the Soviet comedy film.

The recurring theme of late-socialist comedies became the rigidity of social institutions and the people representing them and their inability to be flexible to accommodate the needs and desires of individuals. In his monograph *Laughter, An Essay on the Meaning of the Comic*, Henri Bergson contends that machine-like "automatism . . . makes us laugh" (20), "the comic [is] to be proportioned to the rigidity" (133). He notes that human bodies become comic when they "remind us of [a] mere machine" (32). Indeed, Soviet comedy directors of the 1970s and 1980s focus on the automatism of late-socialist cultural institutions and characters that go through empty rituals without paying any attention to their meaning. Bergson calls such a property of comic characters "absentmindedness," that is, the inability of comic characters to be aware of their machine-like automatism, hence ridiculous for the viewer. Many late-socialist film comedies, in fact, follow the narrative trajectory of characters behaving in a comically automatized way. In the course of the film, via romance, some of them overcome this predicament. Moreover, through the magic power of romance, they acquire individual agency, which in turn allows them to instill empty rituals with new meanings and to reconcile the contradictions of late-socialist life.

In late-socialist comedies characters capable of overcoming rigid social restrictions and revitalizing ossified social relations usually belong to the Soviet intelligentsia. In contrast to Stalinist and even Thaw-era comedies, where working-class characters functioned as markers of a cinema in service to Marxist ideology, the protagonists of comedies of the 1970s are usually college graduates who pursue professional careers. For example, in El'dar Riazanov's films, characters are doctors, teachers, scholars, or college-trained low-level civil servants. Similarly, though Mark Zakharov often set his television films in fantasy locations, his characters remained writers, poets and scholars—in short, people who would belong to the intelligentsia if they lived in the Soviet Union.

If these characters are frozen in their social roles at the beginning of the film, during the course of the narrative they come to life and overcome their social automatism and emotional rigidity. Their comic foils, in contrast, lack self-reflexivity and act like social machines. There are two types of comic characters in the comedies of the period. In the first group are government bureaucrats who mindlessly fulfill their duties. In Riazanov's *Office Romance* (*Sluzhebnyi roman* 1977), for example, the female protagonist, Liudmila Kalugina (Alisa Freindlikh), is a gloomy, humorless head of an unidentified statistical bureau whose machine-like interaction with her subordinates is one of the primary targets of the film's jokes (see Figures 3.1 and 3.2).

The second type of such social automatons are working-class characters who often lack individual identity and appear as a collective hero who does not respect individual characters' privacy and their very right to be individuals. As a boorish and repressive force, this collective hero makes cameo appearances in these comedies as caricatures of the collective working class hero from earlier periods of Soviet cinema. In Riazanov's films, for example, intelligentsia protagonists are often interrupted in the most intimate moments by a faceless group of characters who perform their social role without any regard for others'

Figure 3.1: Kalugina as the gloomy Soviet bureaucrat

Late-Soviet Comedy: Between Rebellion and the Status Quo 111

Figure 3.2: A character mocks the humorless boss

privacy. The comic situation arises out of the protagonists being unable to find private space and the inconsiderate community invading any space that the protagonists try to define as private. In Riazanov's *The Irony of Fate* (*Ironiia sud'by* 1975) a group of drunken neighbors invade a private apartment and interrupt the two main characters as they are trying to understand their feelings toward each other. Notably, the inebriated neighbors are not identified. They are just the collective body celebrating the New Year and end up in the protagonist's apartment because, like a snowball, they try to include in their collective festive body as many individual bodies as possible.

In *Office Romance*, a loud and obnoxious group of workers dressed, significantly, in uniform gray robes invade the office in which two intelligentsia characters are engaged in a highly personal conversation. When the latter protest and insist that the group should respect individuals' privacy, the collective hero first disregards them and then tells them that they are following orders from above to take stock of the office furniture. Furniture matters, while humans, especially "people of intellectual labor" (*rabotniki umstvennogo truda*), as one of the gray-robed characters pejoratively calls them, might want to take their business elsewhere (see Figure 3.3).

Figure 3.3: The individual overshadowed by the body of a nameless working-class character. (Note that the man's face is invisible within the frame, for he is not an individual, but a part of the collective body.)

Working-class characters and other elements of socialist realist aesthetics, such as reeducation, appear in late-Soviet comedies not only as a sign of the state-sponsored oppression of individuals, but also as a concession to state censors, who closely watched for any erroneous interpretations of Soviet life. An example of the latter phenomenon is encountered in *Gentlemen of Fortune* (*Dzhentel'meny udachi* 1971). The director Aleksandr Seryi, using his own recent prison experience, made a comedy about a group of convicts and their boss, who in fact is his look-alike kindergarten teacher aiding the police. The film brims with comically presented details of prison mores and slang. Seryi's picture has been seen by 65 million viewers and enriched the Russian language with numerous comic one-liners evoking prison scenes and using criminal jargon, all of which testified to the success of the director's strategy. By the end, however, the mandatory reeducation plot drained the film of its vitality, replacing it with the sentimental mode as characters end up regretting that they had not started their reeducation earlier and had lost touch with their families.

Some comedies went beyond the limits of the permissible within the Soviet genre system by invoking genres that were not produced by the Soviet film industry. For example, in 1970 Vladimir Motyl' made a comedic parody of a western, *White Sun of the Desert* (*Beloe solntse pustyni*), which inaugurated generic eclecticism as a new trend in Soviet comedy. Inspired by the spaghetti westerns of Sergio Leone and John Sturges's *The Magnificent Seven* (1960), the film depicts a Red Army soldier, Sukhov (Anatolii Kuznetsov), returning from the Russian Civil War to his romantic interest, Katerina. On the way to his Russian beauty Sukhov has to liberate a Central Asian frontier town from local bandits. Several heterosexual romances and homoerotic bonding subplots rely on western conventions to tell the story of individual heroes overcoming standard action-film obstacles.[4]

Many subgenres of late-Soviet comedy, however, shun not only socialist realism but also contemporary life and its Soviet version in particular. The 1970s is the acme of television adaptations of Western literary classics. These productions vary in their approach to the material and in their style. Some are escapist costume spectacles that follow vaudeville aesthetics, where plot intrigue determines the meaning: *The Dog in the Manger* (*Sobaka na sene* 1977), based on a play by Lope de Vega; an adaptation of Shakespeare's *Much Ado about Nothing* (*Mnogo shuma iz nichego* 1973); *The Straw Hat* (*Solomennaia shliapka* 1974), based on a play by Eugène-Marin Labiche. Others are executed in retro style and adopt a minimalist chamber aesthetics and focus on dialogue, e.g., *Three Men in a Boat, To Say Nothing of the Dog* (*Troe v lodke, ne schitaia sobaki* 1979), an adaptation of Jerome K. Jerome's comic travelogue, and *The Adventures of Prince Florizel* (*Prikliucheniia printsa Florizelia* 1979), based on a collection of detective stories by R. L. Stevenson. While the source works for the latter two productions are detective stories, the films focus on romantic plot and an ironic play with both the narrative and the Victorian setting.

Screenplays based on classical literary works played a special role in late-socialist culture. First, reinterpreted classical texts allowed authors to avoid confrontations with censors. Second, teaming up with a scriptwriter (and basically being a co-author) allowed the filmmaker to control the text. Many filmmakers worked with the same scriptwriters for decades. El'dar Riazanov

---

[4] In his correspondence with Goskino, the head of the Studio, Vladimir Pozner Sr., emphasized that the film's serio-comic modality and conventions of a western distinguish this picture from "serious" (aka ideological) films about the Civil War: "[T]he positive heroes of the film [are] are good-looking strong guys (*krasivye sil'nye parni*) who are loyal to their idea" (10). "Beloe solntse pustyni," RGALI, f. 2944, op.4, ed.kh. 1514.

worked with Emil Braginskii, Mark Zakharov with Grigorii Gorin, and both teams wrote flexible scripts that could be adapted for cinema, television, theater, or even radio performance (Golovskoi (2004): 219). Finally, co-writing the script allowed the filmmaker to earn more during the film's production.

What all these productions have in common, apart from very strong acting (which was the norm for late-Soviet television films), is what Iu. Mikheeva calls a special "intonation": "*elevating* character ... above the material in which he exists—and consequently, 'elevating' the viewer above the texture of the plot. Film[s] now offer a chance to sense hidden meanings, an ironic flickering 'between the lines'" (2009: 274). While Mikheeva attributes this quality to what she calls *intelligentnaia komediia*, which addressed and represented the "vacant and restless consciousness" of the Soviet intelligentsia (2009: 280), we argue that the vast majority of late-Soviet comedies keep a certain ironic distance between the literal plot and the meaning of the diegesis. This distance manifests itself in dialogue, the mise-en-scène, soundtrack, and camerawork.

The use of songs and music deserves special attention. On the one hand, the prominence of musical numbers in late-Soviet comedy signals its continuity with 1930s and 1940s musical comedy, with the added advantage of triggering positive associations in the older censors. In fact, the majority of popular Soviet comedies of the 1970s and early 1980s, both for the big screen and for television, belong to the official release genre of "musical comedy." The role of songs in most of these films, however, was radically different from their earlier counterparts. Soviet mass song of Stalin-era productions was loud, choral, and served as the ideological dominanta of the narrative: for instance, "The Song of the Motherland" in *Circus* (*Tsirk* 1936) and "The Harvest Song" in *Cossacks of the Kuban* (*Kubanskie kazaki* 1949).[5] In contrast, songs in the comedies of Gaidai, Riazanov, Zakharov, and many others are low key, personal and, more often than not, work in counterpoint to the narrative or at least add a dimension that is not explicitly part of the plot. Songs convey something that could not be depicted visually and provide a metaphysical, quasi-religious dimension to the visible world of the film. Riazanov, for instance, used poetry by Boris Pasternak, Marina Tsvetaeva, Bella Akhmadulina, Nikolai Zabolotskii and Robert Burns in his "homey" romantic comedies, such as *The Irony of Fate* and *Office Romance*. Zakharov, in

---

[5] On the role of songs in Stalin-era musical comedy, see, for example, Richard Taylor, "Singing on the Steppes for Stalin: Ivan Pyr'ev and the Kolkhoz Musical in Soviet Cinema," *Slavic Review* 58.1 (1999): 143–159 and Rimgaila Salys, *The Musical Comedy Films of Grigorii Aleksandrov: Laughing Matters* (2009).

turn, had songs written for specific characters and scenes, yet these songs often communicate meanings that challenge the straightforward diegetic action.

Rather than talking about a special intonation, which, as Mikheeva herself admits, in the 1970s comedy does not imply a "signature" expression of *auteurs* but a shared *Weltanschauung* (274), we propose that a key development in the Soviet comedy was the appearance of an ironic edge in a comic narrative. Linda Hutcheon links the emergence of the questioning ironic mode with the exhaustion and automatization of tropes that become incompatible with new cultural values. According to her, central to an ironic meaning are relational, inclusive, and differential semantic characteristics. Irony operates between meanings (said, unsaid) and among people (ironists, interpreters, targets) in order to create something new and to endow it with the critical edge of judgment (58); the relational aspect of irony implies a discursive community of an ironist and an interpreter that makes irony possible (92); finally, ironic usage does not replace the said with the unsaid but, rather, superimposes the unsaid on the said (64).

The ironic mode became decisive for late-Thaw and emerging Stagnation culture. By the 1970s, irony had replaced the sincerity of the Thaw years. In a way it marked the border between Thaw culture, which still attempted to refurbish the tropes of socialist realism, and Stagnation culture, which ironized and later satirized tropes that by then were exhausted. During the late Thaw, irony came to signify a discrepancy between the cultural values of the 1950s and 1960s—anti-monumentalism, sincerity, the cult of emotions—and an undercurrent of a new set of cultural values: loss of the heroic, skepticism about the possibility of authenticity (which became the highest form of artifice),[6] a sense of powerlessness over one's fate, and, last but not least, consumerism and a focus on private life. In literature and film of the late 1960s, irony's edge targeted the gap between the lofty values of the Thaw and the actual practices and experiences of the communities in late-Thaw novels and films. The communities continued to proclaim Thaw values, but acted according to the pragmatic concerns of the emerging Stagnation era.

In his article on the late-Soviet stand-up comedian Arkadii Raikin, Sergei Oushakine points to the counterpoint among various performative modes—textual, visual, vocal, gestural—as the source of the "Soviet comic genre" that "unleashed an

---

[6] Vladimir Vysotskii's career as a singer/songwriter constitutes a prime example of such "performance of authenticity." The many masks he assumed in his songs—from a Great Patriotic War soldier to a grouchy wife in front of a TV set—performed the dominant discourses (patriotism, official anti-semitism, etc.) with earnestness, at times comic, at times dramatic.

important affective discharge" (253). Oushakine talks primarily about Soviet satire of the 1920s–1950s rather than the later iterations/genres of the comic, which are often very conscious of the strategies of multi-messaging. While censorship set limits to what could be represented (and to a lesser degree, how), by the 1970s Soviet culture had become simultaneously more open to Western models and aware of its own artistic heritage, both of which challenged the inherited Stalinist narrative. As we argue further in this chapter, the former became all-important for Riazanov's comedy, while the latter, specifically, Vsevolod Meierkhol'd's avant-garde theater of the 1920s, had a direct influence on Zakharov's television films.

The two major comedy directors of the era, El'dar Riazanov and Mark Zakharov, represent two different comedy models and two media. Between 1975 and 1985 each produced half-a-dozen comedies, which share an awareness of societal ills, in particular deadening conformity and the need for individual agency. We argue that Riazanov's aesthetics represented cinematic comedy, while Zakharov's films articulated the new television aesthetics of late-Soviet comedy. Riazanov focused on the romantic plot with a middle-aged protagonist at the center, whereas Zakharov favored fragmented narratives, peppered with musical numbers and marked by theatrical performances. In their aesthetics, his films offered the viewers a proto-sitcom format.

El'dar Riazanov: the trappings and traps of private life

Riazanov was the major comedy director of the 1970s. Most of his comedies were produced for theatrical release and he established the syntax of late-Soviet comedy on screen. His protagonists from the intelligentsia engage in the battle of the sexes in order to find happiness in romance and austere Soviet consumerism. On the one hand, Riazanov did away with the crude politicization of laughter in Soviet cinema. The political agenda of the period's party line and satire as its auxiliary tool play little role in Riazanov's most popular comedies. The middle age of his protagonists and the fact that many of them were on their second marriage perhaps reflected the general ageing of Soviet culture and its institutions, rather than directly celebrating the Brezhnev-era cult of gerontocracy. On the other hand, Riazanov reintroduced the Soviet audience to the genre conventions of Western comedic traditions, in particular Italian-style comedy and Hollywood screwball comedy. From the former, Riazanov borrowed several elements: its focus on the "little man" who is a captive of a social predicament; recognizable settings and situations of everyday life, where modernity coexists with outdated traditions and rituals, which often constitute obstacles; the use of social masks; and what in the Soviet context would be considered risqué situations in the bedroom. Pietro Germi's *Divorce: Italian Style* (1961, Soviet release 1964) and *Seduced and Abandoned* (1963, Soviet release 1966) familiarized viewers in the USSR with the genre and prepared them for Riazanov's appropriations of its conventions.

Hollywood comedy provided Riazanov with the heteronormative romance as an alternative utopia, which completely replaced the official socialist utopia. Moreover, in his films Riazanov connected romance to the consumerist ideal. The display of a modest but comfortable consumerist lifestyle was an indispensable element of the narrative and mise-en-scène in his comedies. For example, the whole plot of *The Irony of Fate* (1976) is motivated by the fact that both major characters have just moved into new apartments and purchased new furniture, a minor drawback being that both apartments and furniture are too standardized. In *Office Romance* (1977) the lion's share of the plot is dedicated to the female protagonist's makeover, with extensive discussions and displays of current clothing and shoe fashions, hairstyles, and body image. The key obstacle in the two lovers' route to happiness is the female protagonist's excessive dedication to her public service.

With the limited access of Soviet viewers to Western comedies, Riazanov successfully exploited their plots and genre conventions to create domestic analogues. He started his career as a feature movie director in 1956 with *Carnival Night*, a remake of the 1938 *Volga, Volga* (dir. Grigorii Aleksandrov), and subsequently established a pattern of parodying genre conventions of Soviet and, what is more important for our argument, Western genres and filmmakers. In 1966 he released his ironic parody of a heist film, *Beware of a Car*, followed in 1971 by another take on the caper movie genre, *Old Men-Robbers* (*Stariki-razboiniki*). The heist film did not exist within the Soviet cinematic tradition, mainly because crime narratives were always represented from the position of the Soviet authorities. Soviet police played the role of state agent and the narrative focalizer. By framing his films as comic parodies of "alien" genres Riazanov deflected any accusations of romanticizing the criminal underworld—a staple in censors' critique of Soviet crime films. In 1973 in his Soviet-Italian co-production *The Extraordinary Adventures of Italians in Russia* (*Neveroiatnye prikliucheniia ital'iantsev v Rossii* 1973), Riazanov remade Stanley Kramer's *It's a Mad, Mad, Mad, Mad World* (1963). The comic premise of cultural misunderstanding between the Soviets and the West came from Lev Kuleshov's film *The Extraordinary Adventures of Mr. West in the Land of Bolsheviks* (*Neobychainye prikliucheniia mistera Vesta v strane bol'shevikov* 1924), while the social critique of capitalist greed, safe within the Soviet context, came from the *commedia all'italiana*. His *Irony of Fate* and *Office Romance* follow the narrative conventions of Hollywood romance, with the plot of *The Taming of the Shrew* as the basic narrative model.

With his last 1970s film, *Garage* (*Garazh* 1979), the satirical tone became more prominent. However, one thing remained constant: the recycling of plots and genre conventions, both Western and Russian. *Garage*, according to the filmmaker, was modeled on Sidney Lumet's *12 Angry Men* (Riazanov 280).[7] Later, *The Train Station for Two* (*Vokzal dlia dvoikh* 1982) exploits elements of *commedia all'italiana*, with the male protagonist trapped in his social circumstances and black humor prominent in the ending: the protagonist's major accomplishment, which promises a happy romance, hinges on his timely return to the prison camp where he is serving his sentence for a crime he did not commit. *Garage* marked the end of Riazanov as a comedy filmmaker. His next film, *Ruthless Romance* (*Zhestokii romans* 1984), was a remake of Iakov Protazanov's 1937 film adaptation of Aleksandr Ostrovskii's play *Without Dowry* (Riazanov 377–379). In it he he shifted from comedy to social satire and melodrama; hence, most of his later films belong to different genre models and cultural values and are beyond the scope of this chapter.

While Riazanov borrowed conventions from both Hollywood romantic comedy and the *commedia all'italiana*, his films had a different function in Soviet culture from the genres' role in American or Italian cultures. Hollywood comedy is driven by characters' individualist motivation and the changing social landscape of modernity, in particular the shifting notions of class, family, gender, and sexuality in contemporary society. *Comedia all'italliana*, in turn, examines the glaring misalliance of modernity and the stagnant feudal traditions of the Italian south. The role and treatment of women in such films as *Divorce Italian Style* appears as the prime social issue and symptom of society's inability to cope with the challenges of modernity. Hollywood comedy celebrates the open-endedness of modernity enacted as an everlasting war of genders, both in the office and in the bedroom, while the Italian comedy embraces an open-endedness resulting from the culture's inability to reconcile the old and the new. As Thomas Schatz notes, the genre film, and romantic comedy in particular, engages viewers by its capacity

---

[7] In post-Soviet times Nikita Mikhalkov returned to Lumet's film and in 2007 made his melodramatic remake of the Hollywood classic titling it *12*.

to celebrate the contradictions within our culture while seeming to do away with them. [...] The role of the assertive, witty, self-reliant woman; the injection of traditional middle-class values (monogamy, democracy, equal opportunity, rugged individualism) into a decadent urban milieu; and the screwball couple's uninhibited "pursuit of happiness"—these three elements offset and ultimately balance the prosocial implications of marital promise.

1981, 159

None of these issues or concerns is central to Riazanov's oeuvre. If anything, his representation of women is quite retrograde. As opposed to female protagonists of such screwball classics as *It Happened One Night* (Frank Capra, 1934)—an inspiration for *The Irony of Fate*—and Howard Hawks's *His Girl Friday* (1940), Nadia in *The Irony of Fate* lacks her Hollywood counterparts' mobility and agency and simply replaces one candidate for a husband with another. In *Office Romance* the androgynous boss-lady morphs into an attractive female who discovers her happiness in heterosexual romance, while becoming softer and more feminine along the way. In contrast to the open-endedness of Western models, the late-socialist romantic comedy embraces and celebrates the cyclical chronotope of the idyll. The middle-aged and often childless couples form their perfect private world. This idyllic private space is separated by the wall of irony from the politicized world of the public sphere. Ultimately, Riazanov successfully incorporates semantic elements of Western genre models into the syntactic structure that unambiguously suggests the conflictless and timeless existence of the community that has achieved its perfect status quo.

The truly innovative feature of Riazanov's romantic comedy is its celebration of private space. In making private spaces discursively visible and central to the narrative, Riazanov's films were revolutionary for the time, capitalizing on the sensibilities of late socialism: a retreat from the public sphere into private space, a celebration of "austere consumption," and a timid fetishizing of Eastern bloc-produced commodities. In her article on the representations of consumerism in late-Soviet cinema, Natalya Chernyshova points to a paradox. Soviet culture, from its very origins, denounced consumerism and generally, the everyday grind (*byt*) as antithetical to the "Soviet way of life." This censure abated after the "culture wars" of the 1920s,[8] but remained prominent in official discourses. Many films of the 1970s equate consumerism with amoral behavior. Yet, the other, equally strong taboo was the "blackening of Soviet reality," which included

---

[8] See, in particular, Chapter 1 of Svetlana Boym's *Common Places: Mythologies of Everyday Life in Russia* (Harvard University Press, 1994).

anything from depictions of economic problems in the present to excessive dwelling on the devastation of the Great Patriotic War. As a result, Chernyshova writes, "[V]isions of material prosperity had to be evoked in a positive context and without the tensions of moral dilemmas, just as the traditional canons of socialist realism had prescribed ... The glossy portrayal of daily life seemed the most acceptable option—but it gave further sanction to acquisitive pursuits" (2013, 68).

Most of the reviews of *The Irony of Fate* focused on the verisimilitude of Riazanov's mise-en-scène.[9] The critics were fascinated with the possibility of depicting the material culture that was socially accurate but had not been present on screen for the preceding fifty years. For the first time since Abram Room's *Bed and Sofa* (*Tret'ia Meshchanskaia* 1927) the apartment space did not serve the bigger goal of the ideological narrative but instead documented the common places of late socialism. For the first time in Russian culture, the film created a proto-soap opera experience by paralleling the existence of the viewers to that of the characters. This perhaps is one of the explanations why *The Irony of Fate* became the biggest New Year's film in the history of Russian cinema. Every year since the film's television premiere on 1 January 1976, Russians celebrate their New Year's Eve by watching the film about celebrating New Year's Eve in the privacy of their apartments.[10]

Mikheeva considers the everyday Soviet settings of 1970s "intelligent(sia) comedies" a radical departure from conventions of the 1950s–1960s, where comic situations resulted from either character-masks (e.g., in Gaidai's films) or extraordinary settings and the marginal social roles that characters occupy.[11] In contrast, in the 1970s "[t]he hero does not need to leave his everyday existence to look comic.... Soviet reality itself generates comedy ... These [films] are *sui generis* 'reality shows' of that time (it is no coincidence that most of them are set in small, closed spaces, in contrast to previous comedies, shot in open or at least vast spaces)"

---

[9] Valerii Golovskoi notes that while the plots of Riazanov's films are often implausible (he focuses on later films with more pronounced satirical features), the details of the social and material environment are not only accurate but also acquire a symbolic dimension (e.g., the train station and the prison camp in *The Train Station for Two* (232–237)). The same holds for private apartments in *The Irony of Fate* and the office life of a research institute in *Office Romance*. Riazanov, for instance, went to great lengths to create a modern office, even borrowing from the Central Statistical Administration a (literally) precious commodity—a desktop computer. The price of this "prop," which proudly sat on Kalugina's desk, was $100,000, and an assistant had to bring it to the set and take it back *every* day of shooting (Tsymbal (2009) Personal Interview).

[10] For a discussion of the Soviet genre of the New Year film, see Alyssa DeBlasio (2008).

[11] For example, *White Sun of the Desert, Thirty Three* (*Tridtsat' tri* 1965), *Kidnapping Caucasian Style* (*Kavkazskaia plennitsa* 1967).

(2009, 292-93). In the case of Riazanov, the choice of closed spaces, culminating in the museum setting in *Garage*, evokes a sitcom rather than the reality-show format, but the mise-en-scène indeed sparked recognition. The effect was both ironic and comforting. Through their ritualistic appearances on television screens, Riazanov's two most famous male protagonists from *The Irony of Fate* and *Office Romance* (both played by Andrei Miagkov) demonstrated that the everyday, middle-brow Soviet environment was adequate and even conducive to romance.

This ideology of private space is in stark contrast both to Georgii Daneliia's melodrama *Autumn Marathon*, where the hero's lack of genuine desire turns private apartments into traps, and to comedies of the 1930s–1950s, where privacy is either negatively marked (as in musical comedies) or is the starting point of the re-education plot. For example, the private apartment in a Stalinist building in Viktor Eisymont's *Good Luck!* (*V dobryi chas!* 1956) may be neutral per se, but the comfort and security of this privileged life affect the young protagonist negatively. By the end of the film he chooses to follow his cousin to Siberia to become a man, rather than study in Moscow.

In Riazanov's 1970s comedies, in contrast, private spaces do not serve a bigger agenda but, rather, signify a shared understanding of a normal, good life and provide a setting for comic situations. Shots of Moscow begin and end both *The Irony of Fate* and *Office Romance*, and in both cases are accompanied by a song about searching for love. The city's benevolent, "homey" feel is thus conveyed by—and reduced to—a desire for private joys. The spatial trajectory of the plot presents a nearly symmetrical structure: Zhenia's Moscow apartment—the bath house—Moscow airport—Leningrad cab—Nadia's Leningrad apartment—Leningrad train station (where Nadia is buying Zhenia a ticket)—Zhenia's Moscow apartment. To emphasize his point to the level of self-parody in *The Irony of Fate*, Riazanov puts a mother in each apartment. The male protagonist leaves his own mother in his Moscow apartment and eventually ends up with his new fiancée's mother in the identical apartment in Leningrad.

The comedies of Riazanov thus can be called the comedies of a pleasurable return to the status quo, where learning that there is no place like home is the key discovery for the protagonists and by extension the viewers. The director takes the ossified social rituals[12] of the late socialism and gives them an emotional

---

[12] Alexei Yurchak argues in *Everything Was Forever, Until It Was No More: The Last Soviet Generation*: (Princeton: Princeton UP, 2005) that after Stalin's death, Soviet society stopped producing ideological discourses and started mimicking and performing them, with rituals hollowing out the "constative" meaning.

boost, while the members of the community enacting these rituals appear to get a rejuvenating facelift. Finally the community of viewers finds comfort in the stability of the good Soviet life and, if desired, the illusion and unearned moral comfort of temporarily breaking with the conformism of this life. As we argue in the chapter on melodrama, this is the same plot as enacted in the so-called "sad comedies" of Daneliia, which, we believe, sooner fit the melodramatic mode. The difference is that Riazanov creates the illusion that this lack of narrative development—plot stagnation on screen and not just in life—is comforting.

Riazanov's *Irony of Fate* is the best and most relevant example of late-socialist comedic syntax. The thirty-six-year-old protagonist, Zhenia Lukashin (Andrei Miagkov), enters the narrative pressured into marriage while continuing to live with his mother (Liubov' Dobrzhanskaia). From the very beginning he is portrayed as the captive of three New Year's Eve routines: spending the evening with his best friend, that is, his mother; his would-be wife (Ol'ga Naumenko); or his buddies (Aleksandr Shirvindt, Georgii Burkov, Aleksandr Beliavskii). Like a machine, he follows social rituals because it is that time of year. As a genuine stagnation male hero he tries to compromise and combine all three in one night. His first stop is a public bath where he bonds with his friends around drinks. Notably, all his three friends are married and are savoring Zhenia's inevitable pull into the routine of married life. Zhenia is neither enamored nor disgusted with his future spouse; rather, he submits to his fiancée's agency and views it as inevitable as characters in the previous decades saw the coming of communism. He is emotionally numb, and his mind gives in halfway through the first glass of vodka-spiked beer at the bathhouse. Most importantly, he completely forgets that he is getting married.

While *The Irony of Fate* successfully integrates the syntax of romantic comedy with late-Soviet social issues (social conformism, the inability of men to commit, and lack of male sexual desire or, for that matter, desire to act in any sphere),[13] the meanings generated by this syntax and even the plot structure are entirely different from the Hollywood and Italian genre models. Everybody belongs to the Soviet middle class, everyone is modestly comfortable, and everyone shares roughly the same values. Hence the filmmaker needed other mechanisms to represent the "battle of the sexes" that moves the plot in a romantic comedy. One such unfailing motivator was alcohol, which functions both as a male bonding

---

[13] See Kaganovsky (2009) especially page 186, for a discussion of the connections between political and social stagnation and its cultural (and personal) effects. We address the issues of desire and agency in more detail in Chapter 4.

device, extricating Zhenia from his earlier life, and as a comic accelerator of the new romance.

The drinking scene in the bathhouse fulfills several functions in the narrative. First, by drinking himself senseless Zhenia paradoxically liberates himself from the constraints of his empty ritualized existence. Second, drinking briefly awakens in Zhenia and his friends a spirit of collectivism. After several bottles of vodka they recollect a song of their youth about flying to the Siberian taiga to build a utopian city (see Figure 3.4).

Pleasurable for the late-Soviet viewer, the singing episode provided a prime example of the safe and contained irony practiced by Riazanov. It was ironic because in the film only in a state of complete inebriation could one relive the utopian dreams of one's youth. Riazanov's Soviet characters, when they get drunk, all of a sudden reveal their deeply hidden utopian identity. In the final analysis, however, this is precisely what Yurchak describes as the late-socialist performance of ideology (2005: 4–8): it does not matter whether or not the characters believe what they sing; they sing it and thereby perform the ideology.

Figure 3.4: Collective identity only in a state of inebriation

Out of this collectivist merging of bodies and voices comes unexpectedly a change in the narrative trajectory and the miraculous acquisition of patriarchal agency by the protagonist. The road to the protagonist's awakening lies in the complete erasure of his social identity. The inebriated friends stop distinguishing between individual members of the group, unable to remember which one of them is to fly from Moscow to Leningrad to see his wife. As a result Lukashin is mistakenly loaded onto a plane and ends up in an apartment in Leningrad with the same street address as his apartment in Moscow. The owner of the Leningrad apartment, a woman named Nadia (short for Nadezhda, which means Hope in Russian; played by a Polish film star Barbara Brylska) is expecting her fiancé, Ippolit (Iurii Iakovlev) who, she hopes, will propose to her on New Year's Eve. Though she doesn't love him, she wants to settle down, and when she discovers Zhenia on her couch, her future also gets derailed.

Riazanov uses a dual narrative structure, which he borrowed from classical screwball comedies, such as *It Happened One Night* and *Twentieth Century* (Howard Hawks, 1934). If characters in Hollywood films are pressured by their families to get married, Riazanov's characters prepare to get married not because they love each other, but mostly because doing so is convenient; they are approaching middle age and therefore, according to social conventions, need to get married. The irony of fate derails this marriage, however, and the characters have to start a new and authentic romance from scratch. As opposed to Hollywood screwball comedies, in which genders fight on a more-or-less equal footing, in Riazanov's late-socialist imitations of the model the narrative focus is on the male protagonist rediscovering his patriarchal agency. Meanwhile, the female lead rediscovers her traditional role in a heteronormative family. Zhenia and Nadia are equal in everything but the implied degree of their social conformity: while at the beginning of the film both are about to get married without love, Zhenia is aware of the price involved (see Figure 3.5), while Nadia is ready to "adjust" for the sake of the safety vouchsafed by marriage. After the first slapstick encounter between Zhenia and Ippolit, Zhenia becomes the meaning-maker of the film. He "exposes" Nadia's fears of being an unmarried woman in her late thirties and lectures Ippolit about the latter's self-serving image of a reliable patriarch.

Zhenia's narrative trajectory, meanwhile, implicitly contradicts his own rhetoric—while simultaneously being culturally accurate. First, he exchanges an active woman for a passive one. Not only does his fiancée, Galia, plan the New Year's Eve celebration *for* Zhenia, but she as much as proposes to him—an assertiveness that prompts him to flee. Nadia, in contrast, makes herself pretty

Figure 3.5: Zhenia visibly suffers but recovers himself and makes a proposal to his fiancée Galia, a woman he does not love

and waits for her man, whoever he may be. Second, as we learn from the very beginning, Zhenia has a *pattern* of running away from women who come too close. While the story of escaping to Leningrad is treated comically in the film, the final scene comes full circle: Nadia shows up in Zhenia's apartment, and his mother skeptically observes the "intruder" (see Figure 3.6).

This pattern is even more pronounced in Riazanov's next film *Office Romance*. The plot motivation here is an anomalous gender reversal: the director of an Institute of Statistics, Kalugina (Alisa Freindlikh), is a masculine woman, and the protagonist, Novosel'tsev (Andrei Miagkov), is a feminine man. She is childless, assertive, unsentimental, and uninterested in her appearance. He is a gentle, submissive, single father. As Kalugina's secretary remarks, even before Novoseltsev's wife left him with two children, he was the mother of the family. Egged on by his best, notably female, friend Olga (Svetlana Nemoliaeva), Novoseltsev asks to be promoted to a better-paying job that he has no chance of getting. Fate appears in the guise of the only negative character in the film, the eloquently named Samokhvalov (Oleg Basilashvili),[14] who was Novosel'tsev and Olga's friend in

---

[14] In Russian, "Samokhvalov" means self-promoter, a mortal sin in a culture celebrating the primacy of the collective over the individual.

Figure 3.6: Zhenia's mother observes the female "intruder"

college but has had a much more successful career than them. Instead of leading a good Soviet life in the form of austere consumption, he owns a luxury sedan *Volga*, a spacious apartment, and a host of goods and trinkets from his job in the West. As Kalugina's second-in-command, he patronizingly suggests that Novosel'tsev should woo Kalugina to advance his career.

A party at Samokhvalov's house is analogous in its function to the bathhouse scene in *The Irony of Fate*. Novoles'tsev's inept attempts at courtship, some "courage-inspiring" alcohol, and Kalugina's dismissive attitude produce a comic rebellion in the normally shy protagonist. He grows rowdy and tells the boss what he really thinks of her, calling her "heartless and cold." But the next day, when he enters her office expecting to be fired, he encounters a crying woman, not a boss. The characters' mutual attraction finds its expression in their transformation: Novosel'tsev rediscovers his sagging patriarchal power, while Kalugina gets in touch with her feminine side. While both have to change, the joke is on the woman. After a discussion about the latest fashions, Kalugina gets a complete make-over, including a flattering new hairdo, and tries a more seductive gait. Heteronormative gender roles finally restored, Novosel'tsev gets to demonstrate his masculinity by slapping Samokhvalov.

Another important feature of late-socialist romantic comedy, in addition to the eventual "gender propriety," is the doubling of the male leads. For example, in *The Irony of Fate* Zhenia has a foil in Ippolit—a rigid, controlling, and jealous type, who cynically tries to purchase himself a wife after he has already purchased a car and a good overcoat. The same pairing appears in *Office Romance*: the protagonist, a true patriarch in the making, who returns the community to its initial status quo by the film's ending, has a cynical double, Samokhvalov, who tries to manipulate the system to his own advantage. The cynic has a bigger car, better clothing, and plenty of Western goods, such as Marlboro cigarettes and imported hard liquor, which he uses to buy favors from his colleagues. He views people as stepping stones for his career goals whom he can "condition," like Ivan Pavlov's dogs, by gifts of Western commodities.

The film's treatment of Samokhvalov's "villainy" is quite symbolic of 1970s culture. From the very beginning he is set in contrast to Novosel'tsev, because his material well-being and a successful public career, while desirable, are somehow morally suspect. The end of the film links this ambiguity with the Stalinist practice of public trials and the denial of privacy: pursued by Ol'ga, who cannot forget their college romance, he "releases" her love letters to the whole institute collective. Samokhvalov thus acquires the features of a villainous bureaucrat,[15] while the protagonist, in contrast, is a member of the Soviet intelligentsia—the main character of the late-socialist private sphere and the main target audience of Riazanov's films.[16]

The production circumstances of *The Irony of Fate* contributed to cultural producers' rethinking of the relationship between the public and private spheres in Soviet culture and the role of television and cinema as its major visual media. Initially Riazanov proposed to make *The Irony of Fate* as a film in two parts, about three hours long, for theatrical release. However, film studios made films in two parts only if the theme of the film was of major ideological significance, such as the October Revolution, the victory of the Soviet Union in the Great Patriotic War, or an epic adaptation of a classical Russian novel. A story about a drunken doctor did not fit any of these ideological requirements, and the administrators of the film studio rejected Riazanov's proposal. Knowing the

---

[15] In Alla Surikova's *Look for a Woman* (*Ishchite zhenshchinu* 1981) the cynical double of the protagonist becomes a criminal and is removed from the narrative via arrest. Before the foils disappear they play the role of a trickster who puts the plot into motion and serves as a foil to foreground the positive qualities of the more status-quo-driven protagonist. Then this trickster-foil is jettisoned from the narrative.

[16] See Mikheeva on "comedy for the intelligentsia" (*intelligentnaia comediia*), especially p. 280.

rivalry between the heads of the film and television industries, the savvy filmmaker brought the script to the Soviet television bosses and obtained the funding. *The Irony of Fate* became the first major Soviet film released for the small screen first, and then picked up by the movie theaters for theatrical release. As the medium linked to the private sphere, television during the 1970s started replacing cinema as the major visual medium of Soviet culture.[17]

In their attempts to account for the popularity of *The Irony of Fate* critics came up with a host of vague genre definitions. The film was deemed a "document of social psychology," "a comedy with a slightly sad smile," a picture that "is not a musical, though it has a lot of songs, not a satirical comedy, but rather a film dialogue that begins very funnily and ends in great seriousness," and a "mix of buffoonery with drama" (qtd. in MacFadyen (2003): 219). In contrast to his colleagues' whimsical definitions, Iurii Khanuitin called Riazanov's films "urban fairy tales" which take place in "standard apartments, at supermarket counters, in cheap photo studios," [...] "at the intersection of an improbable situation and a prosaic setting." These stories recall O. Henry's tales, with their belief in "a miracle, which is needed to help ordinary life" (1976: 4). This description resonates with the films of Mark Zakharov, who ruled Soviet television comedy in the 1970s and early 1980s and whose film *An Ordinary Miracle* (1978) seems to be in a direct dialogue with Riazanov's comedy. If Riazanov created fairy tales masked as contemporary romantic comedy, Zakharov produced a series of topical social commentaries disguised as fanciful fairy tales.

Mark Zakharov's television films: between the romance and the sitcom

Mark Zakharov was instrumental in the production of two proto-sitcom formats: his TV shows and his films for television articulated many devices of the situational comedy genre, which coalesced into the sitcom format during the post-Soviet years. On the one hand, he was a writer for the television show *The Pub Thirteen Chairs* (*Kabachok 13 stul'ev* 1966–80), a popular vaudeville production set in a fictional Polish pub, where the same characters gathered in

---

[17] The television variant was released in 1975 in two parts (Part 1 ran for one hour and forty minutes and Part 2 for one hour and twenty-four minutes). The variant for movie theaters was released in 1976 in two parts (Part 1 lasting one hour and fifteen minutes and Part 2, one hour and forty three minutes) (Sopin (2011–2012): 634).

every episode to perform comic sketches. On the other hand, he created a series of television films: *The Twelve Chairs* (1976), *An Ordinary Miracle* (1978), *That Very Same Munchausen* (1979), *The House that Swift Built* (1982), and *The Formula of Love* (1984).[18] While this television theater aspired to a higher cultural status compared to *The Pub*, the films had an ambiguous status as cultural texts. The choice of the television medium and the use of vaudeville aesthetics suggested popular entertainment; at the same time, each film existed in its own right and possessed an aura of auteurist originality and high culture. Zakharov's films employ a variety of respectable literary sources: novelistic and dramatic texts by Ilya Ilf and Evgeny Petrov, Aleksei Tolstoi, Evgenii Shvarts, and Grigorii Gorin. Zakharov's position as the artistic director of the Lenkom Theater and his casting of prominent theater actors from the Lenkom and the Satire Theaters in his films also firmly places his productions in the realm of "art."[19]

Ilf and Petrov's 1928 novel *The Twelve Chairs* offered Zakharov the trickster characters and the syntax of a sitcom: two protagonists travel through NEP-era Russia chasing after a fortune. The plot comprises their comic encounters with contemporary social types and institutions. Each of these encounters constitutes an independent episode; these are loosely connected through the two protagonists and their ever-receding goal of finding the treasure. No matter where two protagonists travel in Russia, they end up in the same common environment: chaotic Russian life uprooted by the revolution caught between medieval traditions and modernity. Produced in the 1970s and 1980s, Zakharov's series of television films articulated a proto-sitcom syntax in late-Soviet television. The main features of this syntax included: a recurring cast of social types, settings removed from contemporary Soviet reality (but readable as allegorical), and conflicts familiar to viewers from their daily routines. The basic situation of these conflicts recurred in each film, similarly to the basic feature of the sitcom that precludes major narrative development from episode to episode. Just as in a sitcom, Zakharov's characters do not possess any psychological depth. Rather, they are outlined by several prominent features repeated, with few variations, in each film. As in sitcoms, this flatness is by no means an obstacle to an accurate representation of contemporary cultural values.

---

[18] *Dvenadtsat' stul'ev; Obyknovennoe chudo; Tot samyi Miunkhauzen; Dom, kotoryi postroil Svift; Formula liubvi*. Zakharov's last film, *To Kill a Dragon* (*Ubit' drakona* 1987), is a perestorika-era Soviet-German co-production with a much more avert anti-totalitarian message.

[19] Notably both theaters took their inspiration and style from Vsevolod Meyerhold's aesthetics. Zakharov rethought Meyerhold's heritage in his theatrical productions and applied the same devices in his television films.

If Riazanov's films gave the late-Soviet viewer the comfort of seeing private life as a refuge from the cynical and frustrating public sphere devoid of the utopian drive, Zakharov's films for television, ironically, turned out to be edgier. They queried whether these private pleasures sufficed. Zakharov depicts a cynical community bereft of any faith and surviving on mindlessly repeated social rituals. Zakharov's trickster-protagonist appears amidst this graveyard of late socialism masquerading as an ahistorical setting not associated with Soviet contemporaneity. His major talent is the ability to tell stories that challenge the automatized meaning-making processes of the philistine community.

All of Zakharov's television films thus share the same syntactic structure: the conflict between the poetic trickster and a community of conformists who try to maintain the status quo and "domesticate" him. Caught between these two poles are young characters whose choice in life is as yet undetermined and who therefore can potentially join either camp. Unlike Riazanov's middle-aged heroes, Zakharov's lovers are unequivocally young, practically children, whose life choices are entirely open. Although the possibility of young characters' reeducation may be read as a residue of the socialist realist master plot, the narratives do not involve any official ideology and are motivated by the characters' individual choices.

Perhaps the greatest achievement of Zakharov's comedy for television was the reintroduction of a conflict grounded in viewers' social concerns as the primary narrative attraction. Unlike melodrama, Soviet comedy for a long time retained the quintessential conflictlessness of Stalin-era cinema—namely, a taboo on contemporary issues. In his seemingly ahistorical fairy tales and adaptations of the classics, Zakharov raised a number of burning issues central to a late-socialist society, such as social conformity, rising consumerism, and the possibility of individual agency. All his films pit the individual against the repressive, inert, and ossified community, which does not want to be disturbed by a dissenting voice. This community consists of a range of recognizable social types from late-socialist society: the leader in denial of social collapse, cynical manipulators profiteering on the decomposing social body, an intellectual (i.e., a member of the Soviet intelligentsia) who betrayed his/her ideals, and ordinary citizens who sacrifice their moral values for basic comfort.

The eclectic style and the conflict between a creative individual and a corrupt, conformist environment introduced in *The Twelve Chairs* became trademarks of Zakharov's comedy. Probably the single most distinctive feature of Zakharov's proto-sitcom films is the centrality of the poetic trickster. Summarizing approaches to the trickster figure, Mark Lipovetsky lists its four main aspects: ambivalence and mediation; liminality and transgressive vitality; transformation of tricks into an art form; and a connection to the sacred (29–34). We argue that Zakharov's films embrace the poetic trickster as a "messenger from the gods," as opposed to his cynical double. For this poet, the ability to trick for the sake of lofty ideals is more important than either narrative logic or pragmatic considerations. Zakharov's television tricksters—the Writer-Magician, Baron Munchausen, Jonathan Swift, and Count Cagliostro—are agents of imagination and rebellion against the status quo. Like Ostap Bender, they are extreme egotists and individualists who do things on a whim and thereby disturb the swampy everyday life of good, reasonable citizens. While the tricksters themselves are dramatic rather than comic figures, they radicalize the environment around them and, as a result, ordinary life turns out to be a treasure chest of comic situations. Not unlike Riazanov's films, Zakharov's comedy thus pays homage to the intelligentsia's self-imagined role of rousing the nation's conscience, while employing the popular culture format of a serialized comedy of everyday life to deliver the message.

By the 1970s Soviet utopia was formalized yet allowed filmmakers the opportunities to create new meanings. Zakharov's poetic trickster works with the residue of the utopian discourse trying to bridge the profane everyday world of practical concerns and cynical compromises with the world of lofty ideals and genuine emotions. The latter world is never depicted directly, but the trickster makes the viewer aware of its existence. In contrast to Stalinist or early post-Stalinist comedy, in Zakharov's television comedies the conflict is never completely resolved by the film's end. Nobody can reeducate anybody, neither the community the individual, as in Stalinist film, nor the individual the community, as some Thaw comedies proposed. In this respect the basic situation of these conflicts migrates from film to film. Keeping in mind that many actors in Zakharov's film came from the Lenkom Theater, such as Aleksandr Abdulov, Oleg Iankovskii, Evgenii Leonov, and Tat'iana Pel'tser, all his films look like new season's a installments of the same sitcom.

Zakharov's comedy is not as viewer-friendly as Stalin-era fantasy film for children. Instead, it acknowledges its connection with the tradition of experimental theater and even conceptualist art. The director keeps his texts open-ended, which allows for the conflict to re-emerge in the next film. At most the viewer can glimpse the possibility of surmounting apathy and making a change. But even this possibility is predicated on the viewers' interpretation of the final image. For example, *That Very Same Munchausen* ends with the protagonist (Oleg Iankovskii) climbing a rope into the barrel of a canon in order to demonstrate that it is possible to ride the cannon ball to the Moon. Despite reasonable citizens' pleas to abort the suicidal mission, Munchausen carries on, and the film ends with him climbing into the sky. We never learn whether his mission succeeds, but, in a truly Dostoevskian sense of the comedic, this act tests the faith both of those inside the narrative and of the viewers in front of their TV sets. The last frame of Zakharov's film visualizes the same concept as Ilya Kabakov's conceptualist installation *The Man who Flew into Space from His Apartment* (1988), which replicates a Soviet apartment, now boarded up by authorities, from which an ordinary Soviet citizen has just departed into outer space (see Figures 3.7 and 3.8).

The House that Swift Built (1982) pitches the Irish satirist against the English establishment and ordinary philistines. Unlike Zakharov's other trickster characters who are often quite verbose and on occasion fond of pathos, Swift (Oleg Iankovskii) is practically silent throughout the two-episode film. Instead, his characters speak for him. The film's plot thrives on the ambiguity of the border between fantasy and reality, performance and autheticity. Hired actors

Figure 3.7: The last frame of Zakharov's film: Munchausen departs into outer space from his oppressive community

Late-Soviet Comedy: Between Rebellion and the Status Quo   133

Figure 3.8: Ilya Kabakov. *The Man Who Flew into Space from His Apartment.*
Installation. Created in 1984
Source: Photo by James Dee, New York, 1988.

who impersonate characters from Swift's works to entertain the master also appear in musical numbers commenting on the narrative. The audience for these performances turns out to be full of spies who have been hired to keep an eye on Swift. The two female leads are both nurses vying for Swift's attention *and* reincarnations of his two former lovers. Dr. Simpson (Aleksandr Abdulov) is both a less-than-bright medic who is hired by the town leaders to declare Swift insane, *and* Gulliver himself, about to embark on his journey. The plot (in both a literary and a conspiratorial sense) prepared by Swift's opponents to get rid of the troublesome satirist is thus intertwined with the writer's own narratives.

In his films Zakharov captured the potential of the trickster's cultural mobility. Hence while several of his films exploit existing narratives, as well as characters and myths surrounding them (Ostap Bender, Munchausen, Jonathan Swift), these characters acquire a new meaning in late-socialist culture, with their power predicated on their ability to be both inside and outside of the system. The trickster appears in Zakharov's films as a magic agent capable of temporarily restoring listeners' faith in the story he narrates despite its outrageous improbability. Two types of listeners form the audience for the tricksters' stories in Zakharov's films: outright cynics within the text who, despite their disbelief, become mesmerized by the narrator's imaginative power; and the viewers of Zakharov's films, who are the ultimate cynics frustrated by late-socialist reality. They would love to embrace the miracle of the trickster's story and derive their vicarious pleasure by being less cynical than the philistines in the text.

Fantastic and highly stylized settings allowed Zakharov to avoid any major problems with censorship that his topical conflicts might have triggered. Had Zakharov tried to enact the same conflict on contemporary Soviet material and the big screen, he most certainly would have run into problems with Goskino and Gosteleradio censors. The fairy-tale chronotope of the films and their New Year's release ensured the preferred reading of his films as whimsical but safe holiday fare. In *The Twelve Chairs* Zakharov articulated distancing estrangement as his prime mode of narration and as a feature of his films' mise-en-scène and sound design. He used overt theatricality to represent the picture's diegesis, and displaced action into the fictional time and space that is protected from censors by the canonical status of literary originals. For example, in *The Twelve Chairs* the action takes place in 1920s Soviet Russia; in *The Formula of Love*, in eighteenth-century Russia; while in *The Ordinary Miracle* it is a timeless fairy-tale kingdom. *That Very Same Munchausen* and *The House Built by Swift* transport the action to the fictional Western Europe of remote centuries.

In *The Twelve Chairs* Zakharov retains the picaresque plot familiar to a Russian viewer from an earlier film adaptation of the novel, but foregrounds its playful, performative nature through both theatrical and cinematic devices. The film's style is in stark contrast both to Mikhail Shveitser's 1968 adaptation of *The*

Golden Calf and Gaidai's 1971 version of *The Twelve Chairs*. On the one hand, the film uses cinematic means—tracking camera, montage sequences, a mix of diegetic and extra-diegetic sounds, and visual gags. It opens with a direct quote from Gaidai's *Diamond Arm*—a black frame accompanied by an off-screen screaming voice, followed by a close-up of Ostap Bender's eye (see Figure 3.9). The director's playful treatment of what viewers can and cannot see and the self-reflexive treatment of the gaze as a discourse constructing a visual narrative are signature features of Zakharov's films.

On the other hand, the film is shot mostly in the studio, with minimalist sets that provide comic backdrops for the plot, but eschew any claim to realism. The appearance of the same actors (Oleg Iankovskii, Aleksandr Abdulov, Evgenii Leonov, Andrei Mironov) in different narratives attracts the viewer's attention to the celebrity status of these actors, which constantly extrudes through the mask of the character. While his actors assume the personae of his films, they never completely merge with the roles. For example, in *The Twelve Chairs*, Zakharov introduces his characters, played by famous film stars, via the alienating devices of the animation frame and still image. When the Soviet film star Oleg Tabakov

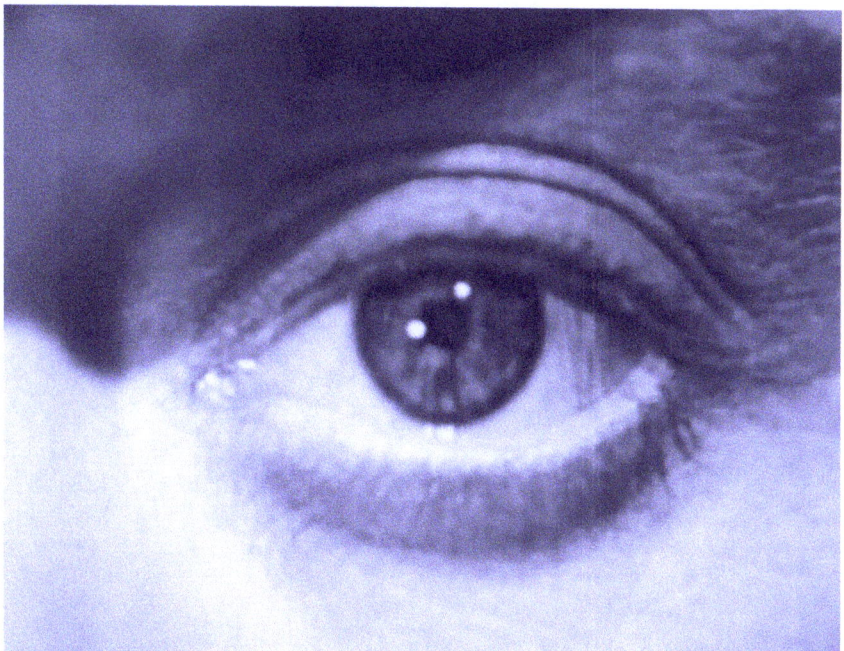

Figure 3.9: Ostap's eye gazing directly at the viewers opens every episode of Zakharov's *Twelve Chairs*

appears on the screen, Zakharov freezes the frame, puts a literal portrait frame around the actor's face, and provides a subtitle on the screen introducing the character. Viewers are invited to suspend their recognition of the screen celebrity for the sake of the character he plays. This onscreen transformation of the film star into a character, however, attracts attention to the artistic convention itself, thus maintaining the distance between the actor's persona and that of the character. To emphasize the conventionality of the medium the acting at times is overly dramatic, especially in the dream sequences that are introduced by the blinking intertitles: "he is imagining this" or "this is his dream" (see Figure 3.10). Moreover, actors frequently converse with the non-diegetic narrator (the voice of Zinovii Gerdt), reacting to his comments, visually illustrating his descriptions, and addressing the viewer/camera directly, in the best traditions of Brechtian aesthetics.

While the sitcom format—episodic structure, recurring characters and conflicts, self-conscious performances—provides the framework and overriding structure for Zakharov's films, his comedy makes use of many other television genres of laughter. Irony and slapstick provide links between the defamiliarizing narratives and settings, on the one hand, and contemporary Soviet conflicts and

Figure 3.10: "And this is his dream as well"

character types, on the other. An ironic mode of narration, which emerged in the late 1960s, becomes the dominant syntactic of the comedy in the 1970s. Zakharov's contrived plots, formulaic settings and characters, and tongue-in-cheek dialogue addressed to the viewer construct diegeses that are not what they seem. Characters of non-Soviet origin and from the most fantastic narratives often deliver one-liners that directly appeal to the viewers' shared knowledge of Soviet and Russian culture. A character looks directly at the viewers and says: "All visitors to Russia perish near Smolensk" (*The Formula of Love*). Indeed, all European invaders, from Napoleon to Hitler, usually stumbled near Smolensk, halfway between Russia's western border and Moscow. In one episode, Ostap Bender declares, "The West is with us" and looks at the TV viewers instead of his fellow characters. He mocks simultaneously the fictional conspirators' hope for mythical Western help and the Soviet idealistic view of the West as a land of plenty behind the Iron Curtain (*The Twelve Chairs*). German city authorities note: "We planned to hold a celebration, followed by arrests, but then we decided to combine the two" (*That Very Same Munchausen*). Soviet viewers immediately recognized a hidden reference to Stalinist campaigns, which in the best medieval traditions combined public festivities with mass arrests, show trials, and at times even public executions. A similar comment by the king appears in *An Ordinary Miracle*: "Executioner, bring the ax and a shot of vodka! Vodka for me, the rest for him." Finally, Swift notes: "We are utterly confused. We say one thing, we think something else entirely, and we write some utter abracadabra" (*The House that Swift Built*)—a clear reference to the Orwellian doublespeak of Soviet society.

Irony fulfilled several functions in Zakharov's repertoire. It operated as a counterpoint to sentimentality and serious pathos. Casting Iankovskii as the Magician, Munchausen, and Swift, Zakharov worked against the grain. The serio-comic effect of his speeches resulted from the gap between the role and the actor's persona: before the trickster-Magician in *An Ordinary Miracle* Iankovskii was cast in the roles of young, straightforward, and earnest characters. Zakharov was not averse to exploiting discourses, but, like his tricksters, he did not allow for a monological reading of the narrative. At the end of *The House that Swift Built*, before the protagonist's death he is asked finally to choose between two loving and sacrificial women. Just as the narrative threatens to slide into a sentimental mode Swift stops the proceedings and notes: "See, love scenes aren't my cup of tea. We rehearsed this scene many times, but it just doesn't work!" Both pathos and Iankovskii's typical screen image are overturned.

The endings of Zakharov's comedies are also profoundly ironic. More often than not they are epilogues following the conclusion of the main plot, with which they have an ambiguous relationship. Typically, they serve as a response, a distancing comment on the themes raised in the film. In *The House that Swift Built*, for example, after several self-staged "deaths," Swift dies on the day that his official biography has recorded for him. This act of "compliance" makes Dr. Simpson rebel and acquire agency. He changes into Gulliver's clothes and boards a ship. As he is struggling against the waves, we hear off-screen directorial remarks: "Go ahead, Aleksandr, do it!" Curiously, this laying bare of the artificiality of the screen world—the director addresses the actor (Aleksandr Abdulov), not the character—in no way destroys the impact of the scene. Rather, the final monologue hints that 1970s Soviet culture is not that far removed from the character's predicament: "Year of death, year of birth ... What is left for a human being to do? Only details ... It's not that little, really."

In short, Zakharov's consistent use of irony and defamiliarization invites viewers not to suspend their disbelief, but, instead, to remain on the border between profane reality and serio-comic fantasy, where contemporary conflicts are acted out in fantastical settings. In *The House that Swift Built*, the giant Glium (Evgenii Leonov) tells his story, which resonates with the fate of individuality in an oppressive society. His height and intellect are so superior to the rest that the mayor orders him to stop growing. The contrast between the short, pudgy, and soft-spoken comic actor and the monologue of a "giant" with a dramatic fate provides comic relief, obfuscating the allegory of stumped creative and personal freedom under socialism (see Figure 3.11). Viewers are thus constantly addressed from inside the diegesis and faced with ambiguous messages that force them to compare the world of the narrative and their own contemporary existence.

The self-reflexive syntax in Zakharov's comedy aligns it with sitcom aesthetics. Jonathan Bignell notes that "television comedy depends more than most kind of television on the self-consciousness of performance, and the willingness of the audience to engage with the excessive speech and behavior of characters that are designed to cue the recognition of the social norm and to surpass it in a manner which becomes funny" (2004, 122). In other words, the sitcom's theatricality works both to lay bare the community's social codes and to carnivalize them in a safe comedic, rather than openly satirical, way. While Zakharov's comedies do not fit neatly into the canonical generic conventions of the sitcom as established by American television, they share with the latter the project of commenting on

Late-Soviet Comedy: Between Rebellion and the Status Quo 139

Figure 3.11: Giant Glium (left), who was ordered by the city mayor to stop growing

social norms via excessively theatrical performance. Arguably the fantasy setting, instead of a contemporary setting, was the feature peculiar to late-Soviet television that existed under the pressure of political censorship.

An Ordinary Miracle offers a good case study of Zakharov's aesthetics and politics. In the film, the Magician (Iankovskii) sets up a fairytale of a bear transformed into a human being who falls in love with a princess (Evgeniia Simonova). To amuse his wife (Irina Kupchenko), the Magician decides that the moment the young man (Aleksandr Abdulov) kisses his beloved he will turn back into a beast. The inevitable meeting of the two young people takes place and they fall in love. Yet, resisting the outcome of the kiss preset by the author, the young man runs away and avoids by all possible means the fatal encounter with love. He even makes a pact with a hunter, who is to kill the young man if he ever meets his princess and turns into a bear. Frustrated with his creation, the Magician loses hope and interest in his protagonist. In fact, he prevents the bear from getting anywhere near the princess, who falls gravely ill. In despair the king (Evgenii Leonov) allows the cynical Minister-Administrator (Andrei Mironov) to take over his affairs and even to propose to the princess. The court drowns in corruption and misery, yet no one dares to confront the king. The film thus displays a full cast of Zakharov's social masks, immediately recognizable to the Soviet TV viewers: the leader in denial, a cynical profiteer, a community of conformists, and a protagonist who has a chance to rebel against the iron logic of the plot.

The character of a trickster plays a central role in *An Ordinary Miracle*. In the film he is both the Magician and the author of the fairy tale unveiled in front of the viewer. As in all Zakharov's fantasy films, the diegesis of *An Ordinary Miracle* is ambiguous and fully at the mercy of his trickster-protagonist. Other characters are the figments of the trickster's imagination, yet he and his wife host the King and his court in their house, and the Minister-Administrator even takes this opportunity to make overtures to the trickster's wife. The Magician-writer seems to be omnipotent and in full control of his story, yet he cannot protect his wife from the verbal assaults and rude sexual advances of the Minister-Administrator. Ultimately, even in the realm of magic, the Magician's power turns out to be limited compared to the power of love. After the bear and the princess suffer enough for their love, they get a chance to kiss for the ultimate test of their feelings and the bear, to everyone's surprise, remains a human being. In other words, the bear adds human emotions to his human appearance only when he learns what true love is about. The Magician-trickster cannot overpower the feelings of his characters but manages to trick his cynical viewers. Instead of concluding with a "logical" anti-climactic denouement the romance narrative ends in the reunification of the couple. The poetic trickster triumphs over late-Soviet cynics in front of their small screens and over cynical characters within the narrative who assure each other that no love can outsmart the iron logic of the author's narrative.

In contrast to Riazanov's films, in which slapstick looks artificial and often unnecessary, Zakharov's slapstick is central to the ideology of his films: retaining the possibility of faith in the sublime in a world devoid of ideals. Slapstick breaks the everyday routine and transgresses social conventions; its clowns often appear in transitional spaces—doorways, windows, picture frames—trying to break through them, just as they break through the fourth wall, addressing the television viewers directly. In *An Ordinary Miracle* the king is one such slapstick clown (see Figure 3.12).

During his first encounter with the Magician and his wife, the king is just a tyrant who explains all his crimes using positivist arguments about the bad environment. When he enters the Magician's house he offers him and his wife poisoned wine, and when the Magician catches him in the act, he claims that he

Figure 3.12: Evgenii Leonov as the king in *An Ordinary Miracle*

poisons so many people not because he is a base person but because it is a feature of his personality inherited from his uncle. The uncle used to like to talk to people when he traveled, but always poisoned his interlocutors at the end of the conversation to keep state secrets safe. The absurd justification of a crime sounds especially ludicrous to the viewer because it is a parody of the textbook Soviet vision of individual identities being mere functions of greater social and biological forces.

In addition to being a ridiculous villain narrating positivist truisms underlying Soviet ideology, the king functions as a slapstick clown who helps to establish the divide between the characters who believe in the miracle of love and those who remain in the purely material world where it is impossible. When the princess falls in love and follows her feelings rather than her father's will, the king realizes that his omnipotence is an illusion. A key scene takes place when the princess promises to shoot anyone who tries to talk to her. The two-tiered mise-en-scène, with the princess in love upstairs and the king's court (mere puppets without personal will or agency) downstairs, marks the divide between those who believe and those who, together with the viewers, are skeptical (see Figure 3.13).

Figure 3.13: The king's court, puzzled by characters who can have both agency and emotions

The king functions as a Bakhtinian clown, who points to the possibility of something other than the familiar profane world. By his very inability to control his daughter and her beloved, as well as his own emotions, he confirms the existence of the sublime world of love beyond his power. His inept attempts to assuage his distress via mass executions and random shooting are presented in a slapstick manner that only confirms the sovereign's impotence. This macabre carnival reveals the very desires and emotions that the king denies himself and others: subjectivity, irrational feelings driving human actions, and freedom of choice.

The narrative never allows the king to sustain epic distance. First, the character includes two mutually contradictory identities—remote royalty and the impulsive, concerned father of a teenage daughter. The pathetic father persona eventually overshadows the tyrannical royal one. Paternal anxieties bring the king into the zone of close contact with the extra-diegetic and contemporary world of the viewer, contributing to the slapstick image of the king/clown and simultaneously motivating the liminality of his discourse. The king constantly switches from his fairytale royal discourse to contemporary colloquial language. For example, he delivers a long monologue about his royal dynasty and how it affected his temper, making an argument about the "class origins" of his terrible behavior. He then switches to a colloquial recasting of a Dostoyevskian counter-argument about the personal responsibility of every human being for his actions, no matter how the social or biological environment conditions him. In Mikhail Zoshchenko's *skaz* manner, right after trying to poison his hosts with "a 300-year-old royal wine," the opinionated king anticipates the interlocutor's objections about his personal choice: "Now you will tell me: 'You should take responsibility and not pin the blame on your comrades, neighbors, or wife.'" The words "comrades" and "neighbors" immediately destroy the epic distance between the action of the fairytale and the viewer, degrading the king to a contemporary bully and, by his own admission, "a pig."

Zakharov also carnivalizes the king via a comic costume that makes his identity unstable. He appears on the doorstep of the writer's house wearing the royal crown, which he immediately takes off and hangs on a nail in the wall as though it were a simple hat. Moreover, when he travels through the mountains, he wears a three-cornered Napoleonic hat (see Figure 3.14). Yet, when he takes it off, underneath he is wearing a Russian babushka kerchief that immediately questions his masculinity (see Figure 3.15). Moreover, the king's royal garb is of an unseemly greenish color that makes him look half-human, half-amphibian.

Figure 3.14: The king's three-cornered Napoleonic hat covers ...

Figure 3.15: ...a Russian babushka kerchief

Songs that function as independent musical numbers frequently suspend and defamiliarize the fairytale narrative.[20] These proto-musical videos comment on the film's narrative, but are not unambiguously continuous with the expectations it sets up. At the lowest point in the narrative, with the bear proven to be a coward and the Magician-Writer refusing to take any more interest in his fate, a clip of a song about the miracle of love interrupts the action. The clip does not have anything to do with the film's story, which is about two equally bad choices, and presents the most irrational third option—that of a miracle. It is up to the viewer to make the connection between the commonsensical narrative and the clip's narrative about faith in the miracle.

The "miracle" does indeed happen at the end. Despite the Writer's ban the bear gets into the house, kisses his princess, and to the joy of some and disappointment of others, remains human. Love triumphs over fear and conformity. Yet, the final song, following the "miracle," is in dissonance with the happy ending and keeps the film open-ended:

Let's part low-key,
Let's part quietly.

[20] Zakharov was a writer for the *Pub 13 Chairs*, the structure of which anticipates his television films: independent skits alternating with musical numbers in which the pub's customers lip-synched to pre-recorded songs by foreign performers.

Let's part with a good feeling.
A week or two,
And we will calm down.
What happened has passed, has gone away.
...
Let's focus on cooking,
Let's focus on tailoring,
Let's focus on the everyday grind.
It's easier this way, isn't it?
It's simpler, isn't it?
It hurts less, doesn't it?

The song, performed in a minor key, seems to suggest that *nothing* has changed (at least not for the viewers, whom the song addresses); the characters slowly pass in front of the camera and depart, and the Magician-Writer burns the set.

The unusual mix of characters, whose behavior evokes parallels with the then-current Soviet life; the fairytale setting, and the Brechtian devices did not escape the attention of Soviet censors, who felt that the contemporary motifs and dialogue threatened the safe distance of the fantasy narrative. In particular, they noted that the actors playing the Magician and the bear did not "get into their characters" sufficiently (33), while the character of the king provoked objections to his intentional crudeness ("Obyknovennoe chudo," 42). Some critics insisted on "simplifying" the Magician's creative line and making clear the fairy-tale nature of the plot. They suggested that the "miracle" be made more expressive and emotional, and the ending of the film, when the Magician burns the set, foregrounding its constructed nature, be changed: "The viewer has just watched a fairy tale, and suddenly the director [the Magician] burns everything, as if cheating the viewer. But the viewer wants to live, to stay with this fairy tale. It is unfair to treat the viewer like this" (52). All these comments are indeed very insightful: *An Ordinary Miracle,* in fact, does want to keep the viewer on the sidelines of the diegesis, uncomfortable with the ending and wondering about the possibility of "miracles."

The censors were also right in pointing out that, instead of celebrating the status quo, these films disturbed the viewer by laying bare the constructed nature of the mise-en-scène and the narrative. Arguably, however, Zakharov's transgressive television fantasy romances offered just a temporary suspension of the status quo for the New Year holiday-week television program. Only during this week of celebration was the Soviet viewer allowed to distance himself a little from his social obligations and even ironize at times about the decline and fall of late-Soviet society.

Whereas Zakharov's films carried a flavor of irony, Riazanov's avoided social commentary and focused primarily on celebrating the possibility of romance as the ultimate proof of society's harmonious status quo. A fantasy about a strong female lead's ability to reignite desire in a male who is devoid of any individual agency or desire constituted the core of late-socialist comedy's syntax.[21] Male desire could be reignited only on New Year's Eve and only with the aid of copious alcohol. The new "romcom" syntax was only about the individual's agency and desire; the happy couple exchanged the cause of building the universal "bright future" for private happiness in the present.

Postscript: the living and the (un)dead

The syntax of late-Soviet comedy—romance between a strong female lead and a weaker male partner, celebration of private life and consumerism—bridges the genres of socialist comedy and the genres of laughter of post-Soviet television and cinema. Two new formats represent the most important tendencies in post-Soviet comedy: (1) situation comedy and (2) remakes and sequels of films from the late-Soviet era. The sitcom provides a major venue for the viewers to reflect on social changes, such as, for example, class and gender inequality. During the economic crisis of the 1990s, when many men lost their jobs, women had to take over as primary breadwinners. Often this meant inventing new ways of earning money, above all managing a private business. By the time Vladimir Putin came to power, these new realities of Russian life, women's independence and agency, found expression in global media formats, such as the television sitcom with a strong female trickster-lead. As Russian cultural critic Vera Zvereva points out, the genre of the sitcom established itself as a global format where new values were negotiated, culminating in the most popular sitcom in Russian television

---

[21] In this respect, *A Forgotten Melody for Flute* (*Zabytaia melodiia dlia fleity* 1987) constitutes a radical break with Stagnation syntax and semantics. Class differences are at the center of the narrative and become the structuring device for the construction of the characters and the mise-en-scène: the apartment of a Party functionary vs the *chernukha*-style communal apartment of the nurse. Moreover, this is the first film by Riazanov where the male hero (Leonid Filatov) truly has to make a choice between love and the security of his comfortable lifestyle. Filimonov's heart attack at the end of the film is an apt metaphor for this internalization of conflict.

history, *My Fair Nanny* (*Moia prekrasnaia niania* 2004–2009), a Russian version of the CBS sitcom *The Nanny* (Zvereva 2007). While this sitcom with a strong female comedienne-lead was an import from US television,[22] its successful adoption became possible because Russian viewers were already familiar with the elements of screwball comedy from Riazanov's comedies and the estrangement effect produced by the flat, sitcom-like characters from Zakharov's television fairy tales. The sitcoms on Russian television continue to integrate the country into global media culture.

The second tendency, the appearance on Russian television and the cinematic release of the remakes and sequels to Soviet comedies, is symptomatic of a cultural backlash against the social and economic changes that Russia underwent in the 1990s. Many of them, such as *The Irony of Fate. A Sequel* (*Ironiia sud'by. Prodolzhenie* 2007), were funded and produced by Russia's Channel One and other state-controlled television channels. The same channels distributed these films in the states of the former Soviet Union. They became part of the Putin-era neo-imperialist project of reintegrating these nations into the Eurasian Union with Russia as its economic and cultural center. Next to adaptations of classical novels that celebrate Russia's great past and its cultural canon, these comedic sequels celebrate the common Soviet past, which is represented, in the case of Bekmambetov's sequel, as a utopian romance with a continuation in the present. As opposed to sitcoms examining Russia's present social issues, these films romanticize the Soviet past and encourage viewers to become nostalgic about the lost family of fraternal nations. While the majority of these releases were box office failures, some of them, such as *The Irony of Fate. A Sequel*, have been quite successful in their celebration of Soviet nostalgia. The film earned $55 million in ticket sales in Russia and the former Soviet states. Which trend in post-Soviet comedy will prevail—escapist nostalgia for the Soviet past or examination of current social issues—remains to be seen.

---

[22] Fran Drescher is both the star and an executive producer of the *Nanny*.

4

Reinventing Desire: Late-Socialist Melodrama

Syntax and semantics of the genre

This chapter discusses the evolution of melodrama from the late 1960s to the early 1980s. The status of this genre in late-Soviet cinema was paradoxical. As Louise McReynolds and Joan Neuberger note, the very existence of melodrama under socialism was denied by "[t]he marginalization of commercial culture [...], the idealization of abstract thought over materialism and consumption, and the widespread suspicion of bourgeois, western individualism" (2002, 4). Though melodrama had lost its earlier ideological label of "bourgeois escapism," neither filmmakers nor critics used the term to reference individual films or to discuss genre conventions.[1] There were no public debates on the "correct way" to make Soviet melodrama, in stark contrast to the lengthy discussions about Soviet comedy or the Soviet adventure film. Yet, of all genres, melodrama most explicitly negotiated the collective/public and individual/private identities in late-Soviet culture, and many individual films provoked heated polemics in the press—usually under the vague names of "contemporary dramas" or "films about our contemporaries."

In socialist realist narratives melodramatic conflicts fulfilled the function of semantic elements, while the films' syntax relied on the extra-textual, ideological discourses that predetermined the meanings. In fact, socialist realist syntax—the primacy of collective interests as well as service to the state and the protagonist's trip to consciousness—constructed the melodramatic conflict and individual identity as something to *overcome*.[2] Because of this, the

---

[1] There were exceptions to this rule, e.g., critic T. Khlopliankina's insightful comments about the distinction between films using melodramatic devices and film-melodramas, which show "love for and interest in their characters" (1973, 8). But the calls not to be shy in using the term usually did not apply to the most significant films of the era, and when they did, as was the case with *Moscow Does Not Believe in Tears* (*Moskva slezam ne verit* 1980) it was to deplore the filmmakers' and the audiences' "poor taste."
[2] Ivan Pyr'ev's *The Party Card* (*Partiinyi bilet* 1936) exemplifies this relationship between the socialist realist syntax and melodramatic semantics. For a detailed discussion see Kaganovsky (2008, 44–48).

stories of individuals and nuclear families offered semantic variations on the same syntactic structure. Whether the melodramatic protagonist was a daredevil pilot (*Valerii Chkalov* 1941), an exploited American single mother victimized by racist society (*Circus/Tsirk* 1936) or an uneducated Russian village woman abused by her husband (*Member of the Government/Chlen pravitel'stva* 1939), their destiny was the same: to become New Soviet men and women; that is, to give up their individual agency and assume the collective identity of the Big Family.

In the films of the 1940s and 1950s, the Great Patriotic War provides an important semantic variation for the socialist realist syntax. War separates families and lovers, creating situations of extreme sacrifice and villainy. The most famous melodrama of the early post-Stalin period, *Cranes Are Flying* (*Letiat zhuravli*, dir. Mikhail Kalatozov, 1957), uses the war setting to assert the existence of individual trauma and the legitimacy of private stories to be told alongside the big story of the country's triumphs. The new type of protagonist (a weak and fallen woman) and neorealist cinematic devices[3] opened up the genre to ambiguities and encouraged its reading in moral and emotional, rather than ideological terms.[4]

In contrast to challenging the syntax of socialist realism via new semantic elements, late-socialist melodramas offer a radical reevaluation of the genre. Not only are private identity and the nuclear family at the center of these films, but more often than not they are incompatible with collectivist goals or state service—the very core of socialist realism. New phenomena—the rise of the urban professional middle class, the role of consumerism in a nuclear family, redefined gender roles in the family and in society—eventually form the structure-bearing conventions that constitute melodramatic syntax, gradually watering down socialist realism and challenging its meanings. Films and TV series discussed in this chapter deal with issues unthinkable just a decade earlier but central to the late-Soviet "melodramatic imagination": conflict between

---

[3] See Aleksandr Prokhorov's analysis of the film in "Soviet Family Melodrama of the 1940s and 1950s: From *Wait for Me* to *The Cranes Are Flying*," in *Imitations of Life: Two Centuries of Melodrama in Russia*, eds. Louise McReynolds and Joan Neuberger, Durham, NC: Duke Uuniversity Press, 202, 208–231.

[4] For a discussion of critics' and audiences' reception of Kalatozov's *Cranes* see Maiia Turovskaia "'Da' i 'net.'" *Iskusstvo kino* 12(1957): 14–18; Rostislav Iurenev, "Vernost'." *Iskusstvo kino* 12 (1957): 5–14; Iurii Bogomolov. *Mikhail Kalatozov: stranitsy tvorcheskoi biografii*. Moscow: Iskusstvo, 1989; Josephine Woll. *The Cranes are Flying*. London: Tauris, 2003; Nancy Condee. "Veronika fuses out: Rape and media specificity in *The Cranes are Flying*." *Studies in Russian and Soviet Cinema* 3.2(2009): 173–183.

public and private desires and identities; masculinity defined by a lack of agency in the present; a female protagonist who challenges the Soviet patriarchal order; and Russian identity prevailing over Soviet identity.

Historically, critics have linked the emergence of melodrama with the rise of the bourgeoisie as a class distinct from the feudal lords and their serfs (Brooks 1985, xii). Even though this chapter examines melodrama in the context of late-Soviet culture, this argument is an appropriate point of departure. The vast majority of 1970s melodramas are set in what arguably can be called a Soviet middle-class milieu, the concerns of which revolve primarily around consumerist demands and the anxieties of the nuclear family. The family becomes the site of crisis and the agent of negotiation between the individual and the state. While the patriarch often tries to preserve the status quo, female members of the family exercise their desires (emotional, consumerist, and even sexual) and thereby acquire agency, which is necessary to provide for the family and for the self by any means possible but which, in the process, undermines both the patriarchy and the status quo.

In addressing the crisis of Soviet patriarchy, many late-Soviet melodramas substituted Russian for Soviet identity or at least blurred the border between the two. Television mini-series portray a history that did not start with the Bolshevik Revolution; rather, the characters are products of both Russian-imperial and Soviet experiences. The historical proto-soaps, such as Vladimir Krasnopol'skii and Valerii Uskov's *Shadows Disappear at Noon* (*Teni ischezaiut v polden'* 1971) and *Eternal Call* (*Vechnyi zov*, 1973–1983), set their narratives in remote locations in Russia, far from the capitals, where the Revolution happened, and infused class struggle with melodramatic motivations. Other films, such as *Officers* (*Ofitsery*, dir. Vladimir Rogovoi, 1971) established a tradition of patriotism and military valor that could be traced from imperial Russian heroic males to Soviet stalwarts, thus enriching masculinity without compromising the "core" Soviet model. The other end of this continuum was Vasilii Shukshin's *Snowball Berry Red* (*Kalina krasnaia* 1973), which was perhaps the most remarkable late-socialist exploration of Russian masculinity. More precisely, by making his protagonist, Egor Prokudin (Vasilii Shukshin), a recent convict who tries to build a life outside prison, Shukshin wanted to look *beyond* the Soviet present, implicitly asking the question: what will happen to the Russian man when Soviet identity disappears? In the film, jail represents both Soviet space and Egor's gang, which attempts to pull him back in; it is a perfect metaphor for Soviet collectivist (and brutal) masculinity.

Meanwhile, many cinematic melodramas defined masculinity by a lack of agency in contemporary society. At the center of these films is the male protagonist whose agency and desires are either out of sync with changing societal expectations, or are absent altogether. The first type appears in such films as *The Lovers' Romance* (*Romans o vliublennykh*) and *Belorussia Station* (*Belorusskii vokzal*, dir. Andrei Smirnov, 1970), which pit ideal Soviet masculinity, inevitably linked to the war trope, against the unheroic present. Their melodramatic pathos emerges out of the clash between the modern, urban, and realistically represented society and the romanticized values and models of male behavior. These films evoke the myth of military service as not only a male duty, but also an identity-shaping experience, a rite of passage into Soviet patriarchy. The warrior experience is singled out as the most valuable aspect of male characters' identity, which, however, has now been relegated to the past and is completely disconnected from their present life. Consequently, the identity of the male protagonist is defined by a painful split between his profane peacetime existence and his memories of epic feats in a military setting. In other words, male melodrama of the 1970s changes the temporality in which the heroic male exists. While the heroic male of Thaw melodrama coped with the losses of the past by reconstituting the nuclear family in order to build the radiant future, the heroic male of the Stagnation era lives with the knowledge of an irreparable break in temporal continuity. The protagonist is forever suspended in a Catch-22: the awareness of a certain deficiency but the impossibility of engaging in a moral quest beyond the confines of socialist realism.

The other typical protagonist of late-socialist melodrama is the man on the run: the unwilling patriarch who finds his responsibilities as a member of society, a citizen of the state, or head of the family simply burdensome. Georgii Daneliia articulated this type of late-socialist masculinity most clearly in his serio-comic films *Afonia* (1976) and *Autumn Marathon* (*Osennii Marafon*, 1979). At the Lenfilm Studio, Vitalii Melnikov depicts this type of dysfunctional masculinity in *Seven Brides of Lance-Corporal Zbruev* (*Sem' nevest efreitora Zbrueva*, 1972), and the made-for-TV films *Elder Son* (*Starshii syn*, 1975) and *Vacation in September* (*Otpusk v sentiabre*, 1979). Daneliia and his scriptwriter, Aleksandr Volodin, called their films "sad comedies": although viewers are aware of the protagonist's flaws they still sympathize with, and even enjoy, his pathetic attempts to fabricate lies. Yet the films trick the viewer via a shift in tone and genre, from a comic beginning to the melodramatic main mode. The man's indecisiveness, apathy, and lies hurt people around him, above all the women in his life; the protagonist gradually spirals into a despair produced by his own emotional impotence.

The nuclear family is the focal point of the films discussed in this chapter. Whereas in the films of the 1930s–1950s, the nuclear family was secondary to the Soviet collective and depicted as benefitting from the generous Soviet state, melodramas of the 1970s problematized both of these assumptions. Films centering on the lives and agency of female protagonists surpassed other subgenres in dismantling the myth of the organic unity between public and collective demands, on the one hand, and individual and family identities and needs, on the other. Even in historical television mini-series—the most ideologically orthodox of the melodrama subgenres examined here—the characters' public lives and official Soviet history constituted a convenient and safe context for the supreme viewer attraction: stories of love, jealousy, betrayal and dark secrets: in short, the material for soap opera narratives.

On the surface, of course, late-Soviet melodrama paid lip-service to the achievements of the socialist state and did not openly challenge its institutions. Many films of the period are set in modest but comfortable households and families want for nothing—at least materially. But this is precisely where late-Soviet melodrama broke the mold of socialist realism, by evoking the spiritual realm beyond the world of Soviet ideology and the everyday—what Peter Brooks calls "the moral occult".[5] The discourse of the moral occult ascribes spiritual power to the vistas of the Russian landscape and to elements of Russian Orthodoxy. A pantheistic view/perception of the Russian countryside features in late-socialist melodramas as a source of agency and hope and as a site of spiritual values beyond the Soviet social world. In such films as *Little Crane* (*Zhuravushka*, dir. Nikolai Moskalenko, 1968) and *Stepmother* (*Machekha*, dir. Oleg Bondarev, 1973), images of fields, rivers, and the sky form persistent motifs linked to the fate of the female protagonists. In *Little Crane*, for example, the shots of cranes in the sky are a visual metaphor for Marfa's longing for her husband missing in the Great Patriotic War, but also acquire a metaphysical dimension: every night, her son asks his mother to read to him his father's last letter from the front, in which he calls Marfa "*Zhuravushka*" (My Little Crane). This ritual is a secular prayer that keeps the father alive in their memories. These moments

---

[5] Brooks defines the "moral occult" as "the domain of operative spiritual values which is both indicated within and masked by the surface of reality" in *The Melodramatic Imagination: Balzac, Henry James, Melodrama, and the Mode of Excess* (New Haven: YaleUniversity Press, 1976) at p. 5.

exist in stark contrast to the collective farm, which is far from nurturing. The villagers—mostly comprising sexually frustrated widows—engage in gossip campaigns against Marfa (Liudmila Chursina), while the chairman sexually harasses her.

Images of churches and icons offer an even more radical departure from the socialist realist canon. Making films about the pre-revolutionary past allowed filmmakers more freedom to represent Orthodox religion as an alternative source of identity. A good example is Vladimir Motyl's 1975 *The Star of Captivating Happiness* (*Zvezda plenitel'nogo schast'ia*), a story of the defeat of the 1825 Decembrists' revolt against Russian imperial autocracy. The film uses the uprising—an iconic event in Soviet ideological narrative—to create a melodrama of strong and noble Russian men (in the film's past) and strong and self-sacrificial Russian women (in the film's present).[6] The latter choose to follow their husbands into exile despite the challenges of the abusive power representatives and their own families. Princess Volkonskaia (Natal'ia Bondarchuk) comes to her decision during prayer. From her tear-stained face (see Figure 4.1) the camera cuts to the icon of the Mother of God (see Figure 4.2). The cut is so abrupt that it disrupts the continuity of the narrative, establishing a spiritual connection between two women and suggesting a melodramatic invocation of "the moral occult" as the only motivation for their actions.

Melodramas set in the present adhere to the late-Soviet visual code, by invariably depicting churches from a point of view where their crosses are invisible. In *Stepmother*, temples are signs of a spiritual, but not necessarily religious worldview; nevertheless, they are prominent in the background shots of the two female protagonists: Shura[7] and her stepdaughter, Sveta (Elena Kostereva) (see Figure 4.3). Unlike her husband, a hero of socialist labor who knows everything about tractors but is emotionally impotent, Shura derives her agency from the family, both her own and the one she has adopted. Children's

---

[6] For Motyl, however, historical accuracy and class issues were secondary to the melodramatic narrative. In his comments, the director made a ritual nod to Lenin's dictum about the progressive meaning of the Decembrists' uprising which "woke up" Russia, but claimed that he was more interested in the dual "paradox" of sacrifice: men sacrificed everything for an idea, while women sacrificed themselves for the husbands whose ideals they did not necessarily share. "And what is most important: if the husbands lost their battle, the wives won theirs" ("Zvezda plenitel'nogo schast'ia," 12).

[7] Shura is played by Tat'iana Doronina, whose melodramatic starring roles also include Niura in *Three Poplar Trees on Pliushchikha Street* (*Tri topolia na Pliushchikhe* 1967) and Natasha in *Once More about Love* (*Eshche raz pro liubov'*, 1968). Nicknamed "the Russian Marilyn Monroe," Doronina brought emotional intensity and validation of private desires to the Soviet screen.

Reinventing Desire: Late-Socialist Melodrama 155

Figure 4.1: Princess Volkonskaia's tear-stained face

Figure 4.2: Panagia Eleousa

Figure 4.3: Shura and her stepdaughter, with a church in the background

bodies, often naked and frail, are constantly on display in the film and are incompatible with the epic dimensions of combines, depicted via propaganda clichés equating harvesting to a military campaign.

The progress-oriented, collectivist public space is portrayed as indifferent at best, but more often hostile to the emotional and ethical needs of the family and the individual. Melodrama thus comes the closest of all genres to questioning the cost of the Soviet political utopia and the toll it exacted from the people. Various modes of articulating this skepticism ranged from the ecological disaster that destroys the living and the dead (the village cemetery) in Andrei Konchalovsky's *Siberiade* (1978), to women's struggle for personal and family happiness amidst the abusive and hypocritical forces of the "collective" and the patriarchy, to the complete erasure of Russian identity in Vasilii Shukshin's *Snowball Berry Red* (1974). Shukshin's film, in fact, captures the crisis of Soviet masculinity as a way to examine the nation's collective guilt. The ruins of the churches that Egor (Vasilii Shukshin) passes on his way from jail; his mother, ruined by her son's negligence and her unbearable life in the *kolkhoz*; and Egor's failed attempt to become a peasant suggest that the damage is irreparable and nothing can be rectified in the present.[8]

---

[8] By making his protagonist a criminal, Shukshin suggested an association with the well-trodden path of the socialist realist reeducation story familiar to viewers (and more importantly, to censors and critics) since Nikolai Ekk's *Road to Life* (*Putevka v zhizn'*, 1931). This plot device, along with the stylized visual mode (the film's mise-en-scène uses a lot of bright primary colors), protected the picture from the censors and defined the discourse about the film in the press. But the film's popularity (60 million tickets sold in the year of release) suggests that viewers, whether they could verbalize it or not, appreciated and identified with precisely the melodramatic excess of the story of Russian masculinity. As one letter from a family put it, the film is "something beyond logic [*chto-to nepostizhimoe*], like a melody, like music" (Pis'ma. *Sovetskii ekran* 13 (1974): 1).

In short, late-Soviet melodrama redefines the future-looking temporality typical of socialist realist narratives.[9] Instead, it captures, celebrates, and mourns the "radiant past," conveying a sense of loss and an unbridgeable gap between utopia and empirical reality. Melodramatic imagination functions as a double-edged device. By using Soviet historical landmarks, visual tropes, and an iconic soundtrack,[10] melodramas confirm their allegiance to the socialist myth and validate Soviet identity. But just as surely they document the death of utopia, which leaves devastation in its stead.

Melodrama is arguably the most important and the most diverse of all late-Soviet genres, as confirmed both by the kinds of issues it tackles and by viewer responses.[11] Each of the three types of melodramas discussed in the following sections responded differently to the cultural shifts. For close analysis we chose texts that are representative of the trend but have been overlooked by scholars. Television mini-series, such as *Shadows Disappear at Noon*, substitute Russian masculinity for its Soviet version, while outwardly conforming to the socialist realist syntax. Cinematic male melodramas, e.g., *A Lovers' Romance*, articulate the crisis of the Soviet patriarchal order and, metaphorically, signal the death of communist utopia. Woman's film, in particular Gleb Panfilov's *I Want the Floor* (*Proshu slova* 1975), engages individual agency and, by focusing on the nuclear family and private identity, outstrips the other subcategories in creating a new syntax of Russian cinematic melodrama.

---

[9] The making of Konchalovskii's *Siberiade* is a perfect example of a socialist realist project metamorphosed into melodrama. The filmmaker and his first scriptwriter, Leonid Agranovich, were commissioned to make a film that was supposed to span the years from 1966 to the almost communist future of the 1990s and to depict the lives of Aleksei Ustiuzhanin, who discovered Siberian oil, and his son, a geo-physicist storming the oil fields of the Arctic Ocean. This socialist-realist production, with the working title *The Continent of Giants*, dedicated to the XXVth Communist Party Congress, transformed, with the help of a new scriptwriter, Valentin Ezhov, into a melodramatic narrative exploring a history of several generations of Siberian dreamers. See Agranovich and Mikhalkov-Konchalovskii, 2–6.

[10] For example, in *Officers*, the soundtrack supports the eclectic visual structure of the picture, punctuated by both diegetic and extradiegetic Soviet hit songs, belonging to various historical periods but united by their nostalgic aura: the revolutionary song "Nash parovoz" (Our Steam Engine), the Civil War song "Ukhodili komsomol'tsy" (Komsomol Members Were Off to the Civil War), and the Great Patriotic War song "Prifrontovoi val's" (Wartime Waltz).

[11] The audience for melodramas was consistently high through the early 1980s: *Moscow Does Not Believe in Tears (Moskva slezam ne verit)* sold 84.4 million tickets, *The Crew (Ekipazh)* 71.1 million, *Gypsies Are Found Near Heaven (Tabor ukhodit v nebo)* 64.9 million, *Snowball Berry Red (Kalina krasnaia)* 62.5 million, *Afonia* 62.2 million, *Stepmother (Machekha)* 59.4 million, etc. See http://kinanet.livejournal.com/689229.html.

Television melodrama

Proto-soap operas in late-Soviet television adhered to the socialist realist syntax (a gesture that in the 1970s was nothing short of anachronistic) but replaced the Soviet masculinity with a Russian ideal of manhood. These mini-series thus combined an ideologically orthodox narrative frame with the novel format of a multi-episodic television production and a melodramatic syntax focused on nuclear families and small communities. The focus on these communities, in turn, was a compromise between a socialist realist story of class struggle and the formation of a utopian collective (*kolkhoz*) on the one hand, and a melodramatic narrative about extended families, where people are connected by blood ties and personal relationships, on the other.

In the late-Soviet context, the story of an extended family[12] represented a compromise between the ideology of collectivity and the value of private life. In their television adaptations of Anatolii Ivanov's novels—*Shadows Disappear at Noon* (1971, seven episodes) and *The Eternal Call* (1973–1983, 19 episodes)— Vladimir Krasnopol'skii and Valerii Uskov managed to create Soviet sagas showcasing the troubled experiences of extended families against the backdrop of twentieth-century Russian history.[13] Other market-savvy filmmakers followed the success of Krasnopol'skii and Uskov. For example, Vladimir Vengerov released an eight-episode saga, *The Strogovs* (*Strogovy,* 1976), Igor' Shatrov produced a seven-episode mini-series of provincial passion and murder, *All This Is About Him* (*I eto vse o nem* 1977), and the same year Vasilii Ordynskii released a 13-episode television version of Aleksei Tolstoi's trilogy, *The Road to Calvary* (*Khozhdenie po mukam* 1977) about the fates of the Russian *intelligentsia* during the First World War, the revolution, and the Civil War. Konchalovskii's four-part, 275-minute *Siberiade* also belongs to this type of narrative, despite its release on the big screen.

---

[12] The model for Soviet TV proto-soaps arrived from the UK: in the early 1970s, Soviet television broadcast the 26-episode *The Forsyte Saga* (1967). It was the first BBC television series sold to the Soviet Union. While this model resembled the soap opera, with its "infinitely expandable middle," three features made it acceptable for Soviet television. First, it was a literary adaptation and thus enjoyed a higher cultural status that the average soap opera. Second, it traced a family history over a long period of time and thus could be grafted onto an epic history of the country. Third, albeit long, the narrative ended with an episode that provided a palpable sense of closure, and therefore, accommodated the requisite Soviet teleology.

[13] *The Shadows* was also one of the first Soviet television series released with closed captions for the hard of hearing. The version with closed captions was shorter and consisted of only four episodes.

Television melodrama of the 1970s developed its own chronotope. Soaps of the period are set far away from political centers, in the villages and small towns of Siberia and the Urals. This setting simultaneously invoked the epic and the heroic socialist realist story (Siberia as a land of Soviet industrial projects), and suggested a connection with nature and tradition that had not been challenged by the forces of modernization. Most importantly, narratives about small peasant communities lost in the wilderness provided a source of Russian character types and values associated with the Russian expanses but which were absent in contemporary urbanized life: decisiveness, responsibility, and desire—in short, male agency as traditional patriarchal culture envisions it.

The narrative time of the melodramatic mini-series was more complex. Television melodrama paid homage to Soviet ideology and the socialist realist tradition, while also appealing to a mass audience.[14] It deployed the temporal backdrop of official Soviet history, with its landmark events, such as the October Revolution, the Civil War, and the Great Patriotic War, but equated this narrative, familiar to every Soviet middle school student, with the natural order of things. In both of their series, Krasnopo'lskii and Uskov used the textbook version of Soviet history as a convenient way to provide a seeming teleology to the narrative that, by itself, had a purely melodramatic meaning and could be set anywhere, from Santa Barbara to Mexico City, from the seventeenth-century slave farm in Brazil to the twentieth-century US suburbs.[15] The narrative of *Shadows*, for instance, traces the life of several generations of Russians in the village Green Valley from the turn of the twentieth century to the 1960s. The series conforms to the official story of the revolution and the building of the happy life in collective farms; at the same time, the characters' present is portrayed as painful retribution for the way they have lived their lives, just as the *telenovela* thrives on dark secrets and repressed memories.[16]

In fact, the Soviet canonical narrative itself rests on melodramatic foundations. For example, in *Shadows*, the revolution chronologically follows two scenes in which female agency is exercised. In the opening scene, the viewer witnesses the

---

[14] This dual task was emphasized in the review of *Shadows* by the Artistic Committee of the Mosfilm studio: "Social conflicts are intertwined with personal and family conflicts, conflicts among relatives. They are resolved dramatically, in striking clashes. [...] Despite its dramatic nature, strong passions and striking conflicts, the picture conveys a profoundly optimistic worldview" ("Teni ischezaiut v polden'," RGALI, fond 2944, op. 4, ed.kh. 2583, 18).
[15] In this sense, 1970s television melodramas paved the way for the enthusiastic reception first, of Latin American *telenovelas*, and then of North American soap operas.
[16] See, for example, Jesús Martín-Barbero 1995, 276.

Men'shikovs, a rich peasant family, in the midst of a drunken orgy. They instigate their buddy, Anisim (Lev Poliakov), to demonstrate his power over Maria (Nina Ruslanova), his mistress and the mother of his child. He tells her that he will marry her and give her a mill if she goes to the forest and kills a bear. A few days later, Maria returns to the village barely alive but proud, throws the bear skin at his feet, and silently walks away and out of his life. From this moment on, she is the one in control of her own fate, while Anisim's life is forever haunted by his guilt. Later in the film, the same Maria brings the revolution to the village and becomes the first chair of the Red Commune in Green Valley (see Figure 4.4).

Males come off no better in the following sequence, set in a neighboring town, where a rich merchant, in a fit of drunkenness, passes his entire gold mining enterprise to his daughter, Serafima (Aleksandra Zav'ialova). She becomes the richest person in the region. Moreover, the father puts her armchair on the table as a throne and orders every male in the room to kiss her boots. Uncomfortable at first, Serafima eventually starts to enjoy humiliating the men. Known from Soviet history books as an outcome of Marxist determinism, "the revolutionary situation" in *Shadows* emerges as a consequence of the degradation of the patriarchy and the rise of women to positions of power.

Figure 4.4: Revolution and love in *Shadows Disappear at Noon*

Maria eventually dies at the hands of the Men'shikov brothers. While her death is portrayed as an act of class-war brutality, it also appears to be a logical development in replacing the romantic stage of the revolution with the status quo stage, during which a patriarch takes over the community and restores the traditional gender hierarchy. The patriarch, Zakhar Bol'shakov (Petr Vel'iaminov), whose appropriate last name evokes the Bolshevik Party, leads the Red Commune to an ever-greater stability from episode two to the series' end. Late-socialist television melodrama thus recasts the Marxist vision of history into a story of the evolution of power from a weak patriarchy of young and volatile males, into the chaos of revolutionary matriarchy, and back to the patriarchy, this time reinforced by the proper class affiliation and, above all, age. By the fourth episode, all the dominant males of Green Valley have progressed from middle to old age. However, they are in control both of their destiny and, by episode seven, of their women.

The patriarchy in *Shadows* is distinctly Russian. It transcends the confines of the nuclear family and embraces the entire village community of Green Valley. The major conflict of the series is between the community, which includes multiple nuclear families but is not limited to them, and the nuclear family of Serafima and Ustin Morozov (Sergei Iakovlev). As heirs to the fortunes expropriated by the revolutionaries, the Morozovs try to undermine Soviet power by any means possible. Interestingly, these do not include wrecking and sabotage, but rather follow the melodramatic tropes of whisper campaigns and the incitement of weak males to irrational and self-destructive behavior that ruins families inside the great collective of Green Valley.

Krasnopol'skii and Uskov sacrifice ideological rigor for entertainment spectacle or, to be more precise, use class struggle as a motivation for what really is a display of popular attractions, the biggest of which is on-screen violence. While the existential threat of enemies to Soviet power is minimal and the 1970s viewer knew that the enemies were doomed, spectacular situations nonetheless arise when enemies strike. The bearded, nasty Men'shikovs kill Maria by smashing her head with a giant stone, towering over the poor woman at the top of a spectacular cliff. To avenge Maria's murder, Anisim throws the murderer over the same cliff. As retribution for the latter murder, the surviving brother ties the kolkhoz leader, Zakhar, by his feet to a horse and drags him through the village streets. The establishment of Soviet power decreases the number of spectacular scenes of violence, but does not eliminate them altogether. The Great Patriotic War is depicted as a scene of filicide: the former kulak Ustin Morozov joins the Nazis and kills his son, a Red Army officer. While all such violent scenes carry some ideological valence, above all class-mindedness, the primary reason for their prominence is to keep the viewers glued to their TV sets.

The moral occult of Soviet television melodrama is the realm of a male quest for spiritual redemption in a post-religious world. Television melodramas avoided Russian Orthodox iconography or presented it in a negative light because of official Soviet atheism and stricter ideological censorship over television as a mass medium. For example, the matriarch of the Morozovs is a religious fanatic who torments her children with senseless prayers and punishes them for refusing to follow Orthodox rituals. Instead of invoking Christian iconography, *Shadows* venerates Russian nature, which it associates with male spirituality. Green Valley sits next to a cliff on which Anisim has planted a birch tree to commemorate Maria, the murdered leader of the Red Commune. This tree carries a dual meaning in the film. It represents the site of the revolutionary struggle but is a reminder of the male characters' personal loss, guilt, and redemption. Anisim hurt Maria, and destroyed her and his chance to have a good family. Frol betrayed Maria's trust and involuntarily became an accomplice in her assassination. The cliff with its birch tree is a quasi-spiritual site, where male characters make important life decisions, reconcile with the greater collective, and maintain the continuity of the patriarchal order.

Shadows Disappear at Noon is a truly melodramatic narrative, but the outcome is not a traditional nuclear family. In the final episode of the feast dedicated to the opening of the new bridge across the local river, the photographer asks Zakhar to select the best hero-workers of the collective farm for a newspaper picture (see Figure 4.5). Instead, Zakhar remarks that the entire village deserves the honor of being in the picture. The final shot is a compromise between the two extremes: the Soviet trope of identity inseparable from heroic sacrifice for the public good and an acknowledgement of the importance of private identity. In the collective picture, the camera identifies all the newly formed young couples as well as the older ones: the nuclear families can survive only within the framework of the greater Russian community. The theme song leaves no doubt that it is precisely *Russian* identity that is at the core of the series' fictional world: "I look into blue lakes, I pick daisies in the fields,/I call you—Russia, the only one for me./Ask me again and again, there is no land more dear./The land where I received my Russian name."

In the final analysis, Krasnopol'skii and Uskov conceive all their male characters as potent, virile, Russian, and dedicated to the cause, be it socialism or capitalism. These melodrama-males are in stark contrast with the cinematic

Figure 4.5: Russian community at the core of Soviet television melodrama *Shadows Disappear at Noon*

representations of Soviet masculinity in the 1970s discussed below. Even the arch-enemy Ustin leaves no doubt that, were he on the right side, he would be the pride of the Green Valley male brotherhood. In this respect, the filmmakers depict a community whose greatest value is not socialist ideology, but a stable, unwavering patriarchy. In the late USSR, such a portrayal of Russian masculinity serves a therapeutic function: it offers an optimistic picture of the strong Russian man to viewers who need reassurance amid the real-life crisis of the Soviet patriarchy and its aging leadership.[17]

Cinematic masculinities

The majority of 1970s melodramas were about men, though within the Russo-Soviet critical discourse, these films have almost never been categorized as

---

[17] Surveys of letters from viewers to Gosteleradio suggest that *Shadows* struck a chord with Soviet audiences. In 1974, there were 715 requests to re-broadcast the series ("Obzor pisem" 61).

melodramas proper. In Stalinist culture Soviet masculinity was entirely defined by heroic service to the state and a self-sacrificial drive.[18] The tumultuous history of the era provided men with never-ending opportunities to fight and die for their country and thus to confirm simultaneously their own and the system's identity. Men's private identity was bookended by the "wait for me" trope (the loving but remote and invisible family) and male camaraderie in the trenches of communism. Family, children, and everyday life were not part of this heroic age.

It is no accident that many of the best films of the Thaw were about men "coming home": from the war, from geological expeditions, or from state construction sites. Freed from their epic public projects, male characters faced the challenges of re-adjusting to peaceful life. Yet most films eschew a direct encounter of these heroic vagabonds with domestic responsibilities or with women. The heroic male of Thaw melodrama coped with the losses of the past by reconstituting the nuclear family in order to build a radiant future. One of the central tropes of early post-Stalin culture—orphans—was also the culture's displacement mechanism, which preserved the heroic image of the Soviet men. Adopting and caring for orphans is a repeated motif in films of the 1950s–1960s: *Fate of a Man* (*Sud'ba cheloveka* 1959), *Serezha* (1960), *When Trees Were Big* (*Kogda derev'ia byli bol'shimi* 1962). Women in this narrative are observers at best, but just as often heartless villains.

Kira Muratova's *Brief Encounters* (*Korotkie vstrechi* 1967) signaled the exhaustion of the "heroic male" model. The male lead Maksim is a prospector— one of the most romanticized professions in the 1960s—played by cult singer and actor Vladimir Vysotskii. His on-screen existence is confined to the two female leads' flashbacks; in the present of the film there is a gaping hole. Likewise, in *White Sun of the Desert* (dir. Vladimir Motyl' 1969) Sukhov (Anatolii Kuznetsov), an itinerant male committed to the revolutionary cause, mentally recites imaginary letters to his wife, "Dear Katerina Matveevna," (Galina Luchai) while accompanying a harem of liberated "women of the East" across the desert. The ironic tone of both films leaves no doubt that the

---

[18] For a discussion of the cultural construction of Stalin-era masculinity see John Haynes, *New Soviet Man: Gender and Masculinity in Stalinist Soviet Cinema*, Manchester, UK: Manchester University Press, 2003 and Lilya Kaganovsky's *How the Soviet Man Was Unmade: Cultural Fantasy and Male Subjectivity under Stalin*, Pittsburgh: University of Pittsburgh Press, 2008.

heroic male model is incompatible with private life, family or, indeed, flesh-and-blood women.[19]

Lilya Kaganovsky claims that during Stagnation, with the utopian project exhausted, late socialism turned into a state "where there is nothing else to want" and the culture engaged in "the production of subjects without desire" (2009, 187). This is certainly true for male melodramas, many of which examine the death of heroic masculinity associated with the socialist utopia. While outwardly many of these films adhere to socialist realism, including the invocation of canonical moments and tropes of the Soviet revolutionary narrative, they make sense of the characters' experiences in ways that are incompatible with socialist realist syntax. First, the forward-looking temporality gives way to the temporality of the "radiant past" which defines masculinity by lack of agency in the present. Second, they explicitly pit ideological discourses of masculinity against the concerns of the family and everyday life. Third, these films, even when they preserve state service as the ideal, privilege Russian over the Soviet identity.[20]

Male melodrama of the 1970s introduced the temporality of a "radiant past" and its irreparable loss as fundamental to the construction of late-Soviet masculinity. These films usually depict men who served a great cause in the past, but whose post-heroic existence makes them confront profane contemporaneity. The sense of loss defines their masculinity and triggers the melodramatic narrative mode. Films such as Andrei Smirnov's *Belorussia Station* (1970) and Andrei Konchalovskii's *A Lovers' Romance* (1974) evoke the myth of military service as an identity-shaping experience, a rite of passage into the Soviet patriarchy. The warrior experience, however, is relegated to the past and is completely disconnected from their present existence.

Konchalovskii's bipartite *A Lovers' Romance* explicitly contrasts the story of idealized Soviet masculinity against the 1970s narrative of the hero's death. In the first part of the film, the romance between Sergei (Evgenii Kindinov)

---

[19] Irony as part of the representation of heroic masculinity in *White Sun of the Desert* also spilled over into the production circumstances of the film. Motyl's film had problems with financing and equipment because all the resources of the Soviet film industy were dedicated to Ozerov's war epic *Liberation*. In order to secure safety for the film crew during the film's production in Turkmenistan, the director had to give a "bad guy" part to the local leader of a criminal gang.

[20] For a discussion of masculinity and identity in *Officers* and *White Sun of the Desert*, see Elena Prokhorova "Mending the Rupture: The War Trope and the Return of the Imperial Father in 1970s cinema." *Cinepaternity: Fathers and Sons in Soviet and Post-Soviet Film*. Eds. Helena Goscilo and Yana Hashamova. Bloomington and Indianapolis: Indiana University Press, 2010. 51–69.

and Tania (Elena Koreneva) promises a nuclear family that will be in perfect harmony with the larger collective of the apartment building where both characters live and the military unit where Sergei serves while he is in the Navy. Emotional excess is central to the effect of *A Lovers' Romance*. The opening scenes are set amid lush nature, dripping with summer rain, the sun reflected in every single drop. The two young lovers, barely dressed, bask in each other's love: whisper nonsense to each other, rush about madly on the beach, and roll on the ground in an embrace. Despite the mise-en-scène of primal scene and the poetic dialogue, the opening—and the entire film—has a distinctly modern feel (see Figure 4.6): the characters are dressed in fashionable, Western-style clothes (for example, he wears jeans), Sergei drives a motorcycle and plays a guitar, and the mise-en-scène of a little cottage on a sandy beach comes straight from a Hollywood movie. The songs for the films were composed and performed by Aleksandr Gradskii—one of the first rock musicians in the Soviet Union.[21]

When Sergei's unit is deployed to help villagers in a disaster area, his armored vehicle is swept away by a tsunami. He is presumed dead, and after grieving, Tanya eventually marries her former classmate, an ice hockey player—that is, a peacetime mock warrior.[22] Yet Sergei not only survives, but saves his commander and eventually returns home a hero. Confronted with a non-heroic reality without Tania, Sergei screams that he has fulfilled his duty to his motherland yet has been deprived of his chance at happiness. At first it seems that the people in Sergei's apartment building can provide a substitute, medium-sized Soviet collective to nurture the hero and help him through his painful return to the present. Yet the film immediately destroys the illusion of a possible return to the harmony of Soviet collectivism. Instead, it offers a different, rather iconoclastic narrative trajectory: if you serve the big family, the price is your personal happiness.

The clash of ideal Soviet masculinity with the everyday finds its outlet in physical violence. Sergei's breakdown is nothing short of male hysteria. He tries to pick a fight with Tania's husband and beats up his own brother, who

---

[21] In 1975 Gradskii's soundtrack for *A Lovers' Romance* earned him a "Music Week Star of the Year Award" from *Billboard* magazine ("Music Week," 57).

[22] As it became obvious in the Brezhnev era that socialism was losing the economic competition with the West, the role of surrogate victories in sport grew proportionately. Ice hockey became the main arena where the Soviets compensated for their loss in the economic war.

Figure 4.6: Sergei and Tania, the Soviet Romeo and Juliet

is trying to stop him. Sergei's passionate nature attempts to reconcile two competing desires: the Stalinist desire to sacrifice oneself for one's country (which he has already done) and the personal, sexual desire for his beloved. Yet 1970s culture, as Kaganovsky notes, has a different economy of desire (2009: 185), and those who try to rein in Sergei's outbursts of violence explain to him that times have changed and that he should be happy with what he has. The first part of the film ends with the hero's symbolic funeral at a train station. The new era does not need a young hero with such powerful desires; they should stay buried in the past. In fact, in the first part of *A Lover's Romance*, Sergei, the hero, dies twice. Though his first funeral seems convincing enough, he survives the physical violence of the elements. By contrast, his second, symbolic, funeral looks theatrical, excessively melodramatic; the deceased is physically alive, but spiritually dead.

Sound and color convey the traumatic gap between heroic masculinity and the everyday. *A Lovers' Romance* chooses a highly stylized, somewhat poetic performance of the dialogue in the first, "heroic" part of the film and a decidedly prosaic one in the second. Color and black-and-white sequences signal the total incompatibility of the epic colorful past, with its heroic public identity, and the profane present, painted in the shades of gray and associated with the everyday and the private identity. Konchalovskii drains the film's world of color in the second part and leaves his protagonist to cope with the crisis alone. While the disappearance of color and poetry establishes a stark contrast between the two parts of the narrative and of Sergei's life, the transition in sound is more complex and even more dramatic—so much so, in fact, that the *Soviet Screen* editorial itself waxed poetic: "The devilish mutation of the dying heart's thumping to the sound of the suburban train and then to the off-screen counting of spoons in the cafeteria pushes the pathos-filled story towards the last trial—the test by the non-illuminated (*neprosvetlennoi*), mundane reality of the everyday (N.a. 1975, 9). The striking epithet "non-illuminated" refers to the good Soviet life of the working class protagonist—an unintentional but symptomatic indictment of late socialism.

It is also no accident that the most dramatic scenes in the second part of the film have a television screen in the background, with the sound off but with programs recognizable to any Soviet citizen: the children's cartoon "Just You Wait!" (*Nu, pogodi!*), the news program "Time" (*Vremia*),[23] with its lead-in image of the Kremlin, a report from a construction site, and an extended clip of the USSR–Sweden ice-hockey match. These black-and-white[24] blinking images of modern but uninspired and official culture substitute for the emotional monologues and human contact at the film's beginning. The witty director makes use of the children's cartoon. He redirects the viewer's gaze, making the cartoon character Volk (Wolf) inside the TV-set stop and look with amazement and horror as if at the male protagonist who has undergone such a dramatic change (see Figure 4.7).

The second part of *A Lovers' Romance* narrates the protagonist's life after his death as a hero. Konchalovskii focuses on the minutiae of Sergei's daily routine, giving the film a Direct Cinema feel. Spatially conveying the constriction in Sergei's life, Konchalovskii shows Sergei working as a bus driver; his bus seems to be going in circles between two stops, which he announces: the school and the hospital. The only other place where we observe the protagonist is at the bus drivers' cafeteria, where Sergei satisfies his only remaining desire: physical

---

[23] *Nu pogodi!* is a Soviet animated series for children, similar in its premise to *Tom and Jerry*, which premiered in 1969. *Vremia* is as evening newscast in the USSR and Russia, which is broadcast nightly at 9 pm, serving as the main source of state propaganda.

[24] Soviet television sets and most shows were black-and-white until the late 1970s. Soviet television experimented with color systems NTSC, PAL, and SECAM throughout the 1960s and early 1970s. In 1967 Central Television of the USSR broadcast nationwide SECAM color coverage of the parade on Red Square dedicated to the fiftieth anniversary of the October Revolution. Central Television transitioned from black-and-white to color broadcasting in 1977.

Reinventing Desire: Late-Socialist Melodrama 169

Figure 4.7: A TV cartoon character "looks" in amazement at the male protagonist who has undergone a dramatic change

hunger. In the midst of his endless, gloomy food consumption, he notices that he is the one being consumed by a female cook's gaze. Devoid of any desire or agency, Sergei follows the girl's lead and marries her (see Figure 4.8).

After the marriage, we observe Sergei mostly in the kitchen, stuffing himself with food just as he stuffs his new apartment with furniture and other consumer goods. Consumerism and the good Soviet life of late socialism appear in Konchalovskii's film as a poor substitute for the authentic desire that the hero experienced in the beginning of *A Lovers' Romance*. One of the key scenes in the second part of the film takes place in a clothing store, where Sergei and his new wife run into a trumpet player from Sergei's old apartment, who was Sergei's spiritual mentor and, through his music, sustained the idealistic spirit of the

Figure 4.8: The good Soviet life after the hero's death

communal apartment building. In this scene, the trumpet player appears without his musical instrument or his ideals, looking for a good coat, just like everyone else. Both men are embarrassed to see each other at a market place rather than in a locus of spiritual values. Sergei claims that he ended up in the store because of his wife, while the trumpet player notes that he hardly plays anymore and is shopping because "everyone now lives well" and nobody wants to be left behind. Konchalovskii chose Innokentii Smoktunovskii for the role of trumpeter, who became an icon of the Thaw hero after he played a heroic Hamlet confronting the oppressive Elsinore in Grigorii Kozintsev's 1964 film adaptation of Shakespeare's tragedy. In the clothing store scene, Smoktunovskii plays a lobotomized Hamlet trying to keep up with a degraded world overrun by the faceless descendants of Elsinore's epic heroes and villains.

The concluding sequence of the film is a celebration in Sergei's apartment of the birth of his child. Unlike his parents, who gave birth in epic times and have three sons, Sergei cannot regenerate the patriarchal order: his progeny is a girl. As if to mock Sergei's warrior past, his wife tells him that his daughter will grow up to be like him. Sergei's response is silence, for how can a woman become a warrior in a traditional patriarchal order? Although the party in honor of the newborn is a festive occasion, people watch the protagonist with worried expressions, as though he were on suicide watch. Among the buzz of voices at the dinner table one stands out: an old woman recollects her family's hardships and losses during the Great Patriotic War. This motif resonates with the war songs playing in the background, their diegetic status unclear. At this stage the heroic male mythology comes full circle, from the crescendo of monologues and documentary clips of Soviet marines in the film's first part to the half-mournful, half-nostalgic echo of the past in the second.

Two images dominate the mise-en-scène of the party. First, the carpet on the wall behind the guests depicts the mountains, which first appeared in the film as an epic, bird's-eye view from the plane when Sergei's mother was flying to reunite with her heroic son, who had returned from the dead after fulfilling his duty. What formerly served as an epic setting for Sergei's epic feat has shrunk to a patch on the wall of Sergei's private apartment, a pale replica of his heroic past. The second key image is an oversized photograph of Sergei's military unit, which Sergei's former commander brings as a gift to the party (see Figure 4.9).

Looking at this pale shadow of the communal harmony and his heroic but irretrievable past, Sergei almost collapses. His ability to sustain himself in the present and to be a husband and a father requires that he repress his former self.

Reinventing Desire: Late-Socialist Melodrama 171

Figure 4.9: Warrior paradise lost/exchanged for the good but uninspiring life

The photograph of the homosocial family of warriors stays outside the protagonist's apartment: it is incompatible with the world of his current family.

Konchalovskii's film became the subject of a heated polemic in the Soviet press. The publication of dozens of letters from viewers in several issues of *Soviet Screen* testified to the cultural impact of Konchalovskii's melodrama. Many young viewers identified with the characters,[25] while older audiences praised the unusual mix of a defamiliarizing style with the surprising authenticity of emotions. Moreover, for the most part they accepted and appreciated the film's expert use of melodramatic conventions: Sergei's "miraculous" survival in the icy water; the logic of "too late,"—that is, Tania's rushed marriage; and the nakedness of the emotional outpourings. It is symptomatic that the film's critics especially objected to the last aspect of the film's representation of Soviet masculinity. In his negative review, critic Iurii Smelkov attacked what he saw as the inconsistency of Sergei's character. While the epic scenes set in the army simply confirm that Sergei "does not need to be re-educated by the army [...] he is completely devoid of infantilism, is reliable and spiritually strong," his breakdown, according to the critic, is completely unmotivated: "A courageous and reliable guy turns into a brute who makes a scene in a public space and hits his own brother in the face. [...] Say what you want, but this [scene] is from a different melodrama (*iz drugogo romansa*)— the one in which characters pound their chest and, smearing tears over their unshaven cheeks, demand pity from friends and strangers" (1975: 12).[26] Smelkov,

---

[25] E.g., a tenth grade student from Moscow writes: "We recognize ourselves in [the characters]." N.a. 1975, 9.
[26] Iu. Smelkov, "Poeziia i pravda," *Sovetskii ekran* 1 (1975), 12–13, 12.

indeed, unwittingly provided an accurate reading of the film: melodramatic excess as a symptom of the death of both socialist realism's model hero and of the Soviet patriarchy.

A clear articulation of the crisis in Soviet masculinity was the sheer number of melodramas where the narrative trajectory suggested suicide. In a progressive and reason-driven socialist ideology, of course, this resolution was impossible—unless the character faced an inevitable capture by the Nazis. As a result, film endings were changed at the script stage by the censors or by the filmmakers themselves in anticipation of objections from film administrators. *Autumn Marathon*, for instance, ends not with the protagonist's suicide, but with his dancing to a pop tune coming from the blank TV screen. In *Snowball Berry Red*, the gang leader kills Egor, the splintered member of the criminal collective. During the round table dedicated to the film, Shukshin claimed that Egor *de facto* commits suicide: "I simply lacked the boldness to do this unambiguously" (qtd. in Dunlop (1992): 233). In Mel'nikov's *Vacation in September* (*Otpusk v sentiabre* 1979) Zilov (Oleg Dal') not only toys with the idea of killing himself, but the very narrative logic suggests this outcome. Viewers can conclude as much when Zilov's friends send him a funeral wreath. This macabre joke is a metaphor for the character's spiritual death; but in Russian culture, which considers such gestures taboo, this is a cypher for Zilov's inevitable suicide. Not surprisingly, the film, finished in 1979, was shelved for the next eight years.[27]

Shukshin's film led the way in rediscovering the male protagonist who yearns to articulate his own identity and to assume his patriarchal responsibilities in the Russian nuclear family. This concern with the national rather than supranational Soviet identity changes the ideology of late-Soviet melodrama and indirectly undermines the "affirmative action" discourse of Soviet nationality policies. This new hero appears, for example, in Iskra Babich's *Guys!* (*Muzhiki!* 1981), Aleksandr Mitta's *The Crew* (*Ekipazh* 1979), as well as the pictures of Vladimir Men'shov, especially in the character of Georgii Ivanovich (Aleksei Batalov), the Prince Charming of the late Stagnation blockbuster *Moscow Doesn't Believe in Tears* (1980). While these men rediscover their desire and family responsibilities, their agency and power are localized. If one assumes that they

---

[27] Melnikov's film is based on Alexander Vampilov's play *Duck Hunting* (*Utinaia okhota* 1970). The film director produced his bipartite television film in 1979 at Lenfilm's Television Film Unit, but the film was banned until Gorbachev's perestroika. It was first broadcast by Soviet television in 1987. See Vitalii Mel'nikov. "Otpusk v sentiabre." *Entsiklopediia otechestvennogo kino*. Ed. Liubov' Arkus. See http://russiancinema.ru/films/film4514/. Accessed June 14, 2012.

need to take charge of the public sphere, then something is not right in the way the country is managed. In Mitta's *The Crew*, for example, three Soviet pilots save their passengers while the local authorities remain completely helpless. It is significant, however, that the film is set in an unnamed foreign country, not the Soviet Union, and the disaster is caused by the inefficiency of non-Soviet authorities.[28] This is the only time in Soviet cinema when men, who are not state agents, are allowed to take charge in the public sphere. In the Soviet Union, these men are allowed to take charge only of their private lives—no small feat, considering the inherited conventions of representing the male hero in Soviet cinema.

Late-Soviet "woman's film"

Mary Ann Doane defines a "woman's film" as a type of melodramatic narrative that puts the female protagonist in a position of agency. She contends that this type of melodrama "obsessively centers and re-centers a female protagonist" and redefines the domestic sphere as socially significant (2002, 293–294). In his analysis of stagnation melodrama, Joshua First argues that in the 1970s the woman's film became a major presence in film critics' discussions and at the box office: *Stepmother* (1973) and *Moscow Doesn't Believe in Tears* sold 60 and 80 million tickets respectively (2008b, 22–23). Most importantly, the "woman's film" emerged as an important harbinger of commercial genre cinema in the Soviet film industry. Concerned with and puzzled by the spectacular success of Indian, Egyptian, and Mexican melodramas with Soviet viewers,[29] the film administration encouraged Soviet filmmakers to venture into these new generic forms that used domestic settings and actors.

Films aimed at women not only adopted the syntax of melodrama (with individual agency and the family as key elements of the narrative), but boldly relegated socialist realist film devices to the role of mere semantic features of the narrative. Moreover, as First notes, the Soviet womens' films of the 1970s made

---

[28] Russian filmmaker Nikolai Lebedev repeats this important narrative model in his 2016 remake of *The Crew*, titled *The Flight Crew*. The creators of the remake emphasized the significance of the story and the continuity between Soviet and post-Soviet films by using cutting-edge 3D IMAX technology. After Bondarchuk's *Stalingrad*, *The Flight Crew* became the second Russian film using the 3D IMAX camera.

[29] The Mexican melodrama *Yesenia* (1971; released in the USSR in 1975) sold 91.4 million tickets— the highest audience for any Soviet or foreign film ever screened in the USSR. Not far behind were Egyptian and Indian films, e.g. *The White Dress* (1973; released in the USSR in 1976) 61 million, and *Bobby* (1973; Soviet release 1975) 62.6 million. See http://kinanet.livejournal.com/13882.html.

an ideological breakthrough by placing the domestic sphere at the center of the narrative and emphasizing its incompatibility with the public sphere (26).

Historically late-Soviet womens' films followed a clear trajectory. Earlier instantiations of the genre were films of post-war reconstruction, with the position of agency forced upon the female protagonist because men had either perished or had never returned home from the war. By the 1970s, women were using their control not only due to the absence of the patriarch, but also because it was an indispensable part of their self-fulfillment as individuals. Most importantly, women's individual self-realization becomes completely separate from the Soviet public sphere, which was usually presented as male-dominated, but simultaneously impotent and corrupt.

The syntax of woman's film emerged initially in films set in post-war Russian villages and often centered on the widows of the Great Patriotic War (*A Simple Story* [*Prostaia istoriia* 1960], *Gypsy* [*Tsygan* 1967], *A Little Crane* [*Zhuravushka* 1969], *Stepmother* [1973]) and enjoyed immediate success with viewers. Initially, however, these films were received poorly by critics because of their excessive sentimentality and "philistine" moral stance—known in Russian as *poshlost*'.[30] Because the genre was new, there was no unified position on the official reception of these films. Evgenii Margolit notes that the editor-in-chief of *Art of Cinema*, Liudmila Pogozheva, who published a poor review of Evgenii Matveev's melodrama *Gypsy* (*Tsygan 1967*), lost her job because the film administration decided to market these films at festival circuits and on the global film market as a peculiar Russian quasi-folk product (2004, 232).

The woman's film set in rural Russia featured the female protagonist as an individual endowed with agency, while representing the male world as sterile and often hostile to the individual. The moral occult in these pictures appeared in the form of the Russian landscape, particularly in images of churches or the sky. Often these scenes were loosely connected to the narrative and emphasized the protagonist's subjectivity as part of spiritual domain beyond the world of Soviet values. Dialog was sparse and secondary to the cinematography and the music. Last, but not least, woman's film articulated sexual desire as an indispensable component of individual identity.

---

[30] Svetlana Boym (1994) defines *poshlost*' as "the Russian version of banality, with a characteristic national flavoring of metaphysics and high morality, and a peculiar conjunction of the sexual and the spiritual. This one word encompasses triviality, vulgarity, sexual promiscuity, and a lack of spirituality. The war against *poshlost*' was a cultural obsession of the Russian and Soviet intelligentsia from the 1860s to 1960s" (41).

As opposed to female melodramas set in the villages, those set in an urban landscape ascribed to the female protagonist a social identity beyond that of a wife and/or a mother. She was a professional, an economically independent individual, and a wife and mother if she so chose. Juggling these multiple identities in a hostile urban environment was the biggest challenge and a miraculous achievement of the 1970s female protagonist. Very often the conflict among these multiple identities and desires was at the heart of the film's narrative. Since the complex identity of the protagonist in the woman's film determined her age, very often she was not a young girl, but a middle-aged woman, with a family and a past.

Just like the identity of the protagonist, the representation of the moral occult became more complex and nuanced in these types of films. Usually the female protagonist was the only character in the picture who refused to compromise and settle for an illusion of happiness. Instead, she fought all the way alone both professionally and personally. The representation of this lonely struggle comprised the moral occult in this type of film. Whereas in rural melodramas, nature and occasional glimpses of churches provided an organic backing for the female protagonist's emotional struggle, in the urban melodramas the cityscape appeared as an antagonistic force challenging the heroine. This confrontation with soulless urban modernity mirrored the female protagonist's relationship with various male characters, who were portrayed as inauthentic, conformist, and emotionally sterile.

One of the best and most complex examples of a late socialist woman's film is Gleb Panfilov's *I Want the Floor*. This picture used a melodramatic plot to examine the nature of women's relationship with the Soviet utopian project. The filmmaker questioned one of the foundational myths of Soviet cinema: the transformation of the female protagonist into a powerful social force driving historical progress toward a radiant future. Panfilov's protagonist, Uvarova (Inna Churikova), a working-class woman and an exemplary sharpshooter,[31] becomes mayor of the city of Zlatograd and wants to build a new city across the river from the old township. To accomplish her utopian plan, she needs to build a bridge.

---

[31] The female protagonist as sharpshooter is a clear reference to Stalin-era female warriors. During the Great Patriotic War, hundreds of women served in the Red Army as sharpshooters. One of them, Liudmila Pavlichenko, who had 309 confirmed kills, became an international celebrity when in 1942 she visited the UK, US, and Canada. She was the first Soviet citizen to be received by President Roosevelt at the White House. Panfilov's reference to Uvarova as a sharpshooter is also ironic. Despite her clear vision, she does not notice her husband's infidelity, completely misses the fact that her fascination with guns will lead to her son's violent death and is oblivious to the growing social collapse in the community she supposedly leads.

The bridge project becomes the ultimate incarnation of Uvarova's drive to connect the present of her city with its radiant future, and she sacrifices everything for this dream. She stops spending time with her children and distances herself from her husband. She hardly communicates with anybody in town apart from Lenin's portraits, which she venerates both in her office and in her study at home. As she becomes increasingly obsessed with her pet project, the film depicts the growing abyss between Uvarova's imaginary world of the future city and the physical world of the present.

Twice, Uvarova comes close to realizing the dream of the communist utopia, and both times she sees this utopia vanish into thin air. The first time, in her official capacity she visits an old Bolshevik on his deathbed and awards him the Order of Lenin. She observes old communists who started the revolution and possibly knew Lenin sing their song, "Full Speed Ahead, My Friends," with fervor and conviction. However, the key episode is the meeting of the sick Bolshevik with another communist, who betrayed him in the past. As Uvarova learns, the heroic past was not as ideal as she would like to believe. When the traitor asks the dying man to forgive him, the old Bolshevik chooses Christian forgiveness over Leninist intolerance towards one's enemies. Fascinated by the fanaticism with which the old communists sing their songs, Uvarova is blind to the interpolation of non-communist tolerance in their relations.

The second time we observe Uvarova getting a clear view of the revolutionary utopia in action is on the television screen. Again, she catches the utopia in its final hour: she watches on the news how leaders of a coup depose Chile's Marxist president, Salvador Allende. The filmmaker does not show us the television screen; instead, the camera shows the living room from behind the TV set, which blocks our view of the physical space in the apartment. One has to be a believer to see the invisible world of utopia and, apparently, neither the viewer nor the filmmaker believes any more.

But the dream world visible only to Uvarova gradually infringes on the physical world of her family apartment. The scene with the family gathered in front of the TV is perhaps the most important one in the film and foreshadows the family tragedy of the son's death and Uvarova's role in it. The four members of the family sit in a row, filmed from just over the edge of the television set, resembling talking heads on TV (see Figure 4.10). Uvarova is upset that a French woman from the delegation she met in the afternoon told her that she dresses too modestly for her position as the mayor. Both the husband and the children agree, and the son mentions that the family could afford a summer house. In

Figure 4.10: Watching the utopia in its final hour

response, Uvarova promises to take the kids to Leningrad and visit Lenin's apartment to see "how modestly he lived." The son calls this modesty hypocrisy, at which point the father decides to play the patriarch, taking the son to the next room offscreen and beating him with a belt. The son's screams don't seem to bother Uvarova, who continues to watch the news. A second later, she starts to cry hysterically: the progressive Chilean leader Salvador Allende is dead. To calm down, Uvarova leaves for the shooting range. The indifference towards the suffering of her own son, in stark contrast with her emotional response to events thousands of miles away, underscores the utter incompatibility of "true socialist" public service and the nuclear family.

The diegetic world of Panfilov's film is not completely devoid of utopian undertones or miraculous coincidences. To the dead utopia of socialism, Panfilov juxtaposes the melodramatic excess of Orthodox churches and monasteries, which appear when Uvarova's dying son is being transported to a hospital. Uvarova, however, does not see this parallel universe of beauty, grace and mercy. She obsessively looks at the empty left bank of the river, trying to envision the future, and is completely blind to the temples of Zlatograd (literally, Golden City) next to her on the "old," right bank. In one remarkable sequence, we first see

Figure 4.11: Uvarova in search of utopia, with the church in the background

Uvarova in focus explaining something to her colleagues about the new bridge to the left bank. The camera then reveals to the viewers a beautiful church in the background, with crosses on its onion domes (see Figure 4.11). We will never learn whether Uvarova will experience the moment of spiritual transcendence achieved by the hero of classical melodrama. At the end of the film she breaks the fourth wall and silently gazes directly at the viewer, who has just witnessed her entire life and her son's death in a personal flashback. Then she requests that she be given the floor, though what she wishes to say remains unknown.

Uvarova's predecessor in the mayor's office, whose pet project was building a city stadium, has a high regard for Uvarova's husband and no faith in Uvarova, in her ability to realize her dreams, or much else. Exasperated by his uncooperativeness and misogynistic humor, Uvarova tells him to stop his buffoonery. Indeed, all the men in *I Want the Floor* act like buffoons and conformists. Unlike Uvarova, however, they are well aware that the utopia is dead and that their goal in life is to avoid initiative and personal responsibility. The long scene between Uvarova and the former mayor is emblematic of Panfilov's pessimistic take on Uvarova, masculinity, and on socialist utopia. Bitter about his forced retirement, the mayor seems completely dispirited and socially castrated, in contrast to the decisive, phallic, but also uncomprehending Uvarova. Yet the mise-en-scène, especially the lonely picture of Lenin staring out of a wall of pale pink—the tired red drained of its revolutionary essence—"sides" with the former mayor's defeatist predictions for Uvarova. All of them eventually come true: she is unable to build a dream city, while the existing apartment buildings fall apart; she destroys the city's sports team and loses its best soccer players because she considers her husband's request to provide the players with apartments favoritism. Unlike her predecessor, she takes a serious interest in the arts. But in her well-meaning zeal, she tramples over the career of a playwright (played in the film by Vasilii Shukshin). Perhaps more importantly, the former mayor's ironic jibe that questions Uvarova's ability to do her job while "kiddies need their mommy" proves prophetic in reverse: she is so dedicated to her projects that she destroys her family.

The filmmaker poses the old Dostoevskian question of whether the end justifies the means. Uvarova is a top Soviet sharpshooter and a city mayor who sees targets and ideological goals all too clearly. For her, progress towards utopia justifies many sacrifices. While purportedly building the radiant future for humanity, she dismisses the opinions of those who express any second thoughts about her proposals. Most importantly, she neglects her own family. The only time we see her spend time alone with her children is at the shooting range—presumably because, in her view, her children need to be as sharp-eyed as their mother. As a result of such an upbringing, they do not nurture a fascination with their mother's ideology, but a fascination with guns does pass on to the new generation.

The accidental death of Uvarova's teenage son from the gun he found in the field next to his house provides the filmmaker's answer to the protagonist's ideology. Indeed, her son's death, which opens the film, establishes the tone of the narrative. The devastating scene of Uvarova's son dying from a pistol wound he receives when he tries to disassemble the pistol using tools given to him by his mother comprises the first of Uvarova's flashbacks as she reconstructs the most important events of her life. The rest of the film is colored by this tragedy, and, empowered by this knowledge, the viewers are free to draw their own conclusions about Uvarova's character. The flashback imbues otherwise neutral details in the film with ominous significance. Viewers observe Uvarova as a champion sharpshooter, "nurturing" her children at the shooting range (see Figure 4.12). At home, she behaves as if at a public forum, making speeches about the town's future and Lenin's personal modesty. Both her son and husband consider this

Figure 4.12: Uvarova mentoring her children

hypocrisy, while her daughter, who shares their desire for consumerist comforts, "agrees" with her mother and grows up a hypocrite. But the fatal flaw in Uvarova's character is not hypocrisy; it is blind faith in communist ideals and her readiness to sacrifice the private for the public good. This dedication to what the film suggests is already dead becomes an obsession that initially is represented with sympathy, but progressively becomes a tragic anomaly.

One of the few of Uvarova's "motherly" acts is to bring her son a tool kit she bought in Moscow. When he asks why she did not buy an imported one, she responds: "Our tools are more dependable." What Uvarova does not know—but the viewer does—is that she has just delivered a deadly weapon to her child: he found a gun in the field, and the tool kit and the obsession with guns she has passed along to her children will kill him. The son's death provoked objections among the censors, who noted that this knowledge communicated to the viewer lent the entire film a tragic overtone. Panfilov, however, refused to move the episode, replying that by not putting this scene at the end, he avoided making the film melodramatic.[32]

---

[32] "Proshu slova." RGALI, F. 2944, op. 4, ed. khran. 3034, 52–53.

In collaboration with his composer, Vadim Bibergan, Panfilov made the soundtrack central to the ideological conflicts of his picture. The filmmaker and the composer claimed that the primary purpose of the soundtrack was to characterize each member of the Uvarov family in the narrative and to convey the major ideological concerns of the era, the atmosphere of the time (Poliakova). Several distinct songs associated with specific family members are juxtaposed with what Bibergan calls noise-music (*shumomuzyka*). The vague, rhythmical humming, imitating the sound of a running engine, emerges during the first shots of the film, when we see Uvarova in the present, attending a session of the Supreme Soviet of the USSR. We get a bird's eye view of the Soviet parliament: in the center of the meeting room stands a gigantic white marble statue of Lenin, next to which people look like black ants, moving over a faded pink carpet. The noise-music then becomes a sound bridge into Uvarova's first flashback: her teenage son finding a pistol in a desolate, snow-covered field. Bringing the pistol home, he accidentally kills himself while playing with it. The gun that the police had earlier searched for in vain is found by a melodramatic coincidence that has all the characteristics of the iron determinism of Marxist dialectics. Uvarova's idealism and her war against the imperfect nature of life find their logical conclusion in the death of her son. The machine-like noise-music that at first appeared from Uvarova's perspective as the internal diegetic sound of state machinery moving full speed ahead into the revolutionary future undergoes a reevaluation after her son's death: the disturbing sounds come to represent her irreparable personal loss and a society moving towards collective suicide.

Within the framework of this ubiquitous noise of social teleology moving toward its tragic denouement, the old Bolsheviks' song, "Full Speed Ahead, My Friends," acquires an ambiguous meaning. On the one hand, both Uvarova and her son are fascinated by the old communists' fanatical conviction. The Bolsheviks perform a song of faith and, just like an Orthodox chant, their song needs no musical accompaniment, only the human voices of true believers. Uvarova and her son listen to the choir but do not participate.[33] At the film's end, after all of Uvarova's projects are terminated by a decree from Moscow, she turns on "Full

---

[33] During the film's discussion at Goskino, I. Sadchikov praises this scene for its precise depiction of the contrast between the characters' revolutionary spirit and their physical frailty ("Proshu slova," 50–51). This comment ignores the scene's real conflict: the old generation of believers is dying while Uvarova and her son are unable to join them.

Speed Ahead, My Friends" on the turntable and, knowing that she cannot do anything for her city, tries at least to clean her own apartment. She listens to the revolutionary song but does not sing herself. Though she wants to believe, her faith in the system has evaporated.

Uvarova's children sing their own song: Paul McCartney's "Obladi Oblada." The older son turns on the song in his room to separate himself from his mother's alien utopian plans, and his younger sister dances when she hears the song. Notably, the Beatles' English-language song separates the parents, who still listen to Russian music, from the children, whose musical preferences symbolize their alienation from their parents' values.

The third "child" in the family, Uvarova's husband (played by Nikolai Gubenko), also likes to listen to "Obladi Oblada." However, his song is a tango performed by Leonid Utesov's jazz band, another example of an internal diegetic sound. We hear it when we see Uvarova recollecting her courtship with her husband and the birth of their son. Most importantly, all the songs in the film (the revolutionary song, the Western hit, and the Soviet tango) recall the past. In the present, there is only the disturbing noise of a society that has lost its ability to generate music.

The film follows the famous *Citizen Kane* narrative structure: it begins with a death, final and irreversible, and develops through a series of flashbacks, which, like a puzzle, reveal the mystery behind one person's rise and fall. Unlike in *Citizen Kane* however, the flashbacks in Panfilov's film are Uvarova's own: they are explorations of female subjectivity. The very first scenes outline the clash between Uvarova's two roles: the public one as a Supreme Soviet delegate, followed by the personal loss of a mother devastated by her son's death. The film is consistent in limiting us to what Uvarova knows: she is either in the scene or the view is restricted to her point of view (shots of the bank and the church over the water) and her subjectivity (the aural leitmotif of her son's death). The one striking break from this subjective narration is the son's death: it is shown in detail, though Uvarova is not in the scene, absent precisely when she needed to be there. What is present, however, is the pistol, the ultimate tool of Uvarova's career as a markswoman, and the tool kit, her gift to her son. Together these two props seal the son's fate.

Goskino censors objected to the original follow-up to Uvarova's defeated return from Moscow: she takes her daughter to a shooting range. Both Igor' Sadchikov, the main editor of the Script Commission, and Boris Pavlenok, the Deputy Chairman of Goskino, referred to the abrupt transition from Uvarova's visit to Gosplan (State Planning Committee) to the shooting range scene as an "editing inaccuracy" that creates an undesirable generalization. "It is unnecessary to escalate the scene to shooting at ambiguous targets ... Throughout the film the protagonist confronts real people, concrete problems ... but after she clashes with an institution shooting appears."[34] Even though the shooting episode is absent from the final cut of the film, both the discussion and the logic of the narrative demonstrate a level of systemic criticism rare for a Soviet film. Unlike male melodramas such as *Belorussia Station*, where characters could escape into the past, and dramas such as *The Bonus* (*Premiia* 1974), where a few good men restored justice and faith in the system, *I Want the Floor* shows the destruction of a person by the system. Uvarova is a pawn of her own beliefs, not their master, and she pays the ultimate price for her misdirected idealism. In this respect, the repeated official praise of Panfilov's film for its representation of "the Soviet way of life" and of the "complex and interesting fate of the Soviet woman, our contemporary"[35] is indeed accurate, albeit in an unintended way.

If Uvarova sacrifices her individual desires for public service and fails in both the public and private spheres, the protagonist of Vladimir Men'shov's *Moscow Does Not Believe in Tears* manages to succeed in both spheres because of the strength of her character, i.e. her individual agency. Men'shov was aware of the rich socialist realist tradition of strong women-protagonists. During the Stalin era, such characters' desires were equivalent to state demands.[36] Film historians often compare Men'shov's picture with its socialist realist predecessors, such as Grigorii Alexandrov's *Radiant Path* (1940) and Vasilii Ordynskii's *A Person Is Born* (*Chelovek rodilsia* 1956) because all three films recycle the Cinderella plot (the Stalin-era film even had the working title *Cinderella*). Both earlier films use the melodramatic plot in order to exemplify the great opportunities for social mobility the Soviet state opened for women, and the socialist realist syntax organizes semantic elements borrowed from melodrama. For example, in *Radiant Path* a backward peasant woman, Tat'iana (Liubov' Orlova), becomes an outstanding worker who is eventually invited to the Kremlin and receives an award, the Order of Lenin, from the Soviet government. The scenes of Tat'iana working on the factory floor serve the same function as the dance numbers in Hollywood musicals. During these scenes she transforms into the new woman.

---

[34] "Proshu slova," 51.
[35] "Proshu slova," 16.
[36] One has only to think of Fedor Gladkov's classical socialist realist novel *Cement* (*Tsement* 1925) with its female lead Dasha Chumalova.

As an afterthought, at film's end she also receives a husband, the young engineer Aleksei Lebedev (Evgenii Samoilov).

The story of Tat'iana's quest for personal happiness provides superficial semantic features borrowed from melodrama in order to decorate the socialist realist narrative of a peasant woman undergoing reeducation into the exemplary Soviet worker. Her service to the state overshadows any significance of her romance with Lebedev. At the film's end Tat'iana literally flies around Moscow in a luxurious car, the flight giving viewers an opportunity to see the skyline of the USSR's new capital. The car lands next to the monumental sculptures of Stalinist Moscow, which both represent the communist future and dwarf Tat'iana and Aleksei, thus establishing the hierarchy of priorities between the socialist cause and the concerns of nuclear family (see Figure 4.13).

Keeping in mind this honored tradition, Men'shov creates a strong female protagonist, Katerina (Vera Alentova), for a new era and with a new economy of desire. While Katerina's story fits neatly into the socialist realist master plot, its treatment in the film challenges this key ideological narrative to the point of eradicating it. First, the story of Katerina's rise from a simple worker to the director of a state chemical conglomerate disappears in an ellipsis between the first and the second parts of the film. Katerina goes to bed a single mother in a dorm room

Figure 4.13: Tat'iana and Aleksei entering the monumental world of the communist paradise (*Radiant Path* 1940)

at the end of part one and wakes up a successful business woman, surrounded by all the trappings of the Soviet middle class: an apartment, a car, fashionable clothes, and a Japanese stereo playing Euro disco. The didactic story of her social mobility happens somewhere off-screen. By the late-Soviet era, the story of the female protagonist's rise to power with the state's help is so commonplace that every viewer can fill in the blanks on her own based on past Soviet films.

Second, the story of the protagonist's quest for personal happiness is not at all affected by her public triumphs. Katerina's happiness is not about a communal cause, but about her individual identity. Men'shov uses an almost Proppian formula in both parts of the film. In part one, the villainy occurs: a man uses Katerina sexually and abandons her, pregnant, leaving her to cry herself to sleep alone with a baby beside her. Part two follows the same pattern despite all her career achievements. Another man uses Katerina sexually—accompaniment by the same soundtrack, "Besame mucho"— and again abandons her to cry herself to sleep. The only improvement is that her daughter now has a room of her own. The private lack (of a loving partner) can by no means be rectified by Katia's public success.

Third, in Men'shov's film, the villains appropriate socialist realist rhetoric and effectively use it to abuse the melodramatic protagonist. In part one, Katerina dates television cameraman Rudolf (Iurii Vasil'ev) and hides from him the fact that she is a fitter, a working-class professional. Instead, she tells him that she is a student and the daughter of a famous professor. By a melodramatic coincidence, Rudolf is assigned to make a program about Katerina's factory and learns her true identity. After discovering, to his disappointment, that he has wasted his efforts on a socially inferior partner, he notes sarcastically that he is quite impressed that she is a true hero of socialist labor. When Katerina later tells him that she is pregnant and begs him to find her a doctor who will perform an abortion, Rudolf dismisses her request and notes that she should go to the factory hospital because the USSR has the best medical care in the world. Finally, when in part two Rudolf (who has now changed his name to the fashionable Russian-style Rodion) runs into the now accomplished Katerina, he is impressed and finally shows up to meet his grown-up daughter. As an ice-breaker, he compliments Katerina and retells her heroic life in terms of a socialist realist masterplot: "It is a remarkable biography: from a simple worker to the director of a chemical conglomerate." Such a consistent delegation of socialist realist rhetoric to the melodramatic villain invalidates the straight reading of socialist realist tropes in Men'shov's picture.

Men'shov thus preserves the socialist realist narrative as a semantic element but builds his film around the female protagonist in a position of individual agency. Katerina exists on the threshold between the needs of her nuclear family and challenges brought to her by Soviet modernity. *Moscow Does not Believe in Tears* uses devices of socialist-realist cinema to enrich the film with familiar semantics, but uses melodramatic syntax to tell a story of its female protagonist.

The woman's film became the only genre in Soviet cinema that allowed sexual content on screen. This trend culminated in *Moscow Does Not Believe in Tears*, where the "quality" of men and relationships, as well as the female protagonist's subjectivity, is measured by the degree of awkwardness in their love-making. Katia is virtually raped by Rodion to the sound of "Besame Mucho"; her later encounter with her married lover is interrupted by the arrival of his mother-in-law. In contrast, scenes of genuine intimacy and desire punctuate her relationship with Gosha. While still conforming to the puritanical mores of late-Soviet culture, the film allows for some degree of freedom in articulating sexual desire and a woman's sexual identity against the grain of patriarchal conventions.

Katerina's main story in the film goes beyond the socialist realist plot and follows the trajectory of a woman's film. She pursues happiness in both the public and private spheres. She chooses a partner who understands her, is capable of responsibility, and, most importantly, awakens her desire. While feminist readings of Katerina's choice, Georgii Ivanovich or Gosha, played by Aleksei Batalov, justifiably argued that he incarnates the worst stereotypes of patriarchy— hierarchical gender relations and the construction of a woman's happiness around the presence of a male in a nuclear family[37]— we should keep in mind the late-socialist cultural backdrop against which this protagonist appears. Aleksei Batalov's Gosha is a new man compared to the heroes of late-socialist cinema: failed men eschewing social and familial responsibilities. Gosha is also a completely different species from the heroic male of Stalin-era cinema who succeeded in the public sphere by following the utopian demands of the Soviet state but who had no personal agency in this respect. Gosha, in contrast, does something much more difficult, for which there is no precedent in Soviet cinema: he exercises his own will, takes on responsibility for the happiness of the two women he loves (Katerina and her daughter), and, in the process, undergoes

---

[37] See, for example, Gillespie 2002, 89.

a profound change himself—learning to respect a strong and independent partner.

In short, Men'shov's film marks the acme of the development of the late-socialist woman's film in its clear-cut articulation of women's agency and desire as central to the protagonist. The film also succeeds in designing a strong partner who breaks with the tradition of ineffectual males characteristic of late-socialist melodrama. It was very insightful of Men'shov and his scriptwriter Valentin Chernykh to endow the new male protagonist with a Russian, not Soviet, identity. He emerges in the film from behind a Russian samovar, which he is carrying for a peasant woman (see Figure 4.14). His first name, Georgii, references the viewer to St. George, the saint-protector of Moscow, while his patronymic, Ivanovich makes him a quintessential Russian.

Two films released at the end of the Brezhnev era signal two opposite perspectives on melodramatic narratives and cultural values that they brought into circulation. In *Moscow Does Not Believe in Tears*, the romance of Katerina and Gosha foregrounds the syntax of melodrama: the family and the fulfillment of the individual protagonist in the face of modernity's forces. The accomplishments of public life, which Soviet cinema was supposed to describe via the socialist realist master plot, were simply left out in the story of Katerina's search for

Figure 4.14: A Russian (not Soviet) male protagonist emerging from behind a Russian samovar

personal happiness. This unexpectedly fresh look at a Russian woman's life and the familiar melodramatic narrative from behind the Iron Curtain earned Men'shov's film an Academy Award for Best Foreign Language Film in 1981.

In 1982, inspired by *Moscow*'s international success, a veteran of Soviet cinema, Iulii Raizman, released his version of melodrama, titled *Private Life*. In contrast to the story of Katerina's private life as one of self-fulfillment, Raizman's film tells the story of an industry manager of the Stalin-era generation whose retirement from public life is presented as a tragedy. Nuclear family and private life give nothing but a sense of incarceration to the protagonist. Raizman's film acknowledges that the socialist realist narrative is no longer viable, but mourns the disappearance of the narrative model that had sustained totalitarian cinema for the past fifty years. Like several other "simulation melodramas"[38] (e.g., Stanislav Rostotskii's *Dawns Are Quiet Here/ A zori zdes' tikhie* 1972 and *White Bim Black Ear/Belyi Bim Chernoe ukho*1977), *Private Life* was nominated for an Oscar, but, unsurprisingly, did not win. While these films demonstrated the maturity of the Soviet film tradition, both as artistic and industrial products, Western audiences and Academy members did not fail to recognize the anachronistic ideology and genre memory of Stalinist cinema. Although the previous Russian film that won an Oscar (*War and Peace*) was an expected win, confirming the power of the Soviet film industry, *Moscow Does Not Believe in Tears* brought a promise of cinema looking beyond the inherited discourse of totalitarian cinema.

Postscript: televised passions

In the late 1980s and early 1990s previously unavailable imported dramas filled Soviet television screens. Latin American *telenovelas* and North American soaps mesmerized audiences in Russia. As reports suggest,[39] viewers identified with characters of *Los Ricos También Lloran* (*The Rich Also Cry*, Televisa/Mexico, 1979–1980; released in the USSR in 1991–1992) and *Santa Barbara* (NBC/USA,

---

[38] We call simulation melodrama films that celebrate the imperial state and the desire to serve it, disguised as melodramatic narrative. For further discussion of the simulation melodrama see Conclusion, pages 194–195.

[39] See, for example, Kate Baldwin's discussion in "Montezuma's Revenge: Reading *Los Ricos También Lloran* in Russia," in *To Be Continued . . . Soap Operas Around the World*, ed. Robert C. Allen, London: Routledge, 1995, 285–300.

1984–1993, released in Russia in 1992–2002), despite foreign locations and less-than perfect voice dubbing. Successful native productions took about a decade to appear, but in the 2000s, Russian melodramas took television by storm; on some channels, such as "Russia Channel," melodramatic narrative constitutes the bulk of daily broadcasts.

There are three types of melodramas, each with its own audiences and agenda. One is licensed remakes of international series, such as the Colombian "dramedy" *Yo soy Betty, la fea* (titled in Russian release *Be Not Born Beautiful*, 2005–2006). The show became a huge success with younger audiences, because of its setting in the fashion industry and its ideology of glamour, which was at its height in the mid-2000s. In the Russian context, the series provided a space for negotiating the problems of transition to a market economy and the fictional reconciling of Soviet and new Russian ideologies. Another type, the most common and varied in format, is the Russian analog to daytime soap opera. Usually set in contemporary Russia, these productions range from several hundred episodes to only a few; many made-for-TV feature films also belong to this category. With titles invoking love and family, these series target (older) female audiences; unlike daytime soaps, however, they are often screened in prime time.

The third category consists of series that are set in the Soviet Union and marketed as adaptations or historical dramas. Often featuring renowned Soviet political, military, and cultural figures and dealing with contested historical moments (such as Stalin-era purges, the Second World War, or Brezhnev's Stagnation), these series adopted the familiar format of a mini-series. Notably, together with the new releases, in 1998 Channel One Russia (ORT at the time) rereleased the 1970s classic *Shadows Disappear at Noon*. The restored and remastered series now consisted of ten shorter episodes because each episode now had to allow extra time for commecials. The past fifteen years of Putin's rule saw dozens of these productions participate in the re-interpretation of Soviet history via melodramatic narratives that turn problematic figures into participants in family dramas and love triangles. In 1972 Thomas Elsaesser wrote that melodrama as a narrative form was inspired by the rise of the European bourgeoisie in the late eighteenth and early nineteenth century. It was an ideological weapon against a corrupt feudal aristocracy. In the late twentieth and early twenty-first century, these aspects of the melodrama as a visual genre have finally become relevant for Russian culture.

Conclusion

The four film and television genres that we discuss in this book address the major ideological and cultural concerns of the late-socialist era. The order of the chapters models the relative proximity of each genre to its origins in the socialist realist masterplot, as we see it. In our concluding remarks we would like to suggest that these genres continue to dominate Russia's television and cinematic landscape today; moreover, they provide a blueprint for dominant ideological narrative of the Putin-era. With the disappearance of socialist realism, the conflicts, anxieties, and pleasures encoded in the genres' syntax were put to new use in the new economic and cultural environment. In the postscript to the four chapters we outline the continuities between the late-socialist genres and their post-socialist descendants, focusing on the legacies of structure-bearing meanings. Two of the genres—sitcom and the police procedural—dominate post-Soviet television schedules, while prestige productions, virtually absent in the 1990s, received a boost as Russia went into a new spiral of imperial nostalgia and expansion under Putin.

The Soviet-era police procedural and prestige films set up narrative models explaining the relationship between the Soviet state and its subjects. The prestige film told the story of origins: victories in global wars (*Liberation, War and Peace*) and other projects enhancing the USSR's global power projection, such as the Soviet space program (*The Taming of Fire* [*Ukroshchenie ognia* 1972]) or the Soviet atomic bomb project (*Choice of Target* [*Vybor tseli* 1974]). In addition to displaying hard power for domestic and international viewers, the film industry used the Russian literary canon to author scripts that explained the origins of the USSR as a world superpower in the sphere of culture: *War and Peace, Father Sergius* (*Otets Sergii* 1978), *Several Days from the Life of I.I.Oblomov* (*Neskol'ko dnei iz zhizni I.I. Oblomova* 1979), *Steppe* (*Step'* 1977), etc. In post-Soviet Russia, the prestige film continues to fulfill a similar function—representing Russia as a great hard and soft power and displaying the Russian film industry's capability to produce technologically advanced visual narratives. Fedor Bondarchuk's war epic *Stalingrad* (2013) released in 2D and 3D for the widescreen and IMAX is a good example of both continuity between late- and post-Soviet Russian genre models and a family tradition of making big-budget war spectacles. Nikita Mikhalkov's recent *Sunstroke* (*Solnechnyi udar* 2014) exemplifies the post-Soviet use of the literary canon for prestige production purposes. Inspired by Ivan Bunin's writing about the Bolshevik Revolution and set in the Crimea, the film applies narratives from classical Russian literature to justify Russia's recent imperial adventure in Ukraine.

The police procedural similarly bridges Soviet and post-Soviet television. State-controlled media represent Russia as a nation that has achieved stability after the "tumultuous nineties," the expression Russia's president likes to use in order to foreground the achievements of his own rule. Endless television police procedurals, such as *Moscow Police, Forever!* (*MUR est' MUR* 2004-2006), *Cop Wars* (*Mentovskie voiny* 2005-to the present), *The Odyssey of Detective Gurov* (*Odisseia syshchika Gurova* 2013), explain how security ministries play the most important role in holding Russia together and how the nation needs a little more policing and authoritarian power to become a fully stable society. Many of these post-Soviet police shows are set in the Soviet past, thus also whitewashing the role of the police in a Soviet-era rule of mass terror. The genre syntax that inspires contemporary television producers of police serials originates in the television procedurals of the 1970s, such as *The Investigation is Conducted by Experts* and *The Meeting Place Cannot be Changed*. During the 1970s, the viewer got used to turning on his TV set and ending up in the police interrogation room. The short, colloquial version of officers' names in *ICE*—Pal Palych, Shurik, Zinochka—became household names in Soviet families of the late-socialist era. The police serials and films of the 1970s played a major role in the USSR's transition from a society managed by political terror to one managed by surveillance and state-controlled media. Instead of the Stalinist secret police terrorizing citizens by regular late-night arrests, late-socialist television reminded its viewers where they would end up if they transgressed the law, the worst crime being economic entrepreneurship. Not surprisingly, in the early years of Putin's rule, together with the return of the Soviet anthem as the official national song, *ICE* was briefly revived, but soon replaced by an historical docudrama, *The Investigation Was Conducted by* . . . (2006 to the present), a serial retelling the most famous cases of primarily the Brezhnev era and narrated by actor Leonid Kanevskii, who became famous playing one of three Experts in the Brezhnev-era police procedural. Indeed, the genre of the police procedural continues to provide one of the main narratives explaining to the current Russian viewer how the relationship between the Russian state and its subjects should be constructed.

Late-Soviet romantic comedy focused on the pleasure of private life and the modest consumption of the Soviet middle class, celebrating and occasionally challenging the status quo of a generally prosperous and stable society. The genre, therefore, carved a space where late-Soviet audiences could recognize, "rehearse," and (with an ironic smirk) respond to the limits of the permissible under late socialism. The syntax of the post-Soviet sitcom originated in 1970s film and television comedies and the proto-sitcom *Pub 13 Chairs*, but was influenced by Western models. Such breakthrough shows as *My Fair Nanny* (*Moia prekrasnaia niania* 2004-2009), *Happy Together* (*Schastlivy vmeste* 2006-2013) or *The Voronins* (*Voroniny* 2009-present), all licensed remakes of American sitcoms,[1] and *Be Not Born Beautiful* (*Ne rodis' krasivoi* 2005-2006), a remake of the Colombian dramedy *Yo soy Betty, la fea*, adapted the serialized format to the new Russian cultural context. Both of Riazanov's hit comedies of the 1970s— *Irony of Fate* and *The Office Romance*—and a score of others were also remade for new audiences, with varying degrees of success.[2] As Vera Zvereva noted, television sitcoms offer the most extreme departure from Soviet-era narratives, incorporating new social realities into comedic formulas. At the same time, they participate, along with police procedurals, in promoting a positive image of Russian society, with police and special forces protecting private citizens from crime and political chaos. Zvereva quotes an STS channel executive who in 2004 said that he sees the priority of Russian television in the portrayal of private values: "How should one live? How to plan one's future? How to achieve happiness? [...] Viewers do not get answers to their questions in political programs and news broadcasts."[3]

What about melodrama? Late-Soviet melodrama attempted to articulate individual agency and examined the family as a site of crisis in the socialist utopia. We would like to propose that while 1970s Soviet melodrama radically departed from the inherited tropes of socialist realism, like romantic comedy it also set up a trap of sorts. In the recent two decades the idea of separation of private and public spheres, which 1970s melodrama had embraced, has turned into an erasure of the latter. In her book on post-1968 Czechoslovakia, Paulina

---

[1] *The Nanny* (CBS, 1993-1999), *Married with Children* (Fox, 1987-1997) and *Everybody Loves Raymond* (CBS, 1996-2005), respectively.
[2] *The Irony of Fate 2* (dir. Timur Bekmambetov, 2007); *An Office Romance. Our Time* (dir. Sarik Andreasian, 2011); *Diamond Arm 2* (dir. Sergei Ivanov, 2010), etc.
[3] Vera Zvereva, "Zakon i kulak: 'rodnye militseiskie serialy," *Novoe literaturnoe obozrenie* 78 (2006); see http://magazines.russ.ru/nlo/2006/78/zver20.html.

Bren argues that what Czech leaders called the period of "normalization" after the Soviet invasion was a time of consensus, of the "quiet life" as the promises of consumption were fulfilled. As Bren points out, the regime succeeded in connecting the "quiet life" to "new notions about socialist 'self-realization' and [...] 'privatized citizenship'" (2010, 111). In the picture that television family dramas portrayed, Bren says, it was "hard to ascertain where official ideology ended and private protest began" (2010, 173). Media, and especially television, were at the heart of this shift, as both the deliverer of good news and itself a fulfilled promise of a modern, "cultured" life.[4]

Under Putin, Russian television and cinema finally caught up with "normalization"-era Czechoslovakia of the 1970s, where melodrama celebrated a new cult of private life, embraced by individual citizens *and* encouraged by the state. What distinguishes Putin-era culture from Russian culture of the 1990s is its ability to imitate political and cultural institutions of democratic societies while simultaneously dismantling them and replacing them with institutions that allow the dictator to rule through pinpoint applications of terror, such as political murders and media trolling. One of the genres of such ideological trolling that took shape in the 1970s and became the mainstay of Putin-era television culture is imitation melodrama. During the late 1960s and 1970s, several filmmakers, above all Sergei Gerasimov, Iulii Raizman, Stanislav Rostotskii, and Evgenii Matveev, developed a special kind of narrative that appropriated melodramatic devices to articulate the ideology of state authority as sacred power. While on the surface these films dealt with individuals and nuclear families, they only masqueraded as melodramas while asserting statist ideology and collectivist values. Such films as Gerasimov's *Daughters and Mothers* (*Dochki-materi* 1974), Rostotskii's *White Bim Black Ear* (*Belyi Bim Chernoe Ukho* 1977) and Raizman's *Private Life* (*Chastnaia zhizn'* 1982) which we call simulation melodramas, often start in a traditional melodramatic mode, with the nuclear family as the site of conflict between individual desires and the pressures of modernity. While in bona fide melodrama individual agency is reasserted in the course of the conflict between the family and larger social forces, in simulation melodrama, in contrast, individual agency is seen as a flawed source of authority and the replacement of individual agency with state authority is viewed as the prime ideological goal. Such films portray the imperfect

---

[4] On the cultural status of television in Soviet culture, see Kristin Roth-Ey, *Moscow Prime Time*, especially "Introduction" and Chapter 4, "Finding a home for television in the USSR."

nuclear family as the major obstacle to this unmediated relationship of harmony between the state and its subjects.[5]

Late-Soviet historical series, such as *Shadows Disappear at Noon* and *Eternal Call*, are another source of continuity. In melodramatizing Soviet history these proto-soap operas anticipated the post-Soviet proliferation of historical dramas dealing with Soviet political, military, cultural figures: *Brezhnev* (2005), *Furtseva* (2011), *The Case of the Grocery Store Number One* (*Delo gastronoma nomer odin* 2011), *The Son of the Father of the People* (*Syn ottsa narodov* 2013), to name just a few. All of these use melodramatic codes to neutralize and rewrite Soviet history. Aleksei Muradov's 2012 serial about Georgii Zhukov, the most famous Soviet military commander of the Second World War, exemplifies imitation melodrama production of this sort. The two plotlines of this Channel One mini-series focus on Zhukov's involvement in high politics under Stalin and Khrushchev, and his relations with his two wives and a mistress—the more difficult and problematic private sphere of his life. Whereas his relations with other high-powered males, such as Stalin, Beria, Khrushchev, and the KGB chief Ivan Serov, constitute the productive masculine aspects of his life, the protagonist's anxiety about being displaced from the public sphere into the "dark continent" of private life constitutes a key narrative complication in the mini-series. Zhukov's relations with multiple females also provide tabloid-style narrative interest for the otherwise boring biopic about the office intrigues of influential, middle-aged men. But the imitation melodrama's bottom line is still the same as it was in the 1970s: the heroic military commander stoically serves his country, no matter how irrational and distracting his women may be, because service to the state provides meaning to his life and helps him to preserve the integrity of his public identity.

Nikita Mikhalkov's career, which bridges the Soviet and post-Soviet eras, provides insight into the resilience of Soviet genre tropes. The films Mikhalkov made during the 1970s recall Hollywood melodramas in their non-Soviet ethos, especially their melodramatic clashes between private desires and historical forces. Whereas Soviet ideology demanded that public service override the private, Mikhalkov's films examined the private life as incomplete. That gap, filled with nostalgia, was where the empire was missing—not the Soviet empire per se, but a larger, more inclusive one. *Burnt by the Sun* (*Utomlennye solntsem* 1994), ostensibly an anti-Stalinist film, was also an "epic melodrama" (Larsen 2003, 492), a masterful merger of the period-piece aesthetics of aristocratic nests and a longing for a strong and noble father figure. In today's Russia, television serials en masse "transform[ed] the political into the non-political" (Bren 2010, 148–149), appealing to audiences as private citizens whose well-being is ensured by the "organic" unity between the state and its subjects. What in the 1970s used to be a rare insight into the usefulness of melodrama for naturalizing politics has become the shared know-how of Putin-era television creators, explaining to the viewers that the "right" agency comes from the benevolent and wise imperial state.

Bibliography

Agranovich, Leonid and Andrei Mikhalkov-Konchalovskii. "Script Proposal for *Siberiade*, Working Title *The Continent of Giants*." RGALI, fond 2944, op. 4, ed. kh. 4322: 2-6.

Altman, Rick. "A Semantic/Syntactic Approach to Film Genre." *Cinema Journal*, 23.3 (Spring 1984): 6-18.

Altman, Rick. *Film/Genre* (London: BFI, 1999).

Arkhangel'skii, Andrei. "Rodnee nekuda: o chem govoriat i progovarivaiutsia rossiiskie serialy?," *Colta*, 15 April 2015; www.colta.ru/articles/media/7020. Accessed 15 April 2015.

Belodubrovskaya, Mariia. "The Jockey and the Horse: Joseph Stalin and the Biopic Genre in Soviet cinema," *Studies in Russian and Soviet Cinema*, 5.1 (2011): 29-53.

"Beloe solntse pustyni." RGALI (Russian State Archive of Literature and Art), fond 2944, op.4, ed.kh. 1514.

Bergson, Henri. *Laughter: An Essay on the Meaning of the Comic* (Kobenhavn: Green Integer, 1999).

Beumers, Birgit. *Nikita Mikhalkov: Between Nostalgia and Nationalism* (London, NY: I.B. Tauris, 2005).

Bignell, Jonathan. *An Introduction to Television Studies* (London/NY: Routledge, 2004).

Bogomolov, Iurii. *Mikhail Kalatozov: Stranitsy tvorcheskoi biografii* (Moscow: Iskusstvo, 1989).

Bondarchuk, Sergei. "Otzyv khudozhestvennogo rukovoditelia tvorheskogo ob"edineniia Vremia (1oe Tvorcheskoe Ob"edinenie) na fil'm *Kalina krasnaia*." RGALI, fond 2944, op. 4, ed. kh. 2369: 3-4.

Bordwell, David. "The Art Cinema as a Mode of Film Practice," in Leo Braudy and Marshall Cohen (eds), *Film Theory and Criticism: Introductory Readings*. 5th edition (New York, NY: Oxford University Press, 1999), 716-724.

Boym, Svetlana. *Common Places: Mythologies of Everyday Life in Russia* (Cambridge, MA/London: Harvard University Press, 1994).

Bren, Paulina. *The Greengrocer and His TV: The Culture of Communism after the 1968 Prague Spring* (Ithaca, NY: Cornell University Press, 2010).

Brooks, Peter. *The Melodramatic Imagination: Balzac, Henry James, Melodrama, and the Mode of Excess* (New York: Columbia University Press, 1985).

Burgoyne, Robert. "Bare Life and Sovereignty in *Gladiator*," in Robert Bugoyne (ed.), *The Epic Film in World Culture* (New York, NY: Routledge, 2011), 82-98.

Cawelti, John. *The Six-Gun Mystique* (Bowling Green, OH: Bowling Green State University Popular Press, 1971).

Cawelti, John. *Adventure, Mystery, and Romance: Formula Stories as Art and Popular Culture* (Chicago: University of Chicago Press, 1976).
Chaikovskaia, Ol'ga. "Vne podozrenii. Prodolzhaem razgovor o detektive," *Sovetskii ekran*, 18 (1973): 9.
Chaikovskaia, Ol'ga. "I eshche neskol'ko tain," *Sovetskii ekran*, 10 (1973): 2–4.
"Chernyi prints," RGALI (Russian State Archive of Literature and Art), f. 2944, op. 4, ed. kh. 2396.
Chernyshova, Natalya. *Soviet Consumer Culture in the Brezhnev Era* (London and NY: Routledge, 2013).
Clark, Katerina. *Soviet Novel: History as Ritual*. 3rd edition (Bloomington: Indiana University Press, 2000).
Condee, Nancy. *The Imperial Trace: Recent Russian Cinema* (New York, NY: Oxford University Press, 2009a).
Condee, Nancy. "Veronika Fuses Out: Rape and Media Specificity in *The Cranes are Flying*," *Studies in Russian and Soviet Cinema*, 3.2 (2009b): 173–183.
Danilov, Andrei. "Kinoepopeia *Osvobozhdenie*: trudnyi put' k zriteliam," *Belorusskaia voiennaia gazeta*, July 21, 2012. http://vsr.mil.by/2012/07/21/kinoepopeya-osvobozhdenie-trudnyj-put-k-zritelyam/. Accessed June 22, 2013.
DeBlasio, Alyssa. "The New-Year Film as a Genre in Post-War Russian Cinema," *Studies in Russian and Soviet Cinema*, 2.1 (2008): 43–61.
Demin, Viktor. "Otmenno dlinnyi, dlinnyi, dlinnyi fil'm." *Sovetskii ekran*, 16 (1975): 7.
Demin, Viktor. "Dostoinstvo stremitel'nogo zhanra," in Andrei S. Plakhov (ed.), *Bol'shie problemy malogo ekrana* (Moscow: Iskusstvo, 1981), 103–122.
Doane, Mary Ann. "The Woman's Film: Possession and Address," in Christine Gledhill (ed.), *Home Is Where the Heart Is: Studies in Melodrama and the Woman's Film*, 3rd edition (London: BFI publishing, 2002), 283–298.
Dubin, Boris. "Pamiat', voina, pamiat' o voine. Konstruirovanie proshlogo v sotsial'noi praktike poslednikh desiatiletii," *Otechestvennye zapiski*, 43.4 (2008): 6–21.
Dubin, Boris. "Staroe i novoe v trekh teleekranizatsiiakh 2005 goda." *Novoe literaturnoe obozrenie*, 78 (2006). http://magazines.russ.ru/nlo/2006/78/du16-pr.html. Accessed 15 October 2014.
Dunlop, John. "Russian Nationalist Themes in Soviet Film of the 1970s," in Anna Lawton (ed.), *The Red Screen: Politics, Society, Art in Soviet Cinema* (London and NY: Routledge, 1992), 231–248.
Dymshits, Nina. *Sovetskaia kinomelodrama vchera i segodnia* (Moscow: Znanie, 1987).
Elsaesser, Thomas. "Tales of Sound and Fury: Observations on the Family Melodrama," *Monogram*, 4 (1972): 2–15.
Feuer, Jane. "Genre Study and Television," in Robert C. Allen (ed.), *Channels of Discourse, Reassembled: Television and Contemporary Criticism* (NY/London: Routledge, 1992), 104–120.

Feuer, Jane. *Seeing through the Eighties: Television and Reaganism* (Durham: Duke University Press, 1995).
First, Joshua. "From Spectator to 'Differentiated' Consumer: Audience Research (1965–1980)," *Kritika*, 9.2 (2008a): 317–344.
First, Joshua. "Making Soviet Melodrama Contemporary: Conveying 'Emotional Information' in the Era of Stagnation," *Studies in Russian and Soviet Cinema*, 2.1 (2008b): 21–42.
Fomin, Valerii. *Kino i vlast'. Sovetskoe kino, 1965–1985 gody: dokumenty, svidetel'stva, razmyshleniia* (Moscow: Materik, 1996).
Fomin, Valerii. "Laboratoriia. Shukshin," in A. Shemiakin and Iu. Mikheeva (Eds), *Posle ottepeli: Kinematograf 1970-kh* (Moscow: NII Kinoiskusstva, 2009), 327–435.
Gilliespie, David. *Russian Cinema* (Harlow, England: Longman, 2002).
Givens, John. "Vasilii Shukshin and the 'Audience of Millions': *Kalina Krasnaia* and the Power of Popular Cinema," *Russian Review*, 58.2 (1999): 268–285.
Golovskoi, Valerii. *Mezhdu ottepel'iu i glasnost'iu: kinematograf 70-kh* (Moscow: Materik, 2004).
Goscilo, Helena. "Widowhood as Genre and Profession à la Russe: Nation, Shadow, Curator, and Publicity Agent," in Helena Goscilo and Andrea Lanoux (Eds), *Gender and National Identity in Twentieth-Century Russian Culture* (DeKalb, IL: Northern Illinois University Press, 2006), 55–74.
Goscilo, Helena. "Putin's Performance of Masculinity: The Action Hero and Macho Sex-Object," in Helena Goscilo (Ed.), *Putin as Celebrity and Cultural Icon* (New York, NY: Routledge, 2013), 180–207.
Govorukhin, Stanislav. "Mesto vstrechi izmenit' nel'zia." Available at: www.kulichki.com/vv/ovys/kino/govoruxin.html. Accessed 8 March, 2014.
Gural'nik, U. "Dostizhenie eposa. *Voina i mir*. Fil'm i ego kritiki," *Iskusstvo kino*, 8 (1969): 102–117.
Haynes, John. *New Soviet Man: Gender and Masculinity in Stalinist Soviet Cinema* (Manchester, UK: Manchester University Press, 2003).
Holdsworth, Nick. "Russian Director Nikita Mikhalkov: Opponents of Russian Annexation of Crimea are the 'Enemy,'" *Hollywood Reporter*, October 9, 2014. Available at: www.hollywoodreporter.com/news/russian-director-nikita-mikhalkov-opponents-739484. Last accessed October 23, 2014.
Hutcheon, Linda. *Irony's Edge: The Theory and Politics of Irony* (New York, NY/London: Routledge, 1985).
Iampolski, Mikhail. "Russia: The Cinema of Anti-Modernity and Backward Progress," in Valentina Vitali and Paul Willemen (Eds), *Theorizing National Cinema* (London: BFI Publishing, 2006), 72–87.
Iurenev, Rostislav. "Vernost'," *Iskusstvo kino*, 12 (1957): 5–14.
Iurenev, Rostislav. *Sovetskaia kinokomediia* (Moscow: Nauka, 1964).

Ivanov, Nikolai. "Iz dnevnika direktora kartiny." *Sergei Bondarchuk v vospominaniiakh sovremennikov* (Moscow: Eksmo, 2003), 140–165.

Ivanov, Oleg. "Solnechnyi udar Mikhalkova: uspekh ili proval v prokate," *Ekspert*, 13 November, 2014. Available at: http://expert.ru/2014/11/13/solnechnyij-udar-mihalkova-uspeh-ili-proval-v-prokate/. Accessed 15 December, 2014.

Kaganovsky, Lilya. *How the Soviet Man was Unmade: Cultural Fantasy and Male Subjectivity under Stalin* (Pittsburgh: University of Pittsburgh Press, 2008).

Kaganovsky, Lilya. "The Cultural Logic of Late Socialism," *Studies in Russian and Soviet Cinema*, 3.2 (2009): 185–199.

Kassis, Vadim. "Velichie podviga: iaponskaia molodezh' o fil'me 'Osvobozhdenie.'" *Sovetskii ekran*, 24 (1973): 15.

Kelly, Catriona. "The Retreat from Dogmatism: Populism under Khrushchev and Brezhnev," in Katriona Kelly and David Shepherd (eds), *Russian Cultural Studies: An Introduction* (Oxford: Oxford University Press, 1998), 249–273.

Khanuitin, Iurii. "Sergei Bondarchuk," *Iskusstvo kino*, 7 (1962): 90–100.

Khanuitin, Iurii. "Skazki dlia raznogo vozrasta," *Sovetskii ekran*, 19 (1976): 4–5.

Khlopliankina, T. "Shura, Shurka i Tat'iana," *Sovetskii ekran*, 20 (1973): 8–9.

Komarov, N. "Informatsionnyi material po kinoepopee 'Osvobozhdenie'. Delo fil'ma Osvobozhdenie" Gosfilmofond Rossii.

Kondratovich, Aleksei. *Novomirskii dnevnik, 1967–70* (Moscow: Sovetskii pisatel', 1991).

Kosinova, M. "Parametry krizisa organizatsionno-ekonomicheskoi sistemy sovetskogo kinematografa," in A. Shemiakin and Iu. Mikheeva (eds), *Posle ottepeli. Kinematograf 70-kh* (Moscow: NII kinoiskusstva, 2009), 9–73.

Kovalov, Oleg. "Vykhodit fil'm Vladimira Men'shova *Shyrli-myrli*. Eshche odna popytka izgotovleniia 'narodnogo fil'ma–na sei raz komedii," *Noveishaia istoriia otechestvennogo kino, 1986–2000. Kino i kontekst*. Vol. 6, 1992–1996 (St Petersburg: Seans, 2004), 591–606.

Krechetnikov, Artem. "Trofeinaia Germaniia." http://news.bbc.co.uk/hi/russian/russia/newsid_6634000/6634155.stm. Accessed April 21, 2015.

"Krieg um 'Krieg um Frieden.'" *Neues Österreich*, July 21 (1965). Gosfilmofond Archive, "War and Peace." Delo 251.

Kudriavtsev, Sergei. "Poseshchaemost' otechestvennykh i zarubezhnykh fil'mov v sovetskom kinoprokate." http://kinanet.livejournal.com/689229.html. Accessed January 4, 2015.

Kudriavtsev, Sergei. "Zarubezhnye fil'my v sovetskom kinoprokate, chast' 1." http://kinanet.livejournal.com/13882.html. Accessed November 15, 2011.

Kurasov, V. "Fil'm o slave russkogo oruzhiia," *Sovetskii ekran*, 17 (1962): 4.

Larsen, Susan. "National Identity, Cultural Authority, and the Post–Soviet Blockbuster: Nikita Mikhalkov and Aleksei Balabanov," *Slavic Review*, 62.3 (Autumn 2003): 491–511.

Leitch, Thomas. *Crime Films* (New York NY: Cambridge University Press, 2002).

Lipovetsky, Mark. "Iskusstvo alibi: *Semnadtsat' mgnovenii vesny* v svete nashego opyta," *Neprikosnovennyi zapas*, 3 (2007): 131-146.
Lipovetsky, Mark. *Charms of the Cynical Reason: Tricksters in Soviet and Post-Soviet Culture* (Boston: Academic Studies Press, 2011).
Lukin, Iurii. "Kak eto bylo," *Iskusstvo kino*, 7 (1970): 8-16.
MacFadyen, David. *The Sad Comedy of El'dar Riazanov: An Introduction to Russia's Most Popular Filmmaker* (Montreal: McGill-Queen's University Press, 2003).
Margolit, Evgenii. "Melodrama v sovetskom kino," in Liubov' Arkus (ed.), *Noveishaia istoriia otechestvennogo kino/Kino i kontekst*, vol. 6 (St. Petersburg: Seans, 2004), 227- 237.
Markulan, Ianina. *Kinomelodrama; Fil'm uzhasov* (Leningrad: Iskusstvo, 1978).
Markulan, Ianina. *Zarubezhnyi kinodetektiv* (Leningrad: Iskusstvo, 1975).
Martín-Barbero, Jesús. "Memory and Form in Latin American Soap Opera," in Robert C. Allen (ed.), *To Be Continued... Soap Operas Around the World* (London: Routledge, 1995), 276-284.
Mashchenko, N. P. and Iu. Z. Moroz. *Dialogi o mnogoseriinom telefil'me*. Kiev: Mistetsstvo, 1986.
McReynolds, Louise and Joan Neuberger. "Introduction," in Louise McReynolds and Joan Neuberber (eds), *Imitations of Life: Two Centuries of Melodrama in Russia* (Durham, NC: Duke University Press, 2002), 1-24.
Merridale, Catherine. *Red Fortress. History and Illusion in the Kremlin* (New York: Picador, 2014).
Mickiewicz, Ellen. *Media and the Russian Public* (NY: Praeger, 1981).
Mikhalkov-Konchalovskii, Andrei. "V poiske," *Iskusstvo kino*, 9 (Sept 1975): 145-157.
Mikheeva, Iu. "Neser'eznoe kino: Sovetskaia intelligentsia v komediiakh 70-kh," in A. Shemiakin and Iu. Mikheeva (eds), *Posle ottepeli. Kinematograf 70-kh* (Moscow: NII Kinoiskusstva, 2009), 271-295.
Morozov, Petr. Petition to the Ministry of Culture, Russia, to Ban Fedor Bondarchuk's film Stalingrad. 1 November 2013. "To ban the exhibition of F. Bondarchuk's film Stalingrad in the Russian Federation; to ban the distribution of this film abroad; to withdraw the bid for Oscar." Change.org
Motyl', Vladimir. "Skvoz' prizmu poezii," *Soveskii ekran*, 19 (1976): 8-9, 9.
"Music Week Sets Awards for Best Acts," *Billboard*, February 22, 1975, 57.
N.a. "Chto takoe prikliuchencheskii fil'm?" *Sovetskii ekran*, 9 (1969a): 7-9.
N.a. "Chto takoe prikliuchencheskii fil'm?" *Sovetskii ekran*, 10 (1969b): 12-13.
N.a. "Chto takoe prikliuchencheskii fil'm?" *Sovetskii ekran*, 18 (1969c): 6-7.
N.a. "Fond kino opredelilsia s proektami kompanii-liderov," *Gazeta.ru*, 30 August 2013; http://www.gazeta.ru/culture/news/2013/08/30/n_3148781.shtml. Accessed 2 November, 2014.
N.a. "Neskol'ko slov v spore," *Sovetskii ekran*, 4 (1975): 9.
N.a. "O khudozhestvennykh printsipakh, vzgliadakh i vkusakh," *Iskusstvo kino*, 10 (1959): 41-46.

Naiman, Eric and Anne Nesbet. "Documentary Discipline: Three Interrogations of Stanislav Govorukhin," in Nancy Condee (ed.), *Soviet Hieroglyphics: Visual Culture in Late Twentieth Century Russia* (Bloomington: Indiana University Press and BFI, 1995), 52–67.

Naremore, James. "American Film Noir: The History of an Idea," *Film Quarterly*, 49.2 (1995–1996): 12–29.

Neale, Steve. *Genre* (London: British Film Institute, 1980).

Nekrasov, Viktor. "Slova 'velikie' i prostye," *Iskusstvo kino*, 5 (1959): 45–61.

Nicholas, Mary A. *Writers at Work: Russian Production Novels and the Construction of Soviet Culture* (Lewisburg: Bucknell University Press, 2010).

Norris, Stephen M. *Blockbuster History in the New Russia: Movies, Memory, and Patriotism* (Bloomington: Indiana University Press, 2012).

Norris, Stephen M. "Tolstoy's Comrades: Sergei Bondarchuk's *War and Peace* (1966–67) and the Origins of Brezhnev Culture," in Lorna Fitzsimmons and Michael A. Denner, (eds), *Tolstoy on Screen* (Evanston: Illinois: Northwestern University Press, 2015), 155–178.

Novikov, V.G. "Posleslovie," in Olga and Aleksandr Lavrov. *Sledstvie vedut znatoki*, (Moscow: Iskusstvo, 1985), 269–270.

Novikov, V.G. "Posleslovie," in Ol'ga and Aleksandr Lavrov, *Sledstvie vedut znatoki Stsenarii televizionnykh fil'mov* (Moscow: Iskusstvo, 1989), 270–71.

"Obyknovennoe chudo." Mosfilm Studio Archive. Fond 209, op. 12, delo 2477.

"Obzor pisem telezritelei za 1975 god." GARF (State Archive of the Russian Federation). Fond 6903, op. 36, ed. kh. 40.

Orlov, Dal'. "Bagration–eto pobeda," *Iskusstvo kino*, 6 (1971): 18–25.

"Osvobozhdenie Evropy." RGALI (Russian State Archive of Literature and Art), fond 2944, op. 4, ed. kh. 1294.

Oushakine, Serguei. "Crimes of Substitution: Detection in Late-Soviet Society," *Public Culture*, 15.3 (2003): 427–451.

Oushakine, Serguei. "Laughter under Socialism: Exposing the Ocular in Soviet Jocularity." *Slavic Review*, 70.2 (Summer 2011): 247–255.

Ozerov, Iurii. "Vosslavit' podvig naroda," *Iskusstvo kino*, 2 (1971): 1–4.

Paramonova, Kira. *V zritel'nom zale deti* (Moscow: Iskusstvo, 1967).

"Petrovka 38." RGALI (Russian State Archive of Literature and Art), fond 2944, op. 4, ed. kh. 5300.

"Pis'ma," *Sovetskii ekran*, 13 (1974): 1.

Plakhov, Andrei (ed.). *Bol'shie problemy malogo ekrana* (Moscow: Iskusstvo, 1981).

Poliakova, Svetlana. "Antinarodnyi kompozitor i narodnaia muzyka," *Novaia gazeta*, 73 (25 September 2006); http://www.novayagazeta.ru/data/2006/73/38.html. Accessed June 21, 2010.

Prokhorov, Alexander. "Cinema of Attractions versus Narrative Cinema: Leonid Gaidai's Comedies and El'dar Riazanov's Satires of the 1960s," *Slavic Review*, 62.3 (Fall 2003): 455–472.

Prokhorov, Alexander. "Russian and Soviet Adventure Film," in Birgit Beumers (ed.), *Directory of World Cinema: Russia 2* (Bristol, UK: Intellect, 2014), 66-70.
Prokhorova, Elena. "Can the Meeting Place Be Changed: Crime and Identity Discourse in the Russian Television Series of the 1990s," *Slavic Review*, 62.3 (Autumn 2003): 512-524.
Prokhorova, Elena. "Mending the Rupture: The War Trope and the Return of the Imperial Father in 1970s Cinema," in Helena Goscilo and Yana Hashamova (eds), *Cinepaternity: Fathers and Sons in Soviet and Post-Soviet Film* (Bloomington and Indianapolis: Indiana University Press, 2010), 51-69.
"Proshu slova." RGALI (Russian State Archive of Literature and Art), fond 2944, op. 4, ed. kh. 3034.
"Protokol sovetsko-amerikanskikh peregovorov po voprosam kino, prokhodivshikh v Moskve v sentiabre-oktiabre 1958 g." RGALI, fond 2918, op. 1. ed. kh. 80.
Putin, Vladimir. "Dlia russkikh na miru i smert' krasna," http://www.regnum.ru/news/polit/1792501.html. Accessed April 20, 2014.
Putin, Vladimir. *Priamaia liniia s Vladimirom Putinym*. Television Program. Channel Russia-1, date of broadcast: December 16, 2010.
Rajagopalan, Sudja. *Indian Films in the Soviet Union: The Culture of Movie-going after Stalin* (Bloomington: Indiana University Press, 2009).
Razzakov, Fedor. *Gibel' sovetskogo kino.* 2 vols. (Moscow: Eksmo: 2008).
Reid, Susan E. and David Crowley. "Style and Socialism: Modernity and Material Culture in post-war Eastern Europe," in David Crowley and Susan E. Reid (eds), *Style and Socialism: Modernity and Material Culture in Post-war Eastern Europe* (Oxford and New York: Berg, 2000), 1-24.
Revich, Vsevolod. "Sviatoi Luka ostaetsia na meste," *Sovetskii Ekran*, 10 (1971): 7.
Riazanov, El'dar. *Nepodvedennye itogi* (Moscow: Vagrius, 2005).
Roth-Ey, Kristin. *Moscow Prime Time: How the Soviet Union Built the Media Empire that Lost the Cultural Cold War* (Ithaca and London: Cornell University Press, 2011).
Schatz, Thomas. *Hollywood Genres: Formulas, Filmmaking, and the Studio System* (NY: Random House, 1981).
Shatsillo, "Klassika na marshe," *Iskusstvo kino*, 8 (1969): 43-76.
Shaw, Tony, and Denise Youngblood. *Cinematic Cold War: The American and Soviet Struggle for Hearts and Minds* (Lawrence: UP of Kansas, 2010).
Shemiakin, Andrei and Iu. Mikheeva (eds). *Posle ottepeli: kinematograf 1970-kh* (Moscow: NII Kinoiskusstva, 2009).
Shilova, Irina. "O melodrame," *Voprosy kinoiskussva*, vol. 17 (Moscow: Iskusstvo, 1976): 112-135.
Shumiatskii, B. *Kinematografiia millionov. Opyt analiza* (Moscow: Kinofotoizdat, 1935).
Sizov, Nikolai. "Letter to Fillipp Ermash about the Script Proposal by Andrei Mikhalkov-Konchalovskii and Leonid Agranovich, working title *The Continent of Giants.*" RGALI (Russian State Archive of Literature and Art), fond 2944, op. 4. ed. kh. 4322, l.

Smelkov, Iu. "Poeziia i pravda," *Sovetskii ekran*, 1 (1975): 12–13.
Smirnov, S. "Prikliuchencheskii—ne vtorosortnyi," *Sovetskii ekran*, 23 (1969): 18.
Sopin, Artem. "Spisok redaktsii sovetskikh i rossiiskikh igrovykh fil'mov," *Kinovedcheskie zapiski*, 100–101(2011–2012): 606–645.
Taylor, Richard. "Ideology as Mass Entertainment: Boris Shumyatsky and Soviet Cinema in the 1930s," in Richard Taylor and Ian Christie (eds), *Inside the Film Factory* (London: Routledge, 1991), 193–216.
Taylor, Richard. "Singing on the Steppes for Stalin: Ivan Pyr'ev and the Kolkhoz Musical in Soviet Cinema," *Slavic Review*, 58.1 (1999): 143–159.
"Tematicheskii plan Tsentral'nogo televideniia na iiun'–avgust, 1974." GARF, f. 6903, op. 33, ed. kh. 45.
"Teni ischezaiut v polden'." RGALI (Russian State Archive of Literature and Art), fond 2944, op.4, ed.kh. 2583.
Tsitriniak, G. "Napravlenie glavnogo udara. Reportazh," *Iskusstvo kino*, 5 (1970): 7–19.
Tsymbal, Evgenii. Personal Interview. 18 November, 2009.
Tumarkin, Nina. *The Living and the Dead: The Rise and Fall of the Cult of World War II in Russia* (New York: Basic Books, 1994).
Turovskaia, Maiia. "'Da' i 'net'," *Iskusstvo kino*, 12 (1957): 14–18.
Turovskaia, Maiia. *Geroi bezgeroinogo vremeni* (Moscow: Iskusstvo, 1971).
"Ukroshchenie ognia," RGALI (Russian State Archive of Literature and Art), fond 2944, op. 4, ed. kh. 2202.
Usachev, Ivan. *Tainy sovetskogo kino. Mesto vstrechi izmenit' nel'zia*. Television program. Channel TV Tsentr, date of broadcast: 9 September, 2013.
Vartanov, Anri. "Otmenno dlinnyi, dlinnyi, dlinnyi fil'm," *Sovetskii ekran*, 6 (1975): 14.
"Versiia polkovnika Zorina." RGALI (Russian State Archive of Literature and Art), fond 2944, op. 4, ed. kh. 2396.
Viktorov, B.A. "Interv'iu vmesto poslesloviia," in Ol'ga and Aleksandr Lavrov. *Sledstvie vedut znatoki. Sbornik telep'es* (Moscow: Iskusstvo, 1974), 270–272.
Viktorov, B.A. "Razmyshleniia nad pochtoi," in Ol'ga and Aleksandr Lavrov, *Sledstvie vedut znatoki* (Moscow: Iskusstvo, 1977), 266–270.
Vishnevskaia, Inna. "Detektiv—liubov' moia," *Sovetskii ekran*, 17 (1980): 9, 12–13.
"Vozvrashchenie Sviatogo Luki." RGALI (Russian State Archive of Literature and Art), fond 2944, op. 4, ed. kh. 1755.
Wilson, Christopher P. *Cop Knowledge: Police Power and Cultural Narrative in Twentieth-Century America* (Chicago: The University of Chicago Press, 2000).
Winston, Robert P. and Nancy Mellerski. *The Public Eye: Ideology and the Police Procedural* (New York, NY: St Martin's Press, 1992).
Woll, Josephine. *The Cranes are Flying* (London: Tauris, 2003).
Wright, Will. *Six Guns and Society: A Structural Study of the Western* (Berkeley/Los Angeles/London: University of California Press, 1975).

Youngblood, Denise. *Russian War Films: On the Cinema Front, 1914–2005* (Lawrence, KS: University Press of Kansas, 2007).

Youngblood, Denise. *Bondarchuk's War and Peace: Literary Classic to Soviet Cinematic Epic* (Lawrence, KS: University Press of Kansas, 2014).

Yurchak, Alexei. *Everything Was Forever, Until It Was No More: The Last Soviet Generation* (Princeton: Princeton University Press, 2005).

"Za kruglym stolom – televizionisty," *Iskusstvo kino*, 3 (1965): 53–67.

Zolotusskii, Igor'. "Dobavlenie k eposu (Tosltoi v romane i Tolstoi v fil'me)," *Novyi mir*, 6 (1968): 269–283.

Zorkaia, Neia. "Otmenno dlinnyi, dlinnyi, dlinnyi fil'm," *Sovetskii ekran*, 1 (1975): 18.

Zorkaia, Neia. *Fol'klor. Lubok. Ekran* (Moscow: Iskusstvo, 1994).

Zorkaia, Neia. Personal Interview. Pittsburgh, May 1, 2001.

Zorkii, A. "Odin raz pro liubov'," *Sovetskii ekran*, 17 (1968): 2.

Zorkii, A. "V chem secret znatokov," in Ol'ga and Aleksandr Lavrov. *Sledstvie vedut znatoki. Sbornik telep'es*. Moscow: Iskusstvo, 1974. 3–9.

Zvereva, Vera. "Zakon i kulak: 'Rodnye' militseiskie serialy," *NLO*, 78 (2006). http://magazines.russ.ru:81/nlo/2006/78/zver20.html. Accessed May 7, 2015.

Zvereva, Vera. "Novye russkie serialy," in N.B. Kirillova (ed.), *Mediakul'tura novoi Rossii. Metodologiia, tekhnologii, praktiki*, vol. 2 (Ekaterinburg/Moscow: Akademicheskii proekt, 2007), 166–181.

"Zvezda plenitel'nogo schast'ia," *Sovetskii ekran*, 11 (1974): 10–12.

Filmography

The 9th Company (*Deviataia rota*). Dir. Fedor Bondarchuk. 2005.
12. Dir. Nikita Mikhalkov. 2007.
12 Angry Men. Dir. Sidney Lumet. 1957.
A Lovers' Romance (*Romans o vliublennykh*). Dir. Andrei Konchalovskii. 1974
A Person Is Born (*Chelovek rodilsia*). Dir. Vasilii Ordynskii. 1956.
A Simple Story (*Prostaia istoriia*). Dir. Iurii Egorov. 1960.
The Adventures of Prince Florizel (*Prikliucheniia printsa Florizelia*). Dir. Evgenii Tatarskii. 1979.
Afonia (*Afonia*). Dir. Georgii Daneliia. 1976.
Alexander Nevsky. Dir. Sergei Eisenstein. 1938.
All This Is About Him (*I eto vse o nem*). Dir. Igor' Shatrov. 1977.
And Quiet Flows the Don (*Tikhii Don*). Dir. Sergei Gerasimov. 1957–58.
And Quiet Flows the Don (*Tikhii Don*). Dir. Sergei Bondarchuk and Fedor Bondarchuk. 2006; 2009.
Andrei Rublev. Dir. Andrei Tarkovskii. 1966.
Aniskin and Fantomas (*Aniskin i Fantomas*). Dir. Mikhail Zharov, Vitalii Ivanov and Vladimir Rapoport. 1974.
Aniskin, Yet Again (*I snova Aniskin*). Dir. Mikhail Zharov and Vitalii Ivanov. 1977.
Anna Karenina. Dir. Aleksandr Zarkhi. 1967.
Autumn Marathon (*Osennii marafon*). Dir. Georgii Daneliia, 1979.
Ballad of a Soldier (*Ballada o soldate*). Dir. Grigorii Chukhrai. 1959.
Barber of Siberia (*Sibirskii tsiriul'nik*). Dir. Nikita Mikhalkov. 1999.
Battle for Moscow (*Bitva za Moskvu*). Dir. Iurii Ozerov. 1985.
Battle of the Bulge. Dir. Ken Annakin. 1965.
Be Not Born Beautiful (*Ne rodis' krasivoi*). STS Channel. 2005–06.
Bed and Sofa (*Tret'ia Meshchanskaia*). Dir. Abram Room. 1927.
Behind the Department Store's Window (*Za vitrinoi univermaga*). Dir. Samson Samsonov. 1955.
Belorussia Station (*Belorusskii vokzal*). Dir. Andrei Smirnov. 1970.
Beware of a Car (*Beregis' avtomobilia*). Dir. El'dar Riazanov. 1966.
The Black Prince (*Chernyi prints*). Dir. Anatolii Bobrovskii. 1973.
Blocade (*Blokada*). Dir. Mikhail Ershov. 1977.
Bobby. Raj Kapoor. 1973.
Boris Godunov. Dir. Sergei Bondarchuk. 1986.
Brezhnev. Channel One. 2005.

Brief Encounters (*Korotkie vstrechi*). Dir. Kira Muratova. 1967.
Brigade (*Brigada*). Dir. Aleksei Sidorov. 2002.
Brother (*Brat*). Dir Aleksei Balabanov. 1997.
Burnt by the Sun (*Utomlennye solntsem*). Dir. Nikita Mikhalkov. 1994.
Burnt by the Sun 2: Exodus (*Predstoianie*); *The Citadel* (*Tsitadel'*). Dir. Nikita Mikhalkov. 2010–11.
Carnival Night (*Karnaval'naia noch'*). Dir. El'dar Riazanov. 1956.
The Case of the Grocery Store Number One (*Delo gastronoma nomer odin*). Channel One. 2011.
Chapaev. Dir. Georgii Vasil'ev and Sergei Vasil'ev. 1934.
Choice of Target (*Vybor tseli*). Dir. Igor' Talankin. 1974.
Circus (*Tsirk*). Dir. Grigorii Aleksandrov. 1936.
Colonel Zorin's Version (*Versiia polkovnika Zorina*). Dir. Andrei Ladynin. 1978.
The Communist (*Kommunist*). Dir. Iulii Raizman. 1957.
Cop Wars (*Mentovskie voiny*). NTV Channel. 2004-to present.
Cops: Streets of Broken Lights (*Menty: Ulitsy razbitykh fonarei*). 1998 to present.
Cossacks of the Kuban (*Kubanskie kazaki*). Dir. Ivan Pyr'ev. 1949.
Cranes Are Flying (*Letiat zhuravli*). Dir. Mikhail Kalatozov. 1957.
The Crew (*Ekipazh*). Dir. Aleksandr Mitta. Mosfilm. 1980.
Cuckoo (*Kukushka*). Dir. Aleksandr Rogozhkin. 2002.
Daughters and Mothers (*Dochki-materi*). Dir. Sergei Gerasimov. 1974.
Dawns Are Quiet Here (*A zori zdes' tikhie*). Dir. Stanislav Rostotskii. 1972.
Deadly Force (*Uboinaia sila*). 2000–2005.
Death Wish. Dir. Michael Winner. 1974.
Diamond Arm (*Brilliantovaia ruka*). Dir. Leonid Gaidai. 1968.
Divorce: Italian Style. Dir. Pietro Germi. 1961.
The Dog in the Manger (*Sobaka na sene*). Dir. Ian Frid. 1977.
Elder Son (*Starshii syn*). Dir. Vitalii Mel'nikov. 1975.
The End of St. Petersburg (*Konets Sankt-Peterburga*). Dir. Vsevolod Pudovkin. 1927.
Engineer Kochin's Mistake (*Oshibka inzhenera Kochina*). Dir. Alexander Macheret. 1939.
Eternal Call (*Vechnyi zov*). Dir. Vladimir Krasnopol'skii and Valerii Uskov. 1973–1983.
A European Story (*Evropeiskaia istoriia*). Dir. Igor' Gostev. 1984.
The Extraordinary Adventures of Italians in Russia (*Neveroiatnye prikliucheniia ital'iantsev v Rossii*). Dir. El'dar Riazanov. 1973.
The Extraordinary Adventures of Mr. West in the Land of Bolsheviks (*Neobychainye prikliucheniia mistera Vesta v strane bol'shevikov*). Dir. Lev Kuleshov. 1924.
The Fall of Berlin (*Padenie Berlina*). Dir. Mikhail Chiaureli. 1949.
Fate of a Man (*Sud'ba cheloveka*). Dir. Sergei Bondarchuk. 1959.
Father Sergius (*Otets Sergii*). Dir. Igor' Talankin. 1978.
Flight Crew (*Ekipazh*). Dir. Nikolai Lebedev. 2016.
A Forgotten Melody for Flute (*Zabytaia melodiia dlia fleity*). Dir. El'dar Riazanov. 1987.

The Formula of Love (*Formula liubvi*). Dir. Mark Zakharov. 1984.
The Forsyte Saga. BBC. 1967.
Front beyond the Frontline (*Front za liniei fronta*). Dir. Igor' Gostev. 1977.
Front beyond the Enemy Lines (*Front v tylu vraga*). Dir. Igor' Gostev. 1981.
Front without Flanks (*Front bez flangov*). Dir. Igor' Gostev. 1975.
Furtseva. Channel One. 2011.
Garage (*Garazh*). Dir. El'dar Riazanov. 1979.
Gentlemen of Fortune (*Dzhentel'meny udachi*). Dir. Aleksandr Seryi. 1971.
A Girl without an Address (*Devushka bez adresa*). Dir. El'dar Riazanov, 1957.
The Gold Mine (*Zolotaia mina*). Dir. Evgenii Tatarskii. 1977.
Good Luck! (*V dobryi chas!*). Dir. Viktor Eisymont. 1956.
Guys! (*Muzhiki!*). Dir. Iskra Babich. 1981.
Gypsies Are Found Near Heaven (*Tabor ukhodit v nebo*). Dir. Emil' Lotianu. 1975.
Gypsy (*Tsygan*). Dir. Evgenii Matveev. 1967.
Hamlet. Dir. Grigorii Kozintsev. 1964.
Happy Together (*Schastlivy vmeste*). TNT Channel. 2006–2013.
His Girl Friday. Dir. Howard Hawks. 1940.
The House that Swift Built (*Dom, kotoryi postroil Svift*). Dir. Mark Zakharov. 1982.
How the Steel Was Tempered (*Kak zakalialas' stal'*). Dir. Nikolai Mashchenko. 1973.
I Want the Floor (*Proshu slova*). Dir. Gleb Panfilov, 1976.
Investigation is Conducted by Bread Rolls (*Sledstvie vedut kolobki*). Dir. Igor' Kovalev and Alexander Tatarskii. 1983.
The Investigation is Conducted by Experts (*Sledstvie vedut znatoki*). Dir. Viacheslav Brovkin et al. 1971–89; 2002–03.
The Investigation Was Conducted by . . . (*Sledstvie veli . . .*). 2006 to the present.
The Irony of Fate (*Ironiia sud'by*). Dir. El'dar Riazanov. 1975.
The Irony of Fate. A Sequel (*Ironiia sud'by. Prodolzhenie*). Dir. Timur Bekmambetov. 2007.
It Happened in Pen'kovo (*Delo bylo v Pen'kove*). Dir. Stanislav Rostotskii. 1957.
It Happened One Night. Dir. Frank Capra. 1934.
It's a Mad, Mad, Mad, Mad World. Dir. Stanley Kramer. 1963.
Ivan's Childhood (*Ivanovo detstvo*). Dir. Andrei Tarkovskii. 1962.
Just You Wait! (*Nu, pogodi!*). Dir. Viacheslav Kotenochkin et al. 1969–2006.
Kamenskaia. NTV Channel. 2000–2011.
Karl Marx. The Younger Years (*Karl Marks. Molodye gody*). Dir. Lev Kulidzhanov. 1980.
Kidnapping Caucasian Style (*Kavkazskaia plennitsa*). Dir. Leonid Gaidai. 1967.
Lenin in October (*Lenin v Oktiabre*). Dir. Mikhail Romm. 1937.
Liberation (*Osvobozhdenie*). Dir. Iurii Ozerov. 1968–72.
Liquidation (*Likvidatsiia*). Dir. Sergei Ursuliak. 2007.
Little Crane (*Zhuravushka*). Dir. Nikolai Moskalenko. 1968.
The Longest Day. Dir. Ken Annakin, Andrew Marton, and Bernhard Wicki. 1962.
Look for a Woman (*Ishchite zhenshchinu*). Dir. Alla Surikova. 1981.

Los Ricos También Lloran (*The Rich Also Cry*). Televisa/Mexico. 1979–80.
Major Whirlwind (*Maior Vikhr'*). Dir. Evgenii Tashkov. 1967.
The Man Who Doubts (*Chelovek, kotoryi somnevaetsia*). Dir. Leonid Agranovich and Vladimir Semakov. 1963.
The Meeting Place Cannot be Changed (*Mesto vstrechi izmenit' nel'zia*). Dir. Stanislav Govorukhin. 1979.
Member of the Government (*Chlen pravitel'stva*). Dir. Aleksandr Zarkhi and Iosif Kheifits. 1939.
Moscow Does Not Believe in Tears (*Moskva slezam ne verit*). Dir. Vladimir Men'shov. 1980.
Moscow Police, Forever! (*MUR est' MUR*). 2004–06.
The Most Important Assignment (*Osobo vazhnoe zadanie*). Dir. Evgenii Matveev. 1980.
Much Ado about Nothing (*Mnogo shuma iz nichego*). Dir Samson Samsonov. 1973.
My Fair Nanny (*Moia prekrasnaia niania*). STS Channel. 2004–2009.
The Nest of Gentlefolk (*Dvorianskoe gnezdo*). Dir. Andrei Konchalovskii. 1969.
Nobody Wanted to Die (*Nikto ne khotel umirat'*). *Dir.* Vitautas Zhalakiavichus. 1966.
The Odyssey of Detective Gurov (*Odisseia syshchika Gurova*). NTV Channel. 2013.
Office Romance (*Sluzhebnyi roman*). Dir. El'dar Riazanov. 1977.
Officers (*Ofitsery*). Dir. Vladimir Rogovoi. 1971.
Ogareva 6. Dir. Boris Grigor'ev. 1980.
Oh, Sport, You are Peace! (*Oh, sport, ty—mir!*). Dir. Iurii Ozerov. 1981.
Old Men-Robbers (*Stariki-razboiniki*). Dir. El'dar Riazanov. 1971.
Once More about Love (*Eshche raz pro liubov'*). Dir. Georgii Natanson. 1968.
An Ordinary Miracle (*Obyknovennoe chudo*). Dir. Mark Zakharov. 1978.
Patton. Dir. Franklin Shaffner. 1970.
A Person Is Born (*Chelovek rodilsia*). Dir. Vasilii Ordynskii. 1956.
Petrovka 38. Dir. Boris Grigor'ev. 1980.
Private Life (*Chastnaia zhizn'*). Dir. Iulii Raizman. 1982.
The Pub Thirteen Chairs (*Kabachok 13 stul'ev*). 1966–80.
Radiant Path (*Svetlyi put'*). Dir. Grigorii Aleksandrov. 1940.
Red Bells (*Krasnye kolokola*). Dir. Sergei Bondarchuk. 1982.
The Return of St. Luke (*Vozvrashchenie 'Sviatogo Luki'*). Dir. Anatolii Bobrovskii. 1970.
The Road to Calvary (*Khozhdenie po mukam*). Dir. Vasilii Ordynskii. 1977.
Road to Life (*Putevka v zhizn'*). Dir. Nikolai Ekk. 1931.
Ruthless Romance (*Zhestokii romans*). Dir. El'dar Riazanov. 1984.
Santa Barbara. NBC. 1984–93.
Seduced and Abandoned. Dir. Pietro Germi. 1963.
Serezha (*Serezha*). Dir. Georgii Daneliia and Igor Talankin. 1960.
Seven Brides of Lance-Corporal Zbruev (*Sem' nevest efreitora Zbrueva*). Dir. Vitalii Mel'nikov. 1972.
Seventeen Moments of Spring (*Semnadtsat' mgnovenii vesny*). Dir. Tat'iana Lioznova. 1973.

Several Days from the Life of I.I. Oblomov (*Neskol'ko dnei iz zhizni I.I. Oblomova*). Dir. Nikita Mikhalkov. 1979.
Shadows Disappear at Noon (*Teni ischezaiut v polden'*). Dir. Vladimir Krasnopol'skii and Valerii Uskov. 1971.
Sharlotta's Necklace (*Kol'e Sharlotty*). Dir. Evgenii Tatarskii. 1984.
She Loves You! (*Ona vas liubit!*). Dir. Semen Derevianskii and Rafail Suslovich. 1957.
Siberiade (*Sibiriada*). Dir. Andrei Konchalovskii. 1979.
The Sleuth (*Syshchik*). Dir. Vladimir Fokin. 1979.
Snowball Berry Red (*Kalina krasnaia*). Dir. Vasilii Shukshin. 1973.
Soldiers of Freedom (*Soldaty svobody*). Dir. Iurii Ozerov. 1977.
The Son of the Father of the People (*Syn ottsa narodov*). Channel One. 2013.
Stalingrad. Dir. Iurii Ozerov. 1989.
Stalingrad. Dir. Fedor Bondarchuk. 2013.
Standoff (*Protivostoianie*). Dir. Semen Aranovich. 1985.
The Star of Captivating Happiness (*Zvezda plenitel'nogo schast'ia*). Dir. Vladimir Motyl'. 1975.
Stepmother (*Machekha*). Dir. Oleg Bondarev. 1973.
The Steppe (*Step'*). Dir. Sergei Bondarchuk. 1977.
The Straw Hat (*Solomennaia shliapka*). Dir. Leonid Kvinikhidze. 1974.
The Strogovs (*Strogovy*). Dir. Vladimir Vengerov. 1976.
Sunstroke (*Solnechnyi udar*). Dir. Nikita Mikhalkov. 2014.
The Taming of Fire (*Ukroshchenie ognia*). Dir. Daniil Khrabrovitskii. 1972.
That Very Same Munchausen (*Tot samyi Miunkhausen*). Dir. Mark Zakharov. 1979.
Thirty Three (*Tridtsat' tri*). Dir. Georgii Daneliia. 1965.
Three Men in a Boat, To Say Nothing of the Dog (*Troe v lodke, ne schitaia sobaki*). Dir. Naum Birman. 1979.
Three Poplar Trees on Pliushchikha Street (*Tri topolia na Pliushchikhe*). Dir. Tat'iana Lioznova. 1967.
Time (*Vremia*). News Broadcast. 1968–.
To Kill a Dragon (*Ubit' Drakona*). Dir. Mark Zakharov. 1989.
Tragedy of a Century (*Tragediia veka*). Dir. Iurii Ozerov. 1993–1994.
The Train Station for Two (*Vokzal dlia dvoikh*). Dir. El'dar Riazanov. 1982.
The Twelve Chairs (*Dvenadtsat' stul'ev*). Dir. Leonid Gaidai. 1971.
The Twelve Chairs (*Dvenadtsat' stul'ev*). Dir. Mark Zakharov. 1976.
Twentieth Century. Dir. Howard Hawks. 1934.
Twenty Hours. Dir. Zoltán Fábri. 1965.
An Unfinished Piece for a Mechanical Piano (*Neokonchennaia p'esa dlia mekhanicheskogo pianino*). Dir. Nikita Mikhalkov. 1977.
Vacation in September (*Otpusk v sentiabre*). Dir. Vitalii Mel'nikov. 1979.
Valerii Chkalov. Dir. Mikhail Kalatozov. 1941.
Victory (*Pobeda*). Dir. Evgenii Matveev. 1984.

Village Detective (*Derevenskii detektiv*). Dir. Ivan Lukinskii. 1968.
Volga, Volga. Dir. Grigorii Aleksandrov. 1938.
The Voronins (*Voroniny*). STS Channel. 2009-present.
The Voroshilov Sharpshooter (*Voroshilovskii strelok*). Dir. Stanislav Govorukhin. 1999.
The Vow (*Kliatva*). Dir. Mikhail Chiaureli. 1946.
War and Peace. Dir. King Vidor and Mario Soldati. 1956.
War and Peace (*Voina i mir*). Dir. Sergei Bondarchuk. 1965–67.
Waterloo (*Vaterloo*). Dir. Sergei Bondarchuk. 1970.
When Trees Were Big (*Kogda derev'ia byli bol'shimi*). Dir. Lev Kulidzhanov. 1962.
White Bim Black Ear (*Belyi Bim Chernoe ukho*). Dir. Stanislav Rostotskii. 1977.
The White Dress. Dir. Hassan Ramzi. 1974.
White Sun of the Desert (*Below solntse pustyni*). Dir. Vladimir Motyl'. 1970.
Yesenia. Dir. Alfredo Crevenna. 1971.
Yo soy Betty, la fea. RCN Televisión. 1999–2001.
Zhukov. Channel One. 2012.

Index

12 (2007), 118
12 Angry Men (2007), 118

Abdulov, Aleksandr, 131, 134–5, 138–9
Academy of Motion Picture Arts and Sciences, 39
Adamov, Arkadii, 78
Adventures of Prince Florizel, The (1979), 113
Afonia (1976), 152, 157
Agranovich, Leonid, 70, 157
Aleksandrov, Aleksandr, 51
Aleksandrov, Grigorii, 17, 107, 114, 117
Alentova, Vera, 184
Alexander Nevsky (1938), 53–5
All This Is About Him (1977), 158
Allen, Woody, 40
Allende, Salvador, 176–177
And Quiet Flows the Don (1957–8), 74
And Quiet Flows the Don (2006, 2009), 7, 60–1
Andrei Rublev (1966), 37
Aniskin and Fantomas (1974), 75
Aniskin, Yet Again (1977), 75
Anna Karenina (1967), 32, 74
Annakin, Ken, 46
anniversary film, 45–6, 48, 52, 59–60, 92
Aranovich, Semen, see *Standoff*
art cinema, 8, 11, 29–30, 37, 115, 129
Art of Cinema, 8–9, 11, 15, 38, 40–1, 44, 46, 55, 57, 174
auteur theory, 2–3, 9
Autumn Marathon (1979), 121, 152, 172

Baba Yaga, 37
Babich, Iskra, 172
Balabanov, Aleksei, 92
Ballad of a Soldier (1959), 23, 51
Barber of Siberia (1999), 25, 61, 63
Batalov, Aleksei, 186
Battle for Moscow (1985), 59–60
Battle of the Bulge (1965), 47

Be Not Born Beautiful (2005–6), 189, 193
Bed and Sofa (1927), 120
Behind the Department Store's Window (1955), 108
Bekmambetov, Timur, 147, 193
Beliavskii, Aleksandr, 87, 91, 94, 122
Belorussia Station (1970), 152, 165, 183
Beware of a Car (1966), 108, 117
Bibergan, Vadim, 181
Biopic, 4, 195
Black Prince, The (1973), 74–5
Blockade (1977), 24
Bobby (1973), 173
Bobrovskii, Anatolii, 74
Bondarchuk, Fedor, 7, 60–1, 64, 173, 191
Bondarchuk, Natal'ia, 154
Bondarchuk, Sergei, 7, 16, 23, 27–38, 40–2, 46, 57, 60, 64, 74
Bondarev, Iurii, 48
Bondarev, Oleg, 153
Boris Godunov (1986), 21
Braginskii, Emil', 114
Brezhnev (2005), 195
Brezhnev, Leonid, 17, 26, 48, 53, 77
Brief Encounters (1967), 164
Brigade (2002), 92
Brother (1997), 92
Brovkin, Viacheslav, 17
Brylska, Barbara, 124
Burov, Georgii, 122
Burnt by the Sun (1994), 62, 196
Burnt by the Sun 2 (2010–11), 62

Capra, Frank, 119
Carnival Night (1956), 108, 117
Case of the Grocery Store Number One, The (2011), 195
Central Committee of CPSU, 3, 26, 28, 41, 43, 46
Channel One, 60, 104, 147, 189, 195
Chapaev (1934), 5, 41

Chernoutsan, Igor', 41
chernukha cinema, 101
Chernykh, Valentin, 187
Chiaureli, Mikhail, 22, 47
Choice of Target (1974), 191
Chukhrai, Grigorii, 24, 28
Churchill, Winston, 47, 50–1, 53, 55
Churikova, Inna, 175
Circus (1936), 114, 150
Citizen Kane (1941), 182
Cold War, 3, 16, 23, 26–7, 29, 46, 49, 105
Colonel Zorin's Version (1978), 74–5
comedy, 5–7, 9–11, 13, 17–18, 58, 107–49, 193
Communist, The (1957), 46
consumerism, 14, 16–17, 23, 68, 71, 75–8, 80, 84, 87–8, 90, 108, 115–19, 120, 126, 130, 146, 149–51, 169, 180, 193–4
Cop Wars (2004– to the present), 192
Cops: Streets of Broken Lights (1998–2015), 90, 103, 105
Cossacks of the Kuban (1949), 114
Cranes Are Flying (1957), 23, 37, 51, 150
Crew, The (1980), 157, 172–3
Cuckoo (2002), 24

Daneliia, Georgii, 121–2, 152
Daughters and Mothers (1974), 194
Dawns Are Quiet Here (1972), 188, 195
Deadly Force (2000–2005), 90
Death Wish (1974), 96
defamiliarization, 134, 136, 138, 144, 147, 171
Demichev, Petr, 13
Diamond Arm (1968), 58, 135
Diez, Fritz, 50
Directorate for Combating the Embezzlement of Socialist Property (OBKhSS), 85
Divorce: Italian Style (1961), 117–18
Dobrzhanskaia, Liubov', 122
Dog in the Manger, The (1977), 113
Doronina, Tat'iana, 154
Dostoevskii, Fedor, 132, 179
Dovzhenko, Aleksandr, 43
dramedy, 189, 193
Drescher, Fran, 147

Dubček, Alexander, 41
Dzhigarkhanian, Armen, 76, 84, 94, 100

Eisenstein, Sergei, 54
Eisymont, Viktor, 121
Ekk, Nikolai, 156
Elder Son (1971), 152
empire, 22, 24, 30–5, 37–8, 48, 60–2, 64, 67, 147, 151, 154, 165, 188, 191–2, 196
End of St. Petersburg, The (1927), 46
Engineer Kochin's Mistake (1939), 70
epic, 7–8, 12–13, 15–16, 21–66, 127, 152, 156, 158–9, 164–5, 167, 170–1, 191, 196
Epishev, Aleksei, 43
Era of Mercy (1975), 91, 100
Ermash, Filipp, 3, 13–14
Ernst, Konstantin, 60
Eternal Call (1973–83), 151, 158, 195
European Story, A (1984), 25
Evstigneev, Evgenii, 94
Extraordinary Adventures of Italians in Russia, The (1973), 117
Extraordinary Adventures of Mr. West in the Land of Bolsheviks, The (1924), 118
Ezhov, Valentin, 157

Fábri, Zoltán, 38
Fairbanks, Douglas, 67
Fall of Berlin, The (1949), 22, 47–8, 53–5
Fate of a Man (1959), 28, 164
Father Sergius (1978), 191
Fedoseeva-Shukshina, Lidiia, 87
female agency, 18–19, 90, 107, 109, 116, 119, 122, 146, 151–4, 157, 159, 173–88
fictional-documentary film, 15, 59
Fokin, Vladimir, 75
Fonda, Henry, 46
Fonda, Jane, 39–40
Forgotten Melody for Flute, A (1987), 146
Formula of Love, The (1984), 129, 134, 137
Forsyte Saga, The (1967), 158
Freindlikh, Alisa, 110, 125
Front beyond the Enemy Lines (1981), 21
Front beyond the Frontline (1977), 21

Index

Front without Flanks (1975), 21, 24, 26
Furtseva (2011), 195
Furtseva, Ekaterina, 28

Gaidai, Leonid, 18, 58, 108, 114, 120, 135
Garage (1979), 118, 121
genre syntax and semantics, 3-6
　of comedy, 107-16
　of melodrama, 149-58
　of police procedural, 67-80
　of prestige production, 21-7
Gentlemen of Fortune (1971), 112
Gerasimov, Sergei, 74, 188, 194
Gerdt, Zinovii, 136
Germi, Pietro, 117
Girl without an Address, A (1957), 108
Goebbels, Joseph, 50
Gold Mine (1977), 75
Golubkina, Larisa, 54
Good Luck! (1956), 121
Gorbachev, Mikhail, 9-10, 64, 80, 87
Gorin, Grigorii, 114, 129
Goskino (State Committee for
　　Cinematography), 3, 10, 13-15,
　　23, 43, 46-7, 78, 113, 134, 181-2
Gosteleradio, 3, 13-15, 75, 81, 134, 163
Govorukhin, Stanislav, 17, 75, 91-2, 94,
　　96-7
Gradskii, Aleksandr, 166
Grigor'ev, Boris, 71
Gubenko, Nikolai, 182
Guys! (1981), 172
Gypsies Are Found Near Heaven
　　(1975), 157
Gypsy (1967), 174

Hamlet (1964), 170
Happy Together (2006-13), 193
Hawks, Howard, 119, 124
Hepburn, Audrey, 38-9
His Girl Friday (1940), 119
historical chronicle, 48
historico-biographical film, 15
historico-revolutionary film, 15
Hitler, Adolf, 22, 45, 47, 50-1, 53-4, 94, 137
House That Swift Built (1982), 129, 132,
　　134, 138-9
How the Steel Was Tempered (1973), 96

I Want the Floor (1976), 19, 157, 175-83
Iakovlev, Iurii, 124
Iakovlev, Sergei, 161
Iankovskii, Oleg, 131-2, 135, 137, 139
identity
　gender and sexual (see female
　　agency, masculinity, patriarchy,
　　sexuality)
　individual, 149-50, 157, 162, 167,
　　174-5, 185-7
　institutional, 73, 80, 97, 105
　Russian, 19, 151, 154, 156, 162, 165,
　　172, 187
　Soviet, 19, 23, 110, 123, 150, 152, 157,
　　162, 164, 167, 172, 195
　state-sponsored nationalist, 27-42, 54,
　　61-4, 92, 195,
ideological approach to film and television
　genres, 2-3
interpretive community, 1, 3, 5, 27, 47,
　　67, 76
Investigation is Conducted by Bread Rolls
　　(1983), 89
Investigation is Conducted by Experts, The
　　(1971-89, 2002-3), 17, 70, 72-4,
　　78, 80-90, 192
Investigation Was Conducted by . . ., The
　　(2006 to the present), 192
irony, 11, 18, 40, 86, 91, 107-48, 164-5,
　　175, 179, 193
Irony of Fate (1975), 18, 111, 114, 116-28,
　　147, 193
Irony of Fate. A Sequel (2007), 147
It Happened in Pen'kovo (1957), 108
It Happened One Night (1934), 119, 124
Italian-style comedy, 116-18, 122
It's a Mad, Mad, Mad, Mad World
　　(1963), 117
Iurskii, Sergei, 91
Ivanov, Anatolii, 158
Ivan's Childhood (1962), 23, 36, 51

Just You Wait! (1969-2006), 168

Kabakov, Ilya, 132-3
Kalatozov, Mikhail, 28, 37, 150
Kalita, Martins, 63
Kamenskaia (2000-11), 90, 105

Kanevskii, Leonid, 80, 192
Karl Marx. The Younger Years (1980), 27
KGB, 3, 7, 13, 17, 25–6, 46–8, 67–9, 77–8, 195
Khodorkovsky, Mikhail, 104
Khrushchev, Nikita, 16–17, 46, 55, 72, 108, 195
Kidnapping Caucasian Style (1967), 120,
Kindinov, Evgenii, 165
Konchalovskii, Andrei, 9–10, 19, 157–8, 165–71
Konev, Ivan, 48
Konkin, Vladimir, 91, 96–7
Koreneva, Elena, 166
Kovalev, Igor', 89
Kozintsev, Grigorii, 170
Kramer, Stanley, 117
Krasnopol'skii, Vladimir and Valerii Uskov, 19, 151, 158, 161–2
Kuleshov, Lev, 117
Kupchenko, Irina, 139
Kuravlev, Leonid, 94
Kurganov, Oskar, 48
Kuznetsov, Anatolii, 113, 164

Ladynin, Andrei, 74
Lapin, Sergei, 3, 13–14
Laurentiis, Dino De, 43
Lavrov, Aleksandr and Ol'ga Lavrova, 79, 83, 89
Lenfilm Studio, 152, 172
Lenin in October (1937), 46
Leone, Sergio, 113
Leonov, Evgenii, 131, 135, 138–9, 141
Lezhdei, El'za, 80
Liberation (1968–72), 7, 16, 21, 24–5, 27, 42, 43–60, 165, 191
    Film 1: *The Fire Bulge*, 43, 51
    Film 2: *Breakthrough*, 43
    Film 3: *The Direction of the Main Blow*, 43, 52, 57
    Film 4: *The Battle for Berlin*, 43
    Film 5: *The Last Assault*, 43
Lioznova, Tat'iana, 26, 51, 103
Liquidation (2007), 103
Little Crane (1968), 153, 174
Liube soft-rock group, 102
Longest Day, The (1962), 46

Look for a Woman (1983), 127
Love and Death (1975), 40
Lover's Romance, A (1974), 10, 19, 152, 157, 165–72
Lukinskii, Ivan, 75

Macheret, Alexander, 70
Magnificent Seven, The (1960), 113
Main Scripts and Editing Commission, 3, 23
Major Whirlwind (1967), 68
Malinovskii, Rodion, 29, 43, 59
Man Who Doubts, The (1963), 70
Martyniuk, Leonid, 80
masculinity, 19, 104, 126, 143, 151–2, 156–8, 163–73, 178
Mashchenko, Nikolai, 96
Mashkov, Vladimir, 103
Matveev, Evgenii, 53, 174, 188, 194
Medinsky, Vladimir, 63
Meeting Place Cannot Be Changed (1979), 17, 75, 78, 90–104, 192
Mel'nikov, Vitalii, 172
melodrama, 5–7, 9–10, 16, 18–19, 27–30, 36, 53, 62, 101–2, 107, 118, 121–2, 130, 149–90, 193–6
Member of the Government (1939), 150
Menglet, Georgii, 76, 85
Men'shov, Vladimir, 172, 183–8
Miagkov, Andrei, 121–2, 125
Mikhalkov, Nikita, 25, 61–4, 118, 192, 195–6
Milliar, Georgy, 37
mini-series (see television mini-series)
Ministry of Culture of the Russian Federation, 65
Ministry of Culture of the USSR, 3, 14, 28, 43
Ministry of Defense of the Russian Federation, 64
Ministry of Defense of the USSR, 29, 43, 59, 64
Ministry of Internal Affairs (MVD), 3, 16–17, 73, 77–9, 85, 97
Mironov, Andrei, 135, 139
Mitta, Alexander, 172–3
modal schizophrenia, 4, 17
moral occult, 153–4, 162, 174–5, 188

Index   217

Moscow Does Not Believe In Tears (1980), 149, 157, 183, 186–8
Moscow International Film Festival, 28, 37–8
Moscow Police, Forever! (2004–6), 192
Mosfilm Studio, 7, 31–2, 43, 46–7, 60, 74–5, 159
Moskalenko, Nikolai, 153
Most Important Assignment, The (1980), 21, 25
Motyl', Vladimir, 68, 113, 154, 164–5
Much Ado About Nothing (1973), 113
Muratova, Kira, 164
Mussolini, Benito, 51
My Fair Nanny (2004–9), 147, 193

Naumenko, Ol'ga, 122
Nekrasov, Viktor, 8
Nest of Gentlefolk, The (1969), 32
New World, 40–1
NKVD, 85
Nobody Wanted to Die (1966), 68
Nosik, Valerii, 86

Odessa Film Studio, 91
Odyssey of Detective Gurov, The (2013), 192
Office Romance (1977), 110–11, 114, 116–28, 193
Officers (1971), 151, 157, 165
Ogareva 6 (1980), 73–4, 77–8
Oh, Sport, You are Peace! (1981), 59
Old Men-Robbers (1971), 117
Olialin, Nikolai, 53
Olympia (1938), 59
Once More about Love (1968), 154
Ordinary Miracle, An (1978), 18, 128–46
Ordynskii, Vasilii, 158, 183
Orlova, Liubov', 183
Ozerov, Iurii, 7, 16, 25, 27, 43–9, 52–4, 59–60, 165

Panfilov, Gleb, 19, 157, 175, 177–8, 180–3
patriarchy, 100, 174, 186
    Russian, 159–163, 187

Soviet, 124, 126–7, 151–2, 156–7, 165, 170, 172, 177, 188
Patton (1970), 48
Pavlenok, Boris, 182
Pel'tser, Tat'iana, 131
Person is Born, A (1956), 183
Petrovka 38 (1962), 73, 78
Petrovka 38 (1980), 71, 73–5, 82
police procedural, 5–7, 16–17, 19, 67–106, 191–3
positivism, 140, 141
Pozner Sr., Vladimir, 113
Pozner, Vladimir, 60
prestige production, 5, 7, 13, 15–17, 21–66, 74, 191–2
private life, 5, 17–18, 71–2, 77, 84, 90, 97, 102, 107–90, 193–6
Private Life (1982), 188, 194–5
Pub Thirteen Chairs, The (1966–80), 128
Putin, Vladimir, 7, 21, 59–62, 64, 103–5, 146–7, 189, 191–2, 194, 196
Pyr'ev, Ivan, 17, 107, 114, 149

Radiant Path (1940), 183–4
Raizman, Iulii, 188, 194
Red Bells (1982), 21, 24
reeducation
    as a semantic element, 71, 93, 109, 112, 130, 156
    as a syntactic element, 17, 73, 82–4, 86, 88, 108, 112, 121, 184
Return of St. Luke, The (1970), 74–5, 78
Riazanov, El'dar, 13, 18, 108–31, 140, 146–7, 193
Ricos También Lloran, Los (1979–80), 189
Riefenstahl, Leni, 24, 37, 59
ritual approach to film and television genres, 2
Road to Calvary, The (1977), 158
Road to Life (1931), 156
Rogovoi, Vladimir, 151
Romanov, Aleksei, 43, 47
Room, Abram, 120
Roosevelt, Eleanor, 53
Roosevelt, Franklin, 47, 51, 53, 175
Rostotskii, Stanislav, 108, 188, 194–5
Ruslanova, Nina, 160

Russian Cinema Fund, 63
Ruthless Romance (1984), 118

Sadal'skii, Stanislav, 94
Sadchikov, Igor', 181–2
Samoilov, Evgenii, 184
Sanaev, Vsevolod, 53, 73–4
Santa Barbara (1984–93), 189
Savel'eva, Liudmila, 31, 38–40
screwball comedy, 18, 116, 119, 124, 147
Seduced and Abandoned (1963), 117
Sekhon, Miriam, 63
Semenov, Iulian, 73–5, 78
Serezha (1960), 164
Seryi, Aleksandr, 112
Seven Brides of Lance-Corporal Zbruev (1972), 152
Seventeen Moments of Spring (1973), 26, 51, 103
Several Days from the Life of I.I. Oblomov (1979), 191
sexuality, 18, 107, 118–19, 122, 140, 151, 154, 167, 174, 185–6
Shadows Disappear at Noon (1971), 19, 151, 157–63, 181, 195
Sharlotta's Necklace (1984), 75
Shatrov, Igor', 158
Shchelokov, Nikolai, 17, 77, 80
She Loves You! (1957), 108
Shirvindt, Aleksandr, 122
Shtemenko, Sergei, 43–4
Shukshin, Vasilii, 151, 156, 172, 179
Shvarts, Evgenii, 129
Siberiade (1979), 10, 156–8
Simonova, Evgeniia, 139
Simple Story, A (1960), 174
simulation melodrama, 188, 194–5
sitcom, 6, 116, 121, 128–31, 136, 138, 146–7, 191, 193
skaz discourse, 143
Slabnevich, Igor', 48
slapstick comedy, 18, 108, 124, 136, 140, 141, 142
Sleuth, The (1979), 75
Smirnov, Andrei, 152, 165
Smoktunovskii, Innokentii, 108, 170
Snowball Berry Red (1975), 151, 156–7, 172

soap opera, 120, 151, 153, 158–9, 188–9, 195
socialist realism, 4, 13, 15, 17, 59, 113, 120, 150, 152–3, 165, 172, 191, 193
Soldati, Mario, 27
Soldiers of Freedom (1977), 21, 24, 53
Solov'eva, Viktoriia, 63
Son of the Father of the People, The (2013), 195
Soviet Screen, 8, 12, 14–15, 38, 57, 67, 168, 171
Stalin, Joseph, 8, 15, 22–3, 28, 46–53, 55, 70, 93, 195
Stalingrad (1989), 59
Stalingrad (2013), 64–65, 173, 191
Standoff (1985), 74
Star of Captivating Happiness, The (1975), 154–5
Stepmother (1973), 153–7, 173–4
Steppe, The (1977), 21, 191
Straw Hat, The (1974), 113
Strogovs, The (1976), 158
STS Channel, 193
Sturges, John, 113
Sunstroke (2014), 62–3, 192
Surikova, Alla, 127

Tabakov, Oleg, 135
Taming of Fire, The (1972), 26, 191
Tarkovskii, Andrei, 3, 28
Tatarskii, Aleksandr, 89
Tatarskii, Evgenii, 75
telenovela, 159, 188
television mini-series, 6–7, 11–12, 19, 26–7, 51, 60, 67–106, 150–1, 153, 157–3, 168, 189, 195
television film, 7, 11–12, 46, 79, 109, 114, 116, 128–46, 172
Telingater, Solomon, 8
temporality
  contemporary, 16, 18, 68–9, 79, 82, 92, 105, 107–8, 113, 118, 134, 136, 138–9, 142, 145, 149, 152, 159, 183, 189
  melodramatic, 149–90
  utopian
    future, 17, 107, 152, 164, 175–6, 179, 183–4
    past, 21–66, 157, 165

That Very Same Munchausen (1979), 129–34, 137
Thirty Three (1965), 120
Three Men in a Boat, To Say Nothing of the Dog (1979), 113
Three Poplar Trees on Pliushchikha Street (1967), 154
Tikhonov, Viacheslav, 30, 103
Time (1968–), 14, 168
Tito, Iosip Broz, 53
Todd, Mike, 42
Tolstoy, Leo, 29–40
Tragedy of a Century (1993–4), 60
Train Station for Two, The (1982), 118, 120
Tvardovskii, Aleksandr, 41
Twelve Chairs, The (1928), 129
Twelve Chairs, The (1971), 135
Twelve Chairs, The (1976), 129–30, 134–5, 137
Twentieth Century (1934), 124
Twenty Hours (1965), 38

Udovichenko, Larisa, 94–5
Ul'ianov, Mikhail, 50
Unfinished Piece for a Mechanical Piano, An (1976), 32
Union of Soviet Writers, 78

Vacation in September (1979), 152, 172
Vainer, Arkadii and Georgii, 75, 78, 91, 100
Valerii Chkalov (1941), 150
Vampilov, Aleksandr, 172
Vasil'ev, Iurii, 185
Veidt, Conrad, 67
Vel'iaminov, Petr, 161
Vengerov, Vladimir, 158

Vertinskii, Aleksandr, 97
Victory (1984), 21
Vidor, King, 27, 29
Village Detective (1968), 75
Vlasov, Andrei, 50
Volga, Volga (1938), 117
Volodin, Aleksandr, 152
Voronins, The (2009–), 193
Voroshilov Sharpshooter, The (1999), 96
Vow, The (1946), 46
Vysotskii, Vladimir, 91, 94–9, 104, 115, 164

War and Peace (1865–9), 28, 32–5, 40
War and Peace (1956), 27, 29
War and Peace (1965–7), 7, 16, 21, 23–4, 27–43, 46–7, 53, 58, 60–1, 64, 74–5, 188, 191
Waterloo (1970), 21, 42
Wayne, John, 46
When Trees Were Big (1962), 164
White Bim Black Ear (1977), 188, 194–5
White Dress, The (1974), 173
White Sun of the Desert (1969), 68, 113, 120, 164–5
woman's film, 157, 173–88

Yesenia (1971), 173

Zaidenberg, Boris, 53
Zakharov, Mark, 18, 109, 114, 116, 128–47
Zarkhi, Aleksandr, 74
Zhalakiavichus, Vitautas, 68
Zharov, Mikhail, 70, 75
Zhukov (2012), 195
Zhukov, Georgii, 48–52, 54–5, 195
Zimianin, Mikhail, 13